Hands-On Reactive Programming with Clojure
Second Edition

Create asynchronous, event-based, and concurrent applications

Konrad Szydlo
Leonardo Borges

BIRMINGHAM - MUMBAI

Hands-On Reactive Programming with Clojure
Second Edition

Commissioning Editor: Richa Tripathi
Acquisition Editor: Denim Pinto
Content Development Editor: Rohit Kumar Singh
Technical Editor: Gaurav Gala
Copy Editor: Safis Editing
Project Coordinator: Vaidehi Sawant
Proofreader: Safis Editing
Indexer: Mariammal Chettiyar
Graphics: Alishon Mendonsa
Production Coordinator: Jyoti Chauhan

First published: March 2015
Second edition: January 2019

Production reference: 1240119

Published by Packt Publishing Ltd.
Livery Place
35 Livery Street
Birmingham
B3 2PB, UK.

ISBN 978-1-78934-613-8

www.packtpub.com

`mapt.io`

Mapt is an online digital library that gives you full access to over 5,000 books and videos, as well as industry leading tools to help you plan your personal development and advance your career. For more information, please visit our website.

Why subscribe?

- Spend less time learning and more time coding with practical eBooks and Videos from over 4,000 industry professionals

- Improve your learning with Skill Plans built especially for you

- Get a free eBook or video every month

- Mapt is fully searchable

- Copy and paste, print, and bookmark content

Packt.com

Did you know that Packt offers eBook versions of every book published, with PDF and ePub files available? You can upgrade to the eBook version at `www.packt.com` and as a print book customer, you are entitled to a discount on the eBook copy. Get in touch with us at `customercare@packtpub.com` for more details.

At `www.packt.com`, you can also read a collection of free technical articles, sign up for a range of free newsletters, and receive exclusive discounts and offers on Packt books and eBooks.

About the authors

Konrad Szydlo has worked with Clojure for the last 7 years. Since January 2016, he has worked as a software engineer and team leader at Retailic, responsible for building a website for the biggest royalty program in Poland. Prior to this, he worked as a developer with Sky, developing e-commerce and sports applications, where he used Ruby, Java, and PHP. He is also listed in the Top 75 Datomic developers on GitHub.

Konrad is a part of the Clojurian Slack community, is very interested in functional programming, and gave a Datomic Database talk at the ClojureD conference in Berlin in 2015. He also gave a talk on *Creating reactive components using ClojureScript React wrappers* during Lambda Days in Kraków in 2016.

> *I would like to thank my family, especially my parents, Dorota and Roman, for their love and support. I would also like to thank my university friends, Joanna, Adam, and Wojtek, for all that we have done together. I am grateful to my colleagues from Sky, who showed me the wonderful world of programming. I also thank my friends from Retailic for the opportunity to work with Clojure. Finally, I thank fellow swimmers from KP Masters Krosno for a world besides programming.*

Leonardo Borges is a programming languages enthusiast who loves writing code, contributing to open source software, and speaking on subjects he feels strongly about. He has used Clojure professionally, both as a lead consultant at ThoughtWorks and as a development team lead at Atlassian, where he helped build real-time collaborative editing technology.

Leonardo is currently the CTO for MODRON. Apart from this book, he contributed a couple of chapters to *Clojure Cookbook*, O'Reilly.

Leonardo founded and currently runs the Sydney Clojure User Group in Australia. He also writes posts about software, with a focus on functional programming, on his website. When he isn't writing code, he enjoys riding motorcycles, weightlifting, and playing the guitar.

About the reviewer

Eduard Bondarenko is a software developer living in Kyiv, Ukraine. He started programming using Basic on a ZX Spectrum a long time ago. Later, he worked in the web development domain. He has used Ruby on Rails for over 8 years. Having used Ruby for a long time, he discovered Clojure in early 2009 and liked the simplicity of the language. Besides Ruby and Clojure, he is interested in Go and ReasonML development.

I want to thank my wonderful wife, kids, and parents, for all the love, support, and help they give me.

Packt is searching for authors like you

If you're interested in becoming an author for Packt, please visit `authors.packtpub.com` and apply today. We have worked with thousands of developers and tech professionals, just like you, to help them share their insight with the global tech community. You can make a general application, apply for a specific hot topic that we are recruiting an author for, or submit your own idea.

Table of Contents

Preface

Highly concurrent applications, such as user interfaces, have traditionally managed state through the mutation of global variables. Various actions are coordinated via event handlers, which are procedural in nature.

Over time, the complexity of a system increases. New feature requests come in, and it becomes harder and harder to reason about the application.

Functional programming presents itself as an extremely powerful ally in building reliable systems by eliminating mutable states and allowing applications to be written in a declarative and composable way.

Such principles gave rise to functional Reactive Programming and **Compositional Event Systems**, programming paradigms that are exceptionally useful in building asynchronous and concurrent applications. They allow you to model mutable states in a functional style.

This book is devoted to these ideas and presents a number of different tools and techniques to help manage the increasing complexity of modern systems.

Who this book is for

This book is for Clojure developers who are currently building or planning to build asynchronous and concurrent applications, and are interested in how they can apply the principles and tools of Reactive Programming to their daily jobs.

Knowledge of Clojure and Leiningen—a popular Clojure build tool—is required.

The book also features several ClojureScript examples, and as such, familiarity with ClojureScript—and web development, in general—will be helpful.

Notwithstanding, the chapters have been carefully written in such a way that as long as you possess knowledge of Clojure, following these examples should only require a little extra effort.

As this book progresses, it lays out the building blocks required by later chapters, and as such, my recommendation is that you start with Chapter 1, *What is Reactive Programming?*, and work your way through subsequent chapters in order.

What this book covers

Chapter 1, *What is Reactive Programming?*, starts by guiding you through a compelling example of a reactive application written in ClojureScript. It then takes you on a journey through the history of Reactive Programming, during which some important terminology is introduced, setting the tone for the following chapters.

Chapter 2, *A Look at Reactive Extensions*, explores the basics of this Reactive Programming framework. Its abstractions are introduced, and important subjects such as error handling and back pressure are discussed.

Chapter 3, *Asynchronous Programming and Networking*, walks you through building a stock market application. It starts by using a more traditional approach and then switches to an implementation based on Reactive Extensions, examining the trade-offs between the two.

Chapter 4, *Introduction to core.async*, describes `core.async`, a library for asynchronous programming in Clojure. Here, you learn about the building blocks of communicating sequential processes and how reactive applications are built with `core.async`.

Chapter 5, *Creating Your Own CES Framework with core.async*, embarks on the ambitious endeavor of building a CES framework. It leverages knowledge gained in the previous chapter and uses `core.async` as the foundation for the framework.

Chapter 6, *Building a Simple ClojureScript Game with Reagi*, showcases a domain where reactive frameworks have been used to great effect in games development.

Chapter 7, *The UI as a Function*, shifts gears and shows how the principles of functional programming can be applied to web UI development through the lens of Om, a ClojureScript binding for Facebook's React.

Chapter 8, *A New Approach to Futures*, presents futures as a viable alternative to some classes' reactive applications. It examines the limitations of Clojure futures and presents an alternative: `imminent`, a library of composable futures for Clojure.

Chapter 9, *A Reactive API to Amazon Web Services*, describes a case study taken from a real project, where a lot of the concepts introduced throughout this book have been put together to interact with a third-party service.

Chapter 10, *Reactive Microservices*, introduces you to microservices, showing when using them gives an advantage over monolithic application design. Next, you see a working example of an API microservice written in Clojure.

`Chapter 11`, *Testing Reactive Apps*, explores various testing methodologies and introduces four Clojure unit testing frameworks.

`Chapter 12`, *Concurrency Utilities in Clojure*, explains why most object-oriented languages are not suited for multi-threaded programming and how Clojure can help developers. Finally, it walks you through available concurrency tools in Clojure.

`Appendix`, *The Algebra of Library Design*, introduces concepts from category theory that are helpful in building reusable abstractions. The appendix is optional and won't hinder learning in the previous chapters. It presents the principles used in designing the futures library seen in `Chapter 8`, *A New Approach to Futures*.

To get the most out of this book

This book assumes that you have a reasonably modern desktop or laptop computer as well as a working Clojure environment with Leiningen (see `http://leiningen.org/`) properly configured. Installation instructions depend on your platform and can be found on the Leiningen website (see `http://leiningen.org/#install`).

You are free to use any text editor of your choice, but popular choices include Eclipse (see `https://eclipse.org/downloads/`) with the Counterclockwise plugin (see `https://github.com/laurentpetit/ccw`), IntelliJ (`https://www.jetbrains.com/idea/`) with the Cursive plugin (see `https://cursiveclojure.com/`), Light Table (see `http://lighttable.com/`), Emacs, and Vim.

Download the example code files

You can download the example code files for this book from your account at `www.packt.com`. If you purchased this book elsewhere, you can visit `www.packt.com/support` and register to have the files emailed directly to you.

You can download the code files by following these steps:

1. Log in or register at `www.packt.com`.
2. Select the **SUPPORT** tab.
3. Click on **Code Downloads & Errata**.
4. Enter the name of the book in the **Search** box and follow the onscreen instructions.

Once the file is downloaded, please make sure that you unzip or extract the folder using the latest version of:

- WinRAR/7-Zip for Windows
- Zipeg/iZip/UnRarX for Mac
- 7-Zip/PeaZip for Linux

The code bundle for the book is also hosted on GitHub at `https://github.com/PacktPublishing/Hands-On-Reactive-Programming-with-Clojure-Second-Edition`. In case there's an update to the code, it will be updated on the existing GitHub repository.

We also have other code bundles from our rich catalog of books and videos available at `https://github.com/PacktPublishing/`. Check them out!

Download the color images

We also provide a PDF file that has color images of the screenshots/diagrams used in this book. You can download it here: `https://www.packtpub.com/sites/default/files/downloads/9781789346138_ColorImages.pdf`.

Conventions used

There are a number of text conventions used throughout this book.

`CodeInText`: Indicates code words in text, database table names, folder names, filenames, file extensions, pathnames, dummy URLs, user input, and Twitter handles. Here is an example: "That's why the next thing we do is call `move-forward!`."

A block of code is set as follows:

```
(fn [ctx val]
  (-> ctx
      canvas/save
      (canvas/translate (:x val) (:y val))
```

When we wish to draw your attention to a particular part of a code block, the relevant lines or items are set in bold:

```
[default]
exten => s,1,Dial(Zap/1|30)
exten => s,2,Voicemail(u100)
exten => s,102,Voicemail(b100)
exten => i,1,Voicemail(s0)
```

Any command-line input or output is written as follows:

```
$ lein repl
```

Bold: Indicates a new term, an important word, or words that you see onscreen. For example, words in menus or dialog boxes appear in the text like this. Here is an example: "Select **System info** from the **Administration** panel."

 Warnings or important notes appear like this.

 Tips and tricks appear like this.

Get in touch

Feedback from our readers is always welcome.

General feedback: If you have questions about any aspect of this book, mention the book title in the subject of your message and email us at customercare@packtpub.com.

Errata: Although we have taken every care to ensure the accuracy of our content, mistakes do happen. If you have found a mistake in this book, we would be grateful if you would report this to us. Please visit www.packt.com/submit-errata, selecting your book, clicking on the Errata Submission Form link, and entering the details.

Piracy: If you come across any illegal copies of our works in any form on the Internet, we would be grateful if you would provide us with the location address or website name. Please contact us at copyright@packt.com with a link to the material.

If you are interested in becoming an author: If there is a topic that you have expertise in and you are interested in either writing or contributing to a book, please visit authors.packtpub.com.

Reviews

Please leave a review. Once you have read and used this book, why not leave a review on the site that you purchased it from? Potential readers can then see and use your unbiased opinion to make purchase decisions, we at Packt can understand what you think about our products, and our authors can see your feedback on their book. Thank you!

For more information about Packt, please visit `packt.com`.

1
What is Reactive Programming?

Reactive Programming is a term that's gaining more and more recognition in the IT community. As we will see in this chapter, it is not a new topic and has been sadly overlooked for many years. Recent advancements in hardware and software, combined with applications requiring more elaborate user interactions, have resulted in the concept of Reactive Programming being rediscovered by a wider audience. Reactive Programming is both an overloaded term and a broad topic. As such, this book will focus on a specific formulation of Reactive Programming called **Compositional Event Systems** (**CES**).

In this chapter, we will cover the following topics:

- A working example of a reactive application in Clojure
- The history of Reactive Programming
- The most common terms in Reactive Programming
- The most common applications of Reactive Programming

A taste of Reactive Programming

Before covering some history and background behind Reactive Programming and CES, I would like to open with a working, and hopefully compelling, example: an animation in which we draw a sine wave onto a web page.

The sine wave is simply a graphical representation of the sine function. It is a smooth, repetitive oscillation, and at the end of our animation, it will look like what's shown in the following screenshot:

This example will highlight how CES does the following:

- Urges us to think about *what* we would like to do as opposed to *how*
- Encourages small, specific abstractions that can be composed together
- Produces terse and maintainable code that is easy to change

The core of this program boils down to four lines of ClojureScript:

```
(-> app-time
    (.pipe (rx-take 700))
    (.subscribe (fn [{:keys [x y]}]
                  (fill-rect x y) "orange")))))
```

Simply by looking at this code, it is impossible to determine precisely what it does. However, do take the time to read and imagine what it *could* do.

First, we have a variable called `app-time`, which represents a sequence of time. The next line gives us the intuition that `app-time` is some sort of collection-like abstraction: we use `rx-take` to retrieve `700` numbers from it.

Finally, we have to `.subscribe` to this *collection* by passing it a callback. This callback will be called for each item in the sine wave, finally drawing out the given sine coordinates using the `fill-rect` function.

This is quite a bit to take in for now, as we haven't seen any other code yet, but that was the point of this little exercise: even though we know nothing about the specifics of this example, we are able to develop an intuition of how it might work.

Let's see what else is necessary to make this snippet animate a sine wave on our screen.

This example is built in ClojureScript and uses HTML5 canvas for rendering and RxJS (see `https://github.com/reactivex/rxjs`), a framework for Reactive Programming in JavaScript.

Before we start, keep in mind that we will not go into the details of these frameworks yet; that will happen in the next chapter. This means I'll be asking you to take quite a few things at face value, so don't worry if you don't immediately grasp how things work. The purpose of this example is to simply get us started in the world of Reactive Programming.

For this project, we will be using `figwheel` (see `https://github.com/bhauman/lein-figwheel`), a Leiningen template for ClojureScript that gives us a sample working application that we can use as a skeleton.

To create our new project, head over to the command line and invoke Leiningen as follows:

```
lein new figwheel sin-wave
cd sin-wave
```

Next, we need to modify a couple of things in the generated project. Open up `sin-wave/resources/index.html` and update it to look like the following:

```
<!DOCTYPE html>
<html>
  <head>
    <meta charset="UTF-8">
    <meta name="viewport" content="width=device-width, initial-scale=1">
    <link href="css/style.css" rel="stylesheet" type="text/css">
    <script src="js/rxjs.umd.js" type="text/javascript"></script></head>
<body>
  <div id="app"></div>
  <script src="js/compiled/sin_wave.js" type="text/javascript"></script>
  <canvas id="myCanvas" width="650" height="200" style="border:1px solid
#d3d3d3;"></canvas>
  </body>
</html>
```

This simply ensures that we import both our application code and RxJS. We haven't downloaded RxJS yet, so let's do that now. Browse to `https://unpkg.com/rxjs/bundles/rxjs.umd.js` and save this file to `sin-wave/resources/public/js`. The previous snippets also add an HTML5 canvas element, onto which we will be drawing.

Now, open `/src/cljs/sin_wave/core.cljs`. This is where our application code will live. You can ignore what is currently there. Make sure you have a clean slate like the following one:

```
(ns sin-wave.core)

(defn on-js-reload[])
```

Finally, go back to the command line under the `sin-wave` folder and start up the following application:

```
lein figwheel
Figwheel: Cutting some fruit, just a sec ...
Figwheel: Validating the configuration found in project.clj
Figwheel: Configuration Valid ;)
Figwheel: Starting server at http://0.0.0.0:3449
Figwheel: Watching build - dev
Figwheel: Cleaning build - dev
Compiling build :dev to "resources/public/js/compiled/sine_wave.js" from
["src"]...
Successfully compiled build :dev to
"resources/public/js/compiled/sine_wave.js" in 16.12 seconds.
Figwheel: Starting CSS Watcher for paths  ["resources/public/css"]
Launching ClojureScript REPL for build: dev
Figwheel Controls:
          (stop-autobuild)                  ;; stops Figwheel autobuilder
          (start-autobuild id ...)          ;; starts autobuilder focused on
optional ids
          (switch-to-build id ...)          ;; switches autobuilder to
different build
          (reset-autobuild)                 ;; stops, cleans, and starts
autobuilder
          (reload-config)                   ;; reloads build config and
resets autobuild
          (build-once id ...)               ;; builds source one time
          (clean-builds id ..)              ;; deletes compiled cljs target
files
          (print-config id ...)             ;; prints out build
configurations
          (fig-status)                      ;; displays current state of
system
          (figwheel.client/set-autoload false)    ;; will turn autoloading
off
          (figwheel.client/set-repl-pprint false) ;; will turn pretty
printing off
  Switch REPL build focus:
          :cljs/quit                        ;; allows you to switch REPL to
another build
     Docs: (doc function-name-here)
     Exit: :cljs/quit
 Results: Stored in vars *1, *2, *3, *e holds last exception object
Prompt will show when Figwheel connects to your application
[Rebel readline] Type :repl/help for online help info
ClojureScript 1.10.238
dev:cljs.user!{:conn 2}=>
```

Once the previous command finishes, the application will be available at `http://localhost:3449/index.html`, where you will find a blank, rectangular canvas. We are now ready to begin.

The main reason we are using the `figwheel` template for this example is that it performs hot-reloading of our application code via WebSockets. This means that we can have the browser and the editor side by side, and as we update our code, we will see the results immediately in the browser without having to reload the page.

To validate that this is working, open your web browser's console so that you can see the output of the scripts on the page. Then, add this to `/src/cljs/sin_wave/core.cljs` as follows:

```
(.log js/console "hello clojurescript")
```

You should have seen the `hello clojurescript` message being printed to your browser's console. Make sure you have a working environment up to this point, as we will be relying on this workflow to interactively build our application.

It is also a good idea to make sure we clear the canvas every time `figwheel` reloads our file. This is simple enough to do by adding the following snippet to our core namespace:

```
(defn canvas []
  (.getElementById js/document "myCanvas"))

(defn ctx []
  (.getContext (canvas) "2d"))
```

The concept of time in RxJS

Now that we have a working environment, we can progress with our animation. It is probably a good idea to specify how often we would like to have a new animation frame.

This effectively means adding the concept of *time* to our application. You're free to play with different values, but let's start with a new frame every 10 milliseconds:

```
(def rx-interval js/rxjs.interval)
(def rx-take js/rxjs.operators.take)
(def rx-map js/rxjs.operators.map)
(def app-time (rx-interval 10))
```

As RxJS is a JavaScript library, we need to use ClojureScript's interoperability to call its functions. For convenience, we will bind the `interval` function of RxJS to a local var. We will use this approach throughout this book when appropriate.

Next, we will create an infinite stream of numbers, starting at 0, that will have a new element every 10 milliseconds. Let's make sure this is working as expected:

```
(-> app-time
    (.pipe (rx-take 5))
    (.subscribe (fn [n]
                    (.log js/console n))))
```

```
;; 0
;; 1
;; 2
;; 3
;; 4
```

I use the term *stream* very loosely here. It will be defined more precisely later in the book.

Remember that time is infinite, so we will use the `take` Rx operator in order to avoid indefinitely printing out numbers to the console.

Our next step is to calculate the 2D coordinate representing a segment of the sine wave we can draw. This will be given by the following functions:

```
(defn deg-to-rad [n]
  (* (/ Math/PI 180) n))

(defn sine-coord [x]
  (let [sin (Math/sin (deg-to-rad x))
        y   (- 100 (* sin 90))]
    {:x   x
     :y   y
     :sin sin}))

(def sine-wave
  (.pipe app-time (rx-map sine-coord)))
```

The `sine-coord` function takes an x point of our 2D canvas and calculates the y point based on the sine of x. The constants `100` and `90` simply control how tall and sharp the slope should be. As an example, try calculating the sine coordinate when x is `50`:

```
(.log js/console (str (sine-coord 50)))
;;{:x 50, :y 31.05600011929198, :sin 0.766044443118978}
```

We will be using `app-time` as the source for the values of x. Creating the sine wave is now only a matter of combining both `app-time` and `sine-coord`:

```
(-> app-time
    (.pipe (rx-take 5) )
    (.subscribe (fn [num]
                  (.log js/console (sine-coord num)))))

;; {:x 0, :y 100, :sin 0}
;; {:x 1, :y 98.42928342064448, :sin 0.01745240643728351}
;; {:x 2, :y 96.85904529677491, :sin 0.03489949670250097}
;; {:x 3, :y 95.28976393813505, :sin 0.052335956242943835}
;; {:x 4, :y 93.72191736302872, :sin 0.0697564737441253}
```

This brings us to the original code snippet that piqued our interest, alongside a function to perform the actual drawing:

```
(defn fill-rect [x y colour]
  (set! (.-fillStyle (ctx)) colour)
  (.fillRect (ctx) x y 2 2))

(-> app-time
    (.pipe (rx-take 700))
    (.subscribe (fn [num]
                  (fill-rect x y "orange"))))
```

As this point, we can save the file again and watch as the sine wave we have just created gracefully appears on the screen.

More colors

One of the points this example sets out to illustrate is how thinking in terms of very simple abstractions and then building more complex ones on top of them make for code that is simpler to maintain and easier to modify.

As such, we will now update our animation to draw the sine wave in different colors. In this case, we would like to draw the wave in red if the sine of x is negative, and blue otherwise.

We already have the sine value coming through the `sine-wave` stream, so all we need to do is transform this stream into one that will give us the colors according to the preceding criteria:

```
(def colour (.pipe sine-wave
                   (rx-map
                    (fn [{:keys [sin]}]
                     (if (< sin 0)
                       "red"
                       "blue")))))
```

The next step is to add the new stream into the main drawing loop—remember to comment the previous one so that we don't end up with multiple waves being drawn at the same time:

```
(-> (js/rxjs.zip sine-wave colour)
    (.pipe (rx-take 700))
    (.subscribe (fn [[{:keys [x y]} colour]]
                  (fill-rect x y colour))))
```

Once we save the file, we should see a new sine wave alternating between red and blue as the sine of x oscillates from -1 to 1.

Making it reactive

As fun as this has been so far, the animation we have created isn't really reactive. Sure, it does react to time itself, but that is the very nature of animation. As we will see later, Reactive Programming is called as such because programs react to external inputs such as a mouse or network events.

We will, therefore, update the animation so that the user is in control of when the color switch occurs: the wave will start off red and switch to blue when the user clicks anywhere within the canvas area. Further clicks will simply alternate between red and blue.

We start by creating infinite—as per the definition of `app-time`—streams for our color primitives as follows:

```
(def red  (.pipe app-time (rx-map (fn [_] "red"))))
(def blue (.pipe app-time (rx-map (fn [_] "blue"))))
```

On their own, `red` and `blue` aren't that interesting, as their values don't change. We can think of them as *constant* streams. They become a lot more interesting when combined with another infinite stream that cycles between them based on user input:

```
(def rx-concat       js/rxjs.concat)
(def rx-defer        js/rxjs.defer)
(def rx-from-event   js/rxjs.fromEvent)
(def rx-takeUntil    js/rxjs.operators.takeUntil)


(def mouse-click (rx-from-event canvas "click"))

(def cycle-colour
  (rx-concat (.pipe red (rx-takeUntil mouse-click))
             (rx-defer #(rx-concat (.pipe blue (rx-takeUntil mouse-click))
                                    cycle-colour))))
```

This is our most complex update so far. If you look closely, you will also notice that `cycle-colour` is a recursive stream; that is, it is defined in terms of itself.

When we first saw the code of this nature, we took a leap of faith in trying to understand what it does. After a quick read, however, we realized that `cycle-colour` closely follows how we might have *talked* about the problem: we will use red until a mouse click occurs, after which, we will use blue until another mouse click occurs. Then, we start the recursion.

The change to our animation loop is minimal:

```
(-> (js/rxjs.zip sine-wave cycle-colour)
    (.pipe (rx-take 700))
    (.subscribe (fn [[{:keys [x y]} colour]]
                    (fill-rect x y colour))))
```

The purpose of this book is to help you develop the instinct required to model problems in the way that's demonstrated here. After each chapter, more and more of this example will make sense. Additionally, a number of frameworks will be used both in ClojureScript and Clojure to give you a wide range of tools to choose from.

Before we move on to that, we must take a little detour and understand how we got here.

Exercise 1.1

Modify the previous example in such a way that the sine wave is drawn using all the colors of the rainbow. The drawing loop should look like the following:

```
(-> (js/rx.zip sine-wave rainbow-colours)
    (pipe (rx-take 700))
    (.subscribe (fn [[{:keys [x y]} colour]]
                    (fill-rect x y colour))))
```

Your task is to implement the `rainbow-colours` stream. As everything up until now has been very light on explanations, you might choose to come back to this exercise later, once we have covered more about CES.

The `repeat`, `scan`, and `flatMap` functions may be useful in solving this exercise. Be sure to consult RxJs' API at `https://rxjs-dev.firebaseapp.com/guide/overview` for more information.

A bit of history

Before we talk about what Reactive Programming is, it is important to understand how other relevant programming paradigms influenced how we develop software. This will also help us understand the motivations behind Reactive Programming.

With a few exceptions, most of us will have been taught imperative programming languages such as C and Pascal or object-oriented languages such as Java and C++; either self-taught or at school/university

In both cases, the imperative programming paradigm of which object-oriented languages are a part dictates that we write programs as a series of statements that modify program state.

To understand what this means, let's look at a short program written in pseudocode that calculates the `sum` and the `mean` value of a list of numbers:

```
numbers := [1, 2, 3, 4, 5, 6]
sum := 0
for each number in numbers
  sum := sum + number
end
mean := sum / count(numbers)
```

The `mean` value is the average of the numbers in the list, which is obtained by dividing the `sum` by the number of elements.

First, we create a new array of integers, called `numbers`, with numbers from 1 to 6, inclusive. Then, we initialize `sum` to `0`. Next, we iterate over the array of integers, one at a time, adding the value of each number to `sum`.

Lastly, we calculate and assign the average of the numbers in the list to the `mean` local variable. This concludes the program logic.

This program would print `21` for the `sum` and `3` for the `mean`, if executed.

Though a simple example, it highlights its imperative style: we set up an application state, `sum`, and then explicitly tell the computer how to modify that state in order to calculate the result.

Dataflow programming

The previous example has an interesting property: the value of `mean` clearly has a dependency on the contents of `sum`.

Dataflow programming makes this relationship explicit. It models applications as a dependency graph through which data flows from operation to operation, and as values change, these changes are propagated to its dependencies.

Historically, dataflow programming has been supported by custom-built languages such as Lucid and BLODI, and as such, have been leaving other general-purpose programming languages out.

Let's see how this new insight would impact our previous example. We know that once the last line gets executed, the value of `mean` is assigned and won't change unless we explicitly reassign the variable.

However, let's imagine for a second that the pseudo-language we used earlier does support dataflow programming. In that case, assigning `mean` to an expression that refers to both `sum` and `count`, such as `sum / count(numbers)`, would be enough to create the directed dependency graph that's shown in the following diagram:

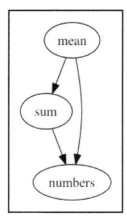

Note that a direct side effect of this relationship is that an implicit dependency from `sum` to `numbers` is also created. This means that if the `numbers` change, the change is propagated through the graph, first updating `sum` and then, finally, updating `mean`.

This is where Reactive Programming comes in. This paradigm builds on dataflow programming and change propagation to bring this style of programming to languages that don't have native support for it.

For imperative programming languages, Reactive Programming can be made available via libraries or language extensions. We don't cover this approach in this book, but should the reader want more information on this subject, please refer to `dc-lib` (see `https://code.google.com/p/dc-lib/`) for an example. It is a framework that adds Reactive Programming support to C++ via dataflow constraints.

Object-oriented Reactive Programming

When designing interactive applications such as desktop **Graphical User Interfaces** (**GUIs**), we are essentially using an object-oriented approach to Reactive Programming. We will build a simple calculator application to demonstrate this style.

Clojure isn't an object-oriented language, but we will be interacting with parts of the Java API to build user interfaces that were developed in an OO paradigm, hence the title of this section.

Let's start by creating a new Leiningen project from the command line:

```
lein new calculator
```

This will create a directory called `calculator` in the current folder. Next, open the `project.clj` file in your favorite text editor and add a dependency on `seesaw`, a Clojure library for working with Java Swing:

```
(defproject calculator "0.1.0-SNAPSHOT"
  :description "FIXME: write description"
  :url "http://example.com/FIXME"
  :license {:name "Eclipse Public License"
            :url "http://www.eclipse.org/legal/epl-v10.html"}
  :dependencies [[org.clojure/clojure "1.8.0"]
                 [seesaw "1.5.0"]]])
```

At the time of writing this book, the latest `seesaw` version that's available is 1.5.0.

Next, in the `src/calculator/core.clj` file, we'll start by requiring the `seesaw` library and creating the visual components we'll be using:

```
(ns calculator.core
  (:require [seesaw.core :refer :all]))

(native!)

(def main-frame (frame :title "Calculator" :on-close :exit))

(def field-x (text "1"))
(def field-y (text "2"))

(def result-label (label "Type numbers in the boxes to add them up!"))
```

The preceding snippet creates a window with the title `Calculator`, which ends the program when closed. We also created two text input fields, `field-x` and `field-y`, as well as a label that will be used to display the results, aptly named `result-label`.

We would like the label to be updated automatically as soon as a user types a new number into any of the input fields. The following code does exactly that:

```
(defn update-sum [e]
  (try
    (text! result-label
          (str "Sum is " (+ (Integer/parseInt (text field-x))
                            (Integer/parseInt (text field-y)))))
    (catch Exception e
      (println "Error parsing input."))))

(listen field-x :key-released update-sum)
(listen field-y :key-released update-sum)
```

The first function, `update-sum`, is our event handler. It sets the text of `result-label` to the sum of the values in `field-x` and `field-y`. We use try/catch here as a really basic way to handle errors, since the key that's being pressed might not have been a number. We then add the event handler to the `:key-released` event of both input fields.

In real applications, we never want a `catch` block such as the previous one. This is considered bad style, and the catch block should do something more useful, such as logging an exception, firing a notification, or resuming the application if possible.

We are almost done. All we need to do now is add the components we have created so far to our `main-frame` and, finally, display it as follows:

```
(config! main-frame :content
         (border-panel
          :north (horizontal-panel :items [field-x field-y])
          :center result-label
          :border 5))

(defn -main [& args]
  (-> main-frame pack! show!))
```

Now, we can save the file and run the program from the command line in the project's root directory:

```
lein run -m calculator.core
```

You should see something like the following screenshot:

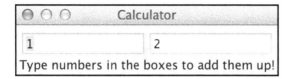

Experiment by typing some numbers into either or both text input fields and watch how the value of the label changes automatically, displaying the sum of both numbers.

Congratulations! You have just created your first reactive application!

As alluded to previously, this application is reactive because the value of the result label *reacts* to user input and is updated automatically. However, this isn't the whole story—it lacks in composability and requires us to specify the how, not the what, of what we're trying to achieve.

As familiar as this style of programming may be, making applications reactive this way isn't always ideal.

Given the previous discussions, we noticed that we still had to be fairly explicit in setting up the relationships between the various components, as evidenced by having to write a custom handler and binding it to both input fields.

As we will see throughout the rest of this book, there is a much better way to handle similar scenarios.

The most widely used reactive program

Both examples in the previous section will feel familiar to some readers. If we call the input text fields `cells` and the result label's handler `formula`, we now have the nomenclature that's used in modern spreadsheet applications such as Microsoft Excel.

The term Reactive Programming has only been in use in recent years, but the idea of a reactive application isn't new. The first electronic spreadsheet dates back to 1969, when Rene Pardo and Remy Landau, then recent graduates from Harvard University, created **LANguage for Programming Arrays at Random (LANPAR)**[1].

It was invented to solve a problem that Bell Canada and AT&T had at the time: their budgeting forms had 2,000 cells that, when modified, forced a software rewrite, taking anywhere from six months to two years to complete.

To this day, electronic spreadsheets remain a powerful and useful tool for professionals in various fields.

The Observer design pattern

Another similarity that the keen reader may have noticed is with the Observer design pattern. It is mainly used in object-oriented applications as a way for objects to communicate with each other without having any knowledge of who depends on its changes.

In Clojure, a simple version of the Observer pattern can be implemented using watches:

```
(def numbers (atom []))

(defn adder [key ref old-state new-state]
  (print "Current sum is " (reduce + new-state)))

(add-watch numbers :adder adder)
```

We will start by creating our program state, which in this case is an atom holding an empty vector. Next, we will create a watch function that knows how to sum all numbers in `numbers`. Finally, we will add our watch function to the `numbers` atom under the `:adder` key (useful for removing watches).

The `adder` key conforms with the API contract required by `add-watch` and receives four arguments. In this example, we only care about `new-state`.

Now, whenever we update the value of `numbers`, its watch will be executed, as demonstrated in the following code:

```
(swap! numbers conj 1)
;; Current sum is  1

(swap! numbers conj 2)
;; Current sum is  3

(swap! numbers conj 7)
;; Current sum is  10
```

The highlighted lines indicate the result that is printed on the screen each time we update the atom.

Though useful, the Observer pattern still requires some amount of work in setting up the dependencies and the required program state, in addition to being hard to compose.

That being said, this pattern has been extended and is at the core of one of the Reactive Programming frameworks we will look at later in this book, Microsoft's **Reactive Extensions** (**Rx**).

Functional Reactive Programming

Just like Reactive Programming, **Functional Reactive Programming** (**FRP**) has unfortunately become an overloaded term.

Frameworks such as RxJava (see `https://github.com/ReactiveX/RxJava`), ReactiveCocoa (see `https://github.com/ReactiveCocoa/ReactiveCocoa`), and Bacon.js (see `https://baconjs.github.io/`) have become extremely popular in recent years and have positioned themselves incorrectly as FRP libraries. This has led to the confusion surrounding the terminology.

As we will see, these frameworks do not implement FRP, but rather are inspired by it.

In the interest of using the correct terminology, as well as understanding what *inspired by FRP* means, we will have a brief look at the different formulations of FRP.

Higher-order FRP

Higher-order FRP refers to the original research on FRP that was developed by Conal Elliott and Paul Hudak in their paper *Functional Reactive Animation*[2] from 1997. This paper presents *Fran*, a domain-specific language embedded in Haskell for creating reactive animations. It has since been implemented in several languages as a library as well as purpose-built reactive languages.

If you recall the calculator example we created a few pages ago, we can see how that style of Reactive Programming requires us to manage state explicitly by directly reading and writing from/to the input fields. As Clojure developers, we know that avoiding state and mutable data is a good principle to keep in mind when building software. This principle is at the core of Functional Programming:

```
(->> [1 2 3 4 5 6]
     (map inc)
     (filter even?)
     (reduce +))
;; 12
```

This short program increments all of the elements in the original list by one filters all even numbers, and adds them up using `reduce`.

Note how we didn't have to explicitly manage local state through each step of the computation.

Different from imperative programming, we focus on what we want to do, for example, iteration, and not how we want it to be done, for example, using a `for` loop. This is why the implementation matches our description of the program closely. This is known as declarative programming.

FRP brings the same philosophy to Reactive Programming. As the Haskell programming language wiki on the subject has wisely put it,

> *"FRP is about handling time-varying values like they were regular values."*

Put another way, FRP is a declarative way of modeling systems that respond to input over time.

Both statements touch on the concept of time. We'll be exploring that in the next section, where we introduce the key abstractions provided by FRP: signals (or behaviors) and events.

Signals and events

So far, we have been dealing with the idea of programs that react to user input. This is, of course, only a small subset of reactive systems, but is enough for the purposes of this discussion.

User input happens several times through the execution of a program: key presses, mouse drags, and clicks are but a few examples of how a user might interact with our system. All of these interactions happen over a period of time. FRP recognizes that time is an important aspect of reactive programs and makes it a first-class citizen through its abstractions.

Both signals (also called behaviors) and events are related to time. Signals represent continuous, time-varying values. Events, on the other hand, represent discrete occurrences at a given point in time.

For example, time is itself a signal. It varies continuously and indefinitely. On the other hand, a key press by a user is an event, that is, a discrete occurrence.

It is important to note, however, that the semantics of how a signal changes need not be continuous. Imagine a signal that represents the current (x,y) coordinates of your mouse pointer.

This signal is said to change discretely, as it depends on the user moving the mouse pointer—an event which isn't a continuous action.

Implementation challenges

Perhaps the most defining characteristic of classical FRP is the use of continuous time.

This means that FRP assumes that signals are changing all the time, even if their value is still the same, leading to needless recomputation. For example, the mouse position signal will trigger updates to the application dependency graph—like the one we saw previously for the mean program—even when the mouse is stationary.

Another problem is that classical FRP is synchronous by default: events are processed in order, one at a time. Harmless at first, this can cause delays, which would render an application unresponsive should an event take substantially longer to process.

Paul Hudak and others furthered research on higher-order FRP[7][8] to address these issues, but that came at the cost of expressivity.

The other formulations of FRP aim to overcome these implementation challenges.

Throughout the rest of this chapter, I'll be using the terms **signals** and **behaviors** interchangeably.

First-order FRP

The most well-known reactive language in this category is Elm (see `http://elm-lang.org/`), an FRP language that compiles to JavaScript. It was created by Evan Czaplicki and presented in his paper *Elm: Concurrent FRP for Functional GUIs*[3].

Elm makes some significant changes to higher-order FRP.

It abandons the idea of continuous time and is entirely event-driven. As a result, it solves the problem of needless recomputation, which was highlighted earlier. First-order FRP combines both behaviors and events into signals, which, in contrast to higher-order FRP, are discrete.

Additionally, first-order FRP allows the programmer to specify when the synchronous processing of events isn't necessary, preventing unnecessary processing delays.

Finally, Elm is a strict programming language, meaning that arguments to functions are evaluated eagerly. This is a conscious decision, as it prevents space and time leaks, which are possible in a lazy language such as Haskell.

 In an FRP library such as Fran, which has been implemented in a lazy language, memory usage can grow unwieldy as computations are deferred to the absolutely last possible moment, therefore causing a space leak. These larger computations, which are accumulated over time due to laziness, can then cause unexpected delays when finally executed, thus causing time leaks.

Asynchronous data flow

Asynchronous data flow generally refers to frameworks such as **Reactive Extensions** (**Rx**), **ReactiveCocoa**, and **Bacon.js**. It is called as such as it completely eliminates synchronous updates.

These frameworks introduce the concept of **Observable Sequences**[4], sometimes called Event Streams.

This formulation of FRP has the advantage of not being confined to functional languages. Therefore, even imperative languages such as Java can take advantage of this style of programming.

Arguably, these frameworks were responsible for the confusion around FRP terminology. Conal Elliott, at some point, suggested the term CES (see `https://twitter.com/conal/status/468875014461468677`).

I have since adopted this terminology (see `http://vimeo.com/100688924`), as I believe it highlights two important factors:

- A fundamental difference between CES and FRP: CES is entirely event-driven
- CES is highly composable via combinators, taking inspiration from FRP

CES is the main focus of this book.

Arrowized FRP

This is the last formulation we will look at. Arrowized FRP[5] introduces two main differences over higher-order FRP: it uses signal functions instead of signals and is built on top of John Hughes' Arrow combinators[6].

It is mostly about a different way of structuring code and can be implemented as a library. As an example, Elm supports Arrowized FRP via its Automaton (see `https://github.com/evancz/automaton`) library.

> The first draft of this chapter grouped the different formulations of FRP under the broad categories of *Continuous and Discrete* FRP. Thanks to Evan Czaplicki's excellent talk, *Controlling Time and Space: understanding the many formulations of FRP* (see
> `https://www.youtube.com/watch?v=Agu6jipKfYw`), I was able to borrow the more specific categories that are used here. These come in handy when discussing the different approaches to FRP.

Applications of FRP

In today's world, the different FRP formulations are being used in several problem spaces by professionals and big organizations alike. Throughout this book, we'll look at several examples of how CES can be applied. Some of these are interrelated, as most modern programs have several cross-cutting concerns, but we will only highlight two main areas.

Asynchronous programming and networking

GUIs are a great example of asynchronous programming. Once you open a web or a desktop application, it simply sits there, idle, waiting for user input.

This state is often called the event or main event loop. It is simply waiting for external stimuli, such as a key press, a mouse button click, new data from the network, or even a simple timer.

Each of these stimuli is associated with an event handler that gets called when one of these events happen, hence the asynchronous nature of GUI systems.

This is a style of programming that we have been used to for many years, but as business and user needs grow, these applications grow in complexity as well, and better abstractions are needed to handle the dependencies between all the components of an application.

Another great example that deals with managing complexity around network traffic is Netflix, which uses CES to provide a reactive API for their backend services.

Complex GUIs and animations

Games are, perhaps, the best example of complex user interfaces, as they have intricate requirements around user input and animations.

The Elm language we mentioned before is one of the most exciting efforts in building complex GUIs. Another example is Flapjax, also targeted at web applications, but it is provided as a JavaScript library that can be integrated with existing JavaScript code bases.

Summary

Reactive Programming is all about building responsive applications. There are several ways in which we can make our applications reactive. Some are old ideas: dataflow programming, electronic spreadsheets, and the Observer pattern are all examples. However, CES in particular has become popular in recent years.

CES aims to bring to Reactive Programming the declarative way of modeling problems that is at the core of Functional Programming. We should worry about what and not about how.

In the following chapters, we will learn how we can apply CES to our own programs.

Further reading

Here is a list of information you can refer to regarding what we have covered in this chapter:

1. *The World's First Electronic Spreadsheet*, Rene Pardo and Remy Landau:
   http://www.renepardo.com/articles/spreadsheet.pdf
2. *Functional Reactive Animation*, Conal Elliott and Paul Hudak:
   http://conal.net/papers/icfp97/icfp97.pdf
3. *Elm: Concurrent FRP for Functional GUIs*, Evan Czaplicki:
   https://www.seas.harvard.edu/sites/default/files/files/archived/Czaplicki.pdf
4. *Subject/Observer is Dual to Iterator*, Erik Meijer:
   http://csl.stanford.edu/~christos/pldi2010.fit/meijer.duality.pdf

5. *Functional Reactive Programming, Continued,* Henrik Nilsson, Antony Courtney, and John Peterson:
   http://haskell.cs.yale.edu/wp-content/uploads/2011/02/workshop-02.pdf

6. *Generalising Monads to Arrows*, John Hughes:
   http://www.cse.chalmers.se/~rjmh/Papers/arrows.pdf

7. *Real-Time FRP*, Zhanyong Wan, Walid Taha, and Paul Hudak:
   http://haskell.cs.yale.edu/wp-content/uploads/2011/02/rt-frp.pdf

8. *Event-Driven FRP*, Walid Taha, Zhanyong Wan, and Paul Hudak: https://www.researchgate.net/publication/2415013_Event-driven_FRP

A Look at Reactive Extensions

2

Reactive Extensions (**Rx**) is a Reactive Programming library from Microsoft that's used for building complex asynchronous programs. It models time-varying values and events as observable sequences and is implemented by extending the Observer design pattern.

Its first target platform was .NET, but Netflix has ported Rx to JVM under the name RxJava. Microsoft also develops and maintains a port of Rx to JavaScript called RxJS, which is the tool we used to build the sine wave application. The two ports work a treat for us, since Clojure runs on JVM and ClojureScript in JavaScript environments.

As we saw in `Chapter 1`, *What is Reactive Programming?*, Rx is inspired by Functional Reactive Programming but uses different terminology. In FRP, the two main abstractions are behaviors and events. Although the implementation details are different, observable sequences represent events. Rx also provides a behavior-like abstraction through another data type, called `BehaviorSubject`.

In this chapter, we will cover the following topics:

- Rx's main abstraction: observables
- The duality between iterators and observables
- Creating and manipulating observable sequences

The observer pattern revisited

In `Chapter 1`, *What is Reactive Programming?*, we saw a brief overview of the Observer design pattern and a simple implementation of it in Clojure using watches. Here's how we did it:

```
(def numbers (atom []))

(defn adder [key ref old-state new-state]
  (print "Current sum is " (reduce + new-state)))

(add-watch numbers :adder adder)
```

In the preceding example, our observable subject is var known as `numbers`. The observer is the `adder` watch. When the observable changes, it *pushes* its changes to the observer *synchronously*.

Now, contrast this to working with sequences:

```
(->> [1 2 3 4 5 6]
     (map inc)
     (filter even?)
     (reduce +))
```

This time around, the vector is the subject being observed and the functions processing it can be thought of as the observers. However, this works in a pull-based model. The vector doesn't push any elements down the sequence. Instead, `map` and friends ask the sequence for more elements. This is a synchronous operation.

Rx makes sequences and other behave like observables so that you can still `map`, `filter`, and compose them just as you would compose functions over normal sequences.

Observer – an iterator's dual

Clojure's sequence operators, such as `map`, `filter`, `reduce`, and so on, support Java iterables. As the name implies, an iterable is an object that can be iterated over. At a low level, this is supported by retrieving an `Iterator` reference from such an object. Java's iterator interface looks like the following:

```
public interface Iterator<E> {
    boolean hasNext();
    E next();
    void remove();
}
```

When passed an object that implements this interface, Clojure's sequence operators pull data from it by using the `next` method, while using the `hasNext` method to know when to stop.

 The `remove` method is required to remove its last element from the underlying collection. This in-place mutation is clearly unsafe in a multithreaded environment. Whenever Clojure implements this interface for the purposes of interoperability, the `remove` method simply throws `UnsupportedOperationException`.

An observable, on the other hand, has observers subscribed to it. Observers have the following interface:

```
public interface Observer<T> {
    void onCompleted();
    void onError(Throwable e);
    void onNext(T t);
}
```

As we can see, an observer implementing this interface will have its `onNext` method called with the next value available from whatever observable it's subscribed to, hence it being a *push*-based notification model.

This duality[1] becomes clearer if we look at both interfaces side by side:

```
Iterator<E> {                          Observer<T> {
    boolean hasNext();                     void onCompleted();
    E next();                              void onError(Throwable e);
    void remove();                         void onNext(T t);
}                                      }
```

Observables provide the ability to have producers push items *asynchronously* to consumers. A few examples will help solidify our understanding.

Creating observables

This chapter is all about Reactive Extensions, so let's go ahead and create a project called `rx-playground` which we will be using in our exploratory tour. We will use RxClojure (see `https://github.com/ReactiveX/RxClojure`), a library that provides Clojure bindings for `RxJava()` (see `https://github.com/ReactiveX/RxJava`):

```
$ lein new rx-playground
```

Open the project file and add a dependency on RxJava's Clojure bindings:

```
(defproject rx-playground "0.1.0-SNAPSHOT"
  :description "FIXME: write description"
  :url "http://example.com/FIXME"
  :license {:name "Eclipse Public License"
            :url "http://www.eclipse.org/legal/epl-v10.html"}
  :dependencies [[org.clojure/clojure "1.9.0"]
                 [io.reactivex/rxclojure "1.0.0"]])
```

Now, fire up a REPL in the project's root directory so that we can start creating some observables:

```
$ lein repl
```

The first thing we need to do is import RxClojure, so let's get this out of the way by typing the following in the REPL:

```
(require '[rx.lang.clojure.core :as rx])
(import '(rx Observable))
```

The simplest way to create a new observable is by calling the `return` function:

```
(def obs (rx/return 10))
```

Now, we can subscribe to it:

```
(rx/subscribe obs
              (fn [value]
                (prn (str "Got value: " value))))
```

This will print the `"Got value:  10"` string to the REPL.

The `subscribe` function of an observable allows us to register handlers for three main things that happen throughout its life cycle: new values, errors, or a notification that the observable is done emitting values. This corresponds to the `onNext`, `onError`, and `onCompleted` methods of the Observer interface, respectively.

In the preceding example, we are simply subscribing to `onNext`, which is why we get notified about the observable's only value, 10.

A single-value observable isn't terribly interesting, though. Let's create and interact with one that emits multiple values:

```
(-> (rx/seq->o [1 2 3 4 5 6 7 8 9 10])
    (rx/subscribe prn))
```

This will print the numbers from 1 to 10, inclusive, to the REPL. `seq->o` is a way to create observables from Clojure sequences. It just so happens that the preceding snippet can be rewritten using Rx's own `range` operator:

```
(-> (rx/range 1 10)
    (rx/subscribe prn))
```

Of course, this doesn't present any advantages to working with raw values or sequences in Clojure yet.

But what if we need an observable that emits an undefined number of integers at a given interval? This becomes challenging to represent as a sequence in Clojure, but Rx makes it trivial:

```
(import '(java.util.concurrent TimeUnit))

(def  repl-out *out*)
(defn prn-to-repl [& args]
  (binding [*out* repl-out]
    (apply prn args)))
(rx/subscribe (Observable/interval 100 TimeUnit/MILLISECONDS)
              prn-to-repl)
```

 RxClojure doesn't provide bindings to all of RxJava's API yet. The `interval` method is one such example of this. We're required to use interoperability and call the method directly on the `Observable` class from RxJava.

`Observable/interval` takes a number and a time unit as arguments. In this case, we are telling it to emit an integer starting from zero every 100 milliseconds. If we type this in a REPL-connected editor, however, two things will happen:

- We will not see any output (depending on your REPL; this is true for Emacs)
- We will have a rogue thread emitting numbers indefinitely

Both issues arise from the fact that `Observable/interval` is the first factory method we have used that doesn't emit values synchronously. Instead, it returns an observable that defers the work to a separate thread.

The first issue is simple enough to fix. Functions such as `prn` will print to whatever the dynamic var `*out*` is bound to. When working in certain REPL environments, such as Emacs, this is bound to the REPL stream, which is why we can generally see everything we print.

However, since Rx is deferring the work to a separate thread, `*out*` isn't bound to the REPL stream anymore, so we don't see the output. To fix this, we need to capture the current value of `*out*` and bind it in our subscription. This will be incredibly useful as we experiment with Rx in the REPL. Let's revisit the `prn-to-repl` helper function which we defined earlier:

```
(def  repl-out *out*)
(defn prn-to-repl [& args]
  (binding [*out* repl-out]
    (apply prn args)))
```

The first thing we do is create var called `repl-out` that contains the current REPL stream. Next, we create a function called `prn-to-repl` which works just like `prn`, except it uses the `binding` macro to create a new binding for `*out*` that is valid within that scope.

This still leaves us with the rogue thread problem. Now is the appropriate time to mention that the `subscribe` method from an observable returns a subscription object. By holding onto a reference to it, we can call its `unsubscribe` method to indicate that we are no longer interested in the values that are produced by that observable.

Putting it all together, our interval example can be rewritten like so:

```
(def subscription (rx/subscribe
                    (Observable/interval 100 TimeUnit/MILLISECONDS)
                    prn-to-repl))

(Thread/sleep 1000)

(rx/unsubscribe subscription)
```

We create a new interval observable and immediately subscribe to it, just as we did before. This time, however, we assign the resulting subscription to a local var. Note that it now uses our helper function, `prn-to-repl`, so we will start seeing values being printed to the REPL straight away.

Next, we sleep the current (the REPL) thread for a second. This is enough time for `Observable` to produce numbers from 0 to 9. That's roughly when the REPL thread wakes up and unsubscribes from that observable, causing it to stop emitting values.

Custom observables

Rx provides many more factory methods to create observables, but it is beyond the scope of this book to cover them all. Interested readers are advised to consult the Rx documentation (see `https://github.com/ReactiveX/RxJava/wiki/Creating-Observables`) which provides examples of other factory methods.

Nevertheless, sometimes, none of the built-in factories are what you want. For such cases, Rx provides the `create` method. We can use it to create a custom observable from scratch.

As an example, we'll create our own version of the `just` observable we used earlier in this chapter:

```
(defn just-obs [v]
  (rx/observable*
    (fn [observer]
      (rx/on-next observer v)
      (rx/on-completed observer))))

(rx/subscribe (just-obs 20) prn)
```

First, we create a function, `just-obs`, which implements our observable by calling the `observable*` function.

When creating an observable in this way, the function passed to `observable*` will get called with an observer as soon as one subscribes to us. When this happens, we are free to do whatever computation—and even I/O—we need in order to produce values and push them to the observer.

We should remember to call the observer's `onCompleted` method whenever we're done producing values. The preceding snippet will print `20` to the REPL.

 While creating custom observables is fairly straightforward, we should make sure that we exhaust the built-in factory functions first, only then resorting to creating our own.

Manipulating observables

Now that we know how to create observables, we should look at what kinds of interesting things we can do with them. In this section, we will see what it means to treat observables as sequences.

We'll start with something simple. Let's print the sum of the first five positive even integers from an observable of all integers:

```
(rx/subscribe (->> (Observable/interval 1 TimeUnit/MICROSECONDS)
                   (rx/filter even?)
                   (rx/take 5)
                   (rx/reduce +))
              prn-to-repl)
```

This is starting to look awfully familiar to us. We create an interval that will emit all positive integers starting at zero every one microsecond. Then, we filter all even numbers in this observable. Obviously, this is too big a list to handle, so we simply take the first five elements from it. Finally, we reduce the value using +. The result is 20.

To drive home the point that programming with observables really is just like operating on sequences, we will look at one more example, where we will combine two different observable sequences. One contains the names of musicians I'm a fan of and the other the names of their respective bands:

```
(defn musicians []
  (rx/seq->o ["James Hetfield" "Dave Mustaine" "Kerry King"]))

(defn bands     []
  (rx/seq->o ["Metallica" "Megadeth" "Slayer"]))
```

We would like to print to a string of the format Musician name - from: band name to the REPL. An added requirement is that the band names should be printed in uppercase for impact.

We'll start by creating another observable that contains the uppercased band names:

```
(defn uppercased-obs []
  (rx/map (fn [s] (.toUpperCase s)) (bands)))
```

While not strictly necessary, this makes a reusable piece of code that can be handy in several places of the program, thus avoiding duplication. Subscribers interested in the original band names can keep subscribing to the bands observable.

With the two observables in hand, we can proceed to combine them:

```
(-> (rx/map vector
            (musicians)
            (uppercased-obs))
    (rx/subscribe (fn [[musician band]]
                    (prn-to-repl (str musician " - from: " band)))))
```

Once more, this example should feel familiar. The solution we were after was a way to `zip` the two observables together. RxClojure provides `zip` behavior through `map`, much like Clojure's core `map` function does. We call it with three arguments: the two observables to `zip` and a function that will be called with both elements, one from each observable, which should return an appropriate representation. In this case, we simply turn them into a vector.

Next, in our subscriber, we simply destructure the vector so that we can access the musician and band names. Finally, we can print the final result to the REPL:

```
"James Hetfield - from: METALLICA"
"Dave Mustaine - from: MEGADETH"
"Kerry King - from: SLAYER"
```

flatmap and friends

In the previous section, we learned how to transform and combine observables with operations such as `map`, `reduce`, and `zip`. However, the two observables that we just looked at—musicians and bands—were perfectly capable of producing values on their own; they did not need any extra input.

In this section, we will examine a different scenario: we'll learn how we can combine observables, where the output of one is the input of another. We encountered `flatmap` before, in `Chapter 1`, *What is Reactive Programming?* If you have been wondering what its role is, this section addresses exactly that.

Here's what we are going to do: given an observable representing a list of all positive integers, we'll calculate the factorial for all even numbers in that list. Since the list is too big, we'll take five items from it. The end result should be the factorials of 0, 2, 4, 6, and 8, respectively.

The first thing we need is a function to calculate the factorial of a number, *n*, as well as our observable:

```
(defn factorial [n]
  (reduce * (range 1 (inc n))))

(defn all-positive-integers []
  (Observable/interval 1 TimeUnit/MICROSECONDS))
```

Using some type of visual aid will be helpful in this section, so we'll start with a marble diagram representing the previous observable:

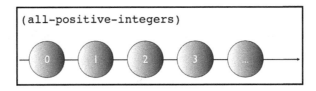

The middle arrow represents time and it flows from left to right. This diagram represents an infinite Observable sequence, as indicated by the use of ellipsis at the end of it.

Since we're combining all the observables now, we'll create one that, given a number, emits its factorial using the helper function that we defined earlier. We'll use Rx's `factorial` method for this purpose:

```
(defn fact-obs [n]
  (rx/observable*
    (fn [observer]
      (rx/on-next observer (factorial n))
      (rx/on-completed observer)))))
```

This is very similar to the `just-obs` observable we created earlier in this chapter, except that it calculates the factorial of its argument and emits the result/factorial instead, ending the sequence immediately thereafter. The following diagram illustrates how this works:

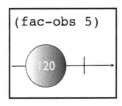

We feed the number 5 to the observable, which in turn emits its factorial, 120. The vertical bar at the end of the timeline indicates that the sequence terminates then.

Running the code for this confirms that our function is correct:

```
(rx/subscribe (fact-obs 5) prn-to-repl)

;; 120
```

So far, so good. Now, we need to combine both observables so that we can achieve our goal. This is where the `flatmap` of Rx comes in. First, we'll see it in action, and then we'll get into the explanation:

```
(rx/subscribe (->> (all-positive-integers)
                   (rx/filter  even?)
                   (rx/flatmap fact-obs)
                   (rx/take 5))
              prn-to-repl)
```

If we run the preceding code, it will print the factorials for 0, 2, 4, 6, and 8, just as we wanted:

```
1
2
24
720
40320
```

Most of the preceding code snippet should look familiar. The first thing we do is filter all even numbers from `all-positive-numbers`. This leaves us with the following observable sequence:

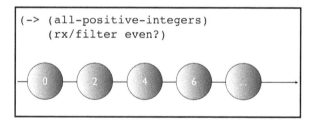

Much like `all-positive-integers`, this, too, is an infinite observable.

However, the next line of our code looks a little odd. We call `flatmap` and give it the `fact-obs` function; a function we know itself returns another observable. `flatmap` will call `fact-obs` with each value it emits. `fact-obs` will, in turn, return a single-value observable for each number. However, our subscriber doesn't know how to deal with observables! It's simply interested in the factorials!

This is why, after calling `fact-obs` to obtain an observable, `flatmap` flattens all of them into a single observable we can subscribe to. This is quite a mouthful, so let's visualize what this means:

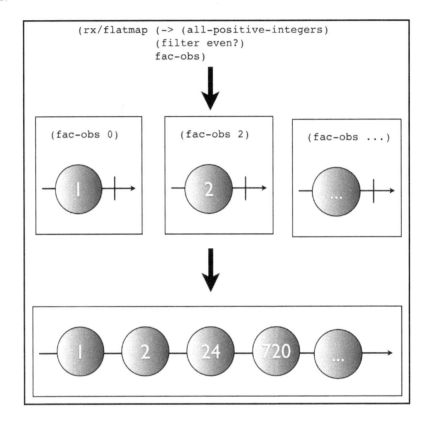

As you can see in the preceding diagram, through the execution of `flatmap`, we end up with a list of observables. However, we don't care about each observable, but rather about the values they emit. `flatmap`, then, is the perfect tool as it combines—that is, *flattens*—all of them into the observable sequence, like the one that's shown at the bottom of the diagram.

You can think of `flatmap` as `mapcat` for observable sequences.

The rest of the code is straightforward. We simply take the first five elements from this observable and subscribe to it, as we have been doing so far.

One more flatmap for the road

You might be wondering what would happen if the observable sequence we're *flatmapping* emitted more than one value. What then?

We'll look at one last example before we begin the next section so that we can illustrate the behavior of `flatMap` in such cases.

Here's an observable that emits its argument twice:

```
(defn repeat-obs [n]
  (rx/seq->o (repeat 2 n)))
```

Using it is straightforward, as demonstrated in the following code block:

```
(-> (repeat-obs 5)
    (rx/subscribe prn-to-repl))

;; 5
;; 5
```

As we did previously, we'll now combine this observable with the one we created earlier, `all-positive-integers`. Before reading on, think about what you expect the output to be for, say, the first three positive integers.

The code is as follows:

```
(rx/subscribe (->> (all-positive-integers)
                   (rx/flatmap repeat-obs)
                   (rx/take 6))
              prn-to-repl)
```

The output is as follows:

```
0
0
1
1
2
2
```

The result might be unexpected for some readers. Let's have a look at the marble diagram for this example and make sure we understand how it works:

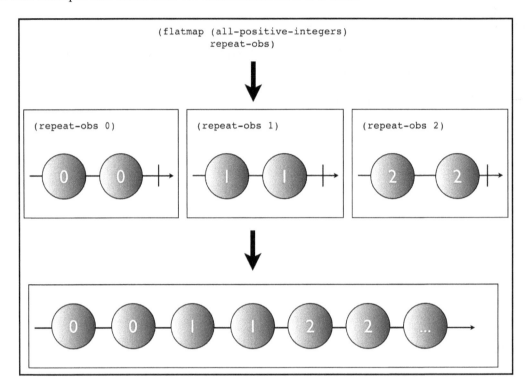

Each time `repeat-obs` gets called, it emits two values and terminates. `flatmap` then combines them all in a single observable, making the previous output clearer.

One last thing worth mentioning about `flatmap`—and the title of this section—is that its *friends* refer to the several names by which `flatmap` is known.

For instance, Rx.NET calls it `selectMany`. RxJava and Scala call it `flatMap`, though RxJava has an alias for it—`mapMany`. The Haskell Community calls it **bind**. Though they have different names, these function's semantics are the same and are part of a higher-order abstraction called a Monad. We don't need to know anything about Monads to proceed.

The important thing to keep in mind is that when you're sitting at the bar talking to your friends about **Compositional Event Systems (CES)**, all these names mean the same thing.

Error handling

A very important aspect of building reliable applications is knowing what to do when things go wrong. It is naive to assume that the network is reliable, that hardware won't fail, or that we, as developers, won't make mistakes.

RxJava embraces this fact and provides a rich set of combinators to deal with failure, a few of which we will examine here.

OnError

Let's get started by creating a badly behaved observable that always throws an exception:

```
(defn exceptional-obs []
  (rx/observable*
    (fn [observer]
      (rx/on-next observer (throw (Exception. "Oops. Something went
wrong")))
      (rx/on-completed observer))))
```

Now, let's watch what happens if we subscribe to it:

```
(rx/subscribe (->> (exceptional-obs)
                   (rx/map inc))
              (fn [v] (prn-to-repl "result is " v)))

;; Exception Oops. Something went wrong  rx-playground.core/exceptional-
obs/fn--1505
```

The exception thrown by `exceptional-obs` isn't caught anywhere, so it simply bubbles up to the REPL. If this was a web application, our users would be presented with a web server error such as the **HTTP code 500 - Internal Server Error**. Those users would probably not use our system again.

Ideally, we would like to get a chance to handle this exception gracefully, possibly rendering a friendly error message that will let ours users know we care about them.

As we saw earlier in this chapter, the `subscribe` function can take up to three functions as arguments:

- The first, the `onNext` handler, is called when the observable emits a new value
- The second, `onError`, is called whenever the observable throws an exception

- The third and final function, `onComplete`, is called when the observable has completed and will not emit any new items

For our purposes, we are interested in the `onError` handler, and using it is straightforward:

```
(rx/subscribe (->> (exceptional-obs)
                   (rx/map inc))
              (fn [v] (prn-to-repl "result is " v))
              (fn [e] (prn-to-repl "error is " e)))

;; "error is " #<Exception java.lang.Exception: Oops. Something went wrong>
```

This time, instead of throwing the exception, our error handler gets called with it. This gives us the opportunity to display an appropriate message to our users.

Catch

The use of `onError` gives us a much better experience overall, but it isn't very flexible.

Let's imagine a different scenario, where we have an observable retrieving data from the network. What if, when this observer fails, we would like to present the user with a cached value instead of an error message?

This is where the `catch` combinator comes in. It allows us to specify a function to be invoked when the observable throws an exception, much like `OnError` does.

Differently from `OnError`, however, `catch` has to return a new observable that will be the new source of items from the moment the exception was thrown:

```
(rx/subscribe (->> (exceptional-obs)
                   (rx/catch Exception e
                       (rx/return 10))
                   (rx/map inc))
              (fn [v] (prn-to-repl "result is " v)))

;; "result is " 11
```

In the previous example, we are essentially specifying that, whenever `exceptional-obs` throws, we should return the value `10`. We are not limited to single values, however. In fact, we can use any observable we like as the new source:

```
(rx/subscribe (->> (exceptional-obs)
                   (rx/catch Exception e
                       (rx/seq->o (range 5)))
```

```
                    (rx/map inc))
          (fn [v] (prn-to-repl "result is " v)))
```

```
;; "result is " 1
;; "result is " 2
;; "result is " 3
;; "result is " 4
;; "result is " 5
```

Retry

The last error handling combinator we'll examine is retry. This combinator is useful when we know that an error or exception is only transient, so we should probably give it another shot by resubscribing to the observable.

First, we'll create an observable that fails when it is subscribed to for the first time. However, the next time it is subscribed to, it succeeds and emits a new item:

```
(defn retry-obs []
  (let [errored (atom false)]
    (rx/observable*
      (fn [observer]
        (if @errored
          (rx/on-next observer 20)
          (do (reset! errored true)
              (throw (Exception. "Oops. Something went wrong"))))))))
```

Let's see what happens if we simply subscribe to it:

```
(rx/subscribe (retry-obs)
              (fn [v] (prn-to-repl "result is " v)))
```

```
;; Exception Oops. Something went wrong  rx-playground.core/retry-obs/fn-
-1476
```

As expected, the exception simply bubbles up, as in our first example. However, we know—for the purposes of this example—that this is a transient failure. Let's see what changes if we use retry:

```
(rx/subscribe (->> (retry-obs)
                   (.retry))
              (fn [v] (prn-to-repl "result is " v)))
```

```
;; "result is " 20
```

Now, our code is responsible for retrying the observable and, as expected, we get the correct output.

It's important to note that `retry` will attempt to resubscribe indefinitely until it succeeds. This might not be what you want, so Rx provides a variation, called `retryWith`, which allows us to specify a predicate function that controls when and if retrying should stop.

All of these operators give us the tools we need to build reliable reactive applications, and we should always keep them in mind since they are, without a doubt, a great addition to our toolbox. The RxJava wiki on the subject should be referred to for more information: `https://github.com/ReactiveX/RxJava/wiki/Error-Handling-Operators`.

Backpressure

Another issue we might be faced with is observables that produce items faster than we can consume them. The problem that arises in this scenario is to do with the ever-growing backlog of items.

As an example, think about zipping two observables together. The `zip` operator (or `map` in RxClojure) will only emit a new value when all observables have emitted an item.

So, if one of these observables is a lot faster at producing items than the others, `map` will need to buffer these items and wait for the others, which will most likely cause an error, as shown here:

```
(defn fast-producing-obs []
  (rx/map inc (Observable/interval 1 TimeUnit/MILLISECONDS)))

(defn slow-producing-obs []
  (rx/map inc (Observable/interval 500 TimeUnit/MILLISECONDS)))

(rx/subscribe (->> (rx/map vector
                          (fast-producing-obs)
                          (slow-producing-obs))
                   (rx/map (fn [[x y]]
                             (+ x y)))
                   (rx/take 10))
              prn-to-repl
              (fn [e] (prn-to-repl "error is " e)))

;; "error is " #<MissingBackpressureException
rx.exceptions.MissingBackpressureException>
```

As we can see in the preceding code, we have a fast-producing observable that emits items 500 times faster than the slower observable. Clearly, we can't keep up with it and, surely enough, Rx throws `MissingBackpressureException`.

What this exception is telling us is that the fast-producing observable doesn't support any type of backpressure—what Rx calls *Reactive pull backpressure*—that is, consumers can't tell it to go slower. Thankfully, Rx provides us with combinators, which are helpful in these scenarios.

Sample

One such combinator is `sample`, which allows us to sample an observable at a given interval, thus throttling the source observable's output. Let's apply it to our previous example:

```
(rx/subscribe (->> (rx/map vector
                           (.sample (fast-producing-obs) 200
                                    TimeUnit/MILLISECONDS)
                           (slow-producing-obs))
                   (rx/map (fn [[x y]]
                             (+ x y)))
                   (rx/take 10))
              prn-to-repl
              (fn [e] (prn-to-repl "error is " e)))

;; 204
;; 404
;; 604
;; 807
;; 1010
;; 1206
;; 1407
;; 1613
;; 1813
;; 2012
```

The only change is that we call `sample` on our fast producing observable before calling `map`. We will sample it every 200 milliseconds.

By ignoring all other items emitted in this time slice, we have mitigated our initial problem, even though the original observable doesn't support any form of backpressure.

The sample combinator is only one of the combinators that's useful in such cases. Others include `throttleFirst`, `debounce`, `buffer`, and `window`. One drawback of this approach, however, is that a lot of the items generated end up being ignored.

Depending on the type of application we are building, this might be an acceptable compromise. But what if we are interested in all of the items?

Backpressure strategies

If an observable doesn't support backpressure but we are still interested in all of the items it emits, we can use one of the built-in backpressure combinators provided by Rx.

As an example, we will look at one such combinator, `onBackpressureBuffer`:

```
(rx/subscribe (->> (rx/map vector
                        (.onBackpressureBuffer (fast-producing-obs))
                        (slow-producing-obs))
                    (rx/map (fn [[x y]]
                               (+ x y)))
                    (rx/take 10))
              prn-to-repl
              (fn [e] (prn-to-repl "error is " e)))

;; 2
;; 4
;; 6
;; 8
;; 10
;; 12
;; 14
;; 16
;; 18
;; 20
```

This example is very similar to the one where we used `sample`, but the output is fairly different. This time, we get all of the items that have been emitted by both observables.

The `onBackpressureBuffer` strategy implements a strategy that simply buffers all of the items that are emitted by the slower Observable, emitting them whenever the consumer is ready. In our case, this happens every 500 milliseconds.

Other strategies include `onBackpressureDrop` and `onBackpressureBlock`.

It's worth noting that Reactive pull backpressure is still a work in progress and the best way to keep up to date with progress is on the RxJava wiki on the subject: `https://github.com/ReactiveX/RxJava/wiki/Backpressure`.

Summary

In this chapter, we took a deep dive into RxJava, a port form of Microsoft's Reactive Extensions from .NET. We learned about its main abstraction, the observable, and how it relates to iterables.

We also learned how to create, manipulate, and combine observables in several ways. The examples shown here were contrived to keep things simple. Nevertheless, all of the concepts that have been presented are extremely useful in real applications and will come in handy for our next chapter, where we will put them to use in a more substantial example.

Finally, we finished by looking at error handling and backpressure, both of which are important characteristics of reliable applications that should always be kept in mind.

In the next chapter we will create a stock market monitoring application using observable sequences and RxClojure. They will help us reduce the complexity when dealing with stateful computations.

Further reading

Here is a list of information you can refer to regarding what we covered in this chapter:

1. *Subject/Observer is Dual to Iterator*, Erik Meijer:
   `http://csl.stanford.edu/~christos/pldi2010.fit/meijer.duality.pdf`

Asynchronous Programming and Networking

3

Several business applications need to react to external stimuli such as network traffic—asynchronously. An example of such software might be a desktop application that allows us to track a company's share prices on the stock market.

We will build this application using a more traditional approach. In doing so, we will be able to do the following:

- Identify and understand the drawbacks of the first design
- Learn how to use RxClojure to deal with stateful computations such as rolling averages
- Rewrite the example in a declarative fashion using observable sequences, thus reducing the complexity found in our first approach

Building a stock market monitoring application

Our stock market program will consist of three main components:

- A function simulating an external service from which we can query the current price—this would likely be a network call in a real setting
- A scheduler that polls the preceding function at a predefined interval
- A display function that's responsible for updating the screen

We'll start by creating a new Leiningen project, where the source code for our application will live. Type the following on the command line and then switch into the newly created directory:

```
lein new stock-market-monitor
cd stock-market-monitor
```

As we'll be building a GUI for this application, go ahead and add a dependency on seesaw to the dependencies section of your project.clj:

```
[seesaw "1.5.0"]
```

Next, create a src/stock_market_monitor/core.clj file in your favorite editor. Let's create and configure our application's UI components:

```
(ns stock-market-monitor.core
  (:require [seesaw.core :refer :all])
  (:import (java.util.concurrent ScheduledThreadPoolExecutor
                                 TimeUnit)))

(native!)

(def main-frame (frame :title "Stock price monitor"
                       :width 200 :height 100
                       :on-close :exit))

(def price-label      (label "Price: -"))

(config! main-frame :content price-label)
```

As you can see, the UI is fairly simple. It consists of a single label that will display a company's share price. We also imported two Java classes, ScheduledThreadPoolExecutor and TimeUnit, which we will use shortly.

The next thing we need is our polling machinery so that we can invoke the pricing service on a given schedule. We'll implement this via a thread pool so as not to block the main thread:

```
(def pool (atom nil))

(defn init-scheduler [num-threads]
  (reset! pool  (ScheduledThreadPoolExecutor. num-threads)))
(defn run-every [pool millis f]
  (.scheduleWithFixedDelay pool
                           f
                           0 millis TimeUnit/MILLISECONDS))
```

```
(defn shutdown [pool]
  (println "Shutting down scheduler...")
  (.shutdown pool))
```

User interface SDKs such as Swing have the concept of a main—or UI—thread. This is the thread that's used by the SDK to render the UI components to the screen. As such, if we have blocked, or even simply slow-running, operations executing in this thread, the user's experience will be severely affected, hence the use of a thread pool to offload expensive function calls.

The init-scheduler function creates ScheduledThreadPoolExecutor with the given number of threads. That's the thread pool in which our periodic function will run. The run-every function schedules a function, f, in the given pool to run at the interval specified by millis. Finally, shutdown is a function that will be called on program termination and thus will shut down the thread pool gracefully.

The rest of the program puts all of these parts together:

```
(defn share-price [company-code]
  (Thread/sleep 200)
  (rand-int 1000))


(defn -main [& args]
  (show! main-frame)
  (.addShutdownHook (Runtime/getRuntime)
                    (Thread. #(shutdown @pool)))
  (init-scheduler 1)
  (run-every @pool 500
             #(->> (str "Price: " (share-price "XYZ"))
                   (text! price-label)
                   invoke-now)))
```

The share-price function sleeps for 200 milliseconds to simulate network latency and returns a random integer between 0 and 1,000, representing the stock's price.

The second line of our -main function adds a shutdown hook to the runtime. This allows our program to intercept termination, such as pressing *Ctrl* + *C* in a Terminal window, and gives us the opportunity to shut down the thread pool.

The ScheduledThreadPoolExecutor pool creates non-daemon threads by default. A program cannot terminate if there are any non-daemon threads alive in addition to the program's main thread. This is why the shutdown hook is necessary.

Next, we initialize the scheduler with a single thread and schedule a function to be executed every 500 milliseconds. This function asks the `share-price` function for XYZ's current price and updates the label.

 Desktop applications require all rendering to be done in the UI thread. However, our periodic function runs on a separate thread and needs to update the price label. This is why we use `invoke-now`, which is a `seesaw` function that schedules its body to be executed in the UI thread as soon as possible.

Let's run the program by typing the following command in the project's `root` directory:

```
lein trampoline run -m stock-market-monitor.core
```

 Trampolining tells Leiningen not to nest our program's JVM within its own, thus freeing us to handle uses of *Ctrl + C* ourselves through shutdown hooks.

A window like the one shown in the following screenshot will be displayed, with the values on it being updated as per the schedule that we implemented earlier:

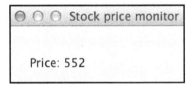

This is a fine solution. The code is relatively straightforward and satisfies our original requirements. However, if we look at the big picture, there is a fair bit of noise in our program. Most of its lines of code are dealing with creating and managing a thread pool, which, while necessary, isn't central to the problem we're solving—it's an implementation detail.

We'll keep things as they are for the moment and add a new requirement: rolling averages.

Rolling averages

Now that we can see the up-to-date stock price for a given company, it makes sense to display a rolling average of the past, say, five stock prices. In a real scenario, this would provide an objective view of a company's share trend on the stock market.

Let's extend our program to accommodate this new requirement.

First, we'll need to modify our namespace definition:

```
(ns stock-market-monitor.core
  (:require [seesaw.core :refer :all])
  (:import (java.util.concurrent ScheduledThreadPoolExecutor
                                 TimeUnit)
           (clojure.lang PersistentQueue)))
```

The only change is a new import clause for Clojure's `PersistentQueue` class. We will be using that later.

We'll also need a new label to display the current running average:

```
(def running-avg-label (label "Running average: -"))
(config! main-frame :content
           (border-panel
            :north  price-label
            :center running-avg-label
            :border 5))
```

Next, we need a function to calculate rolling averages. A rolling—or moving—average is a calculation in statistics where you take the average of a subset of items in a dataset. This subset has a fixed size and it shifts forward as data comes in. This will become clear with an example.

Suppose you have a list with numbers from 1 to 10, inclusive. If we use 3 as the subset size, the rolling averages are as follows:

```
[1 2 3 4 5 6 7 8 9 10] => 2.0
[1 2 3 4 5 6 7 8 9 10] => 3.0
[1 2 3 4 5 6 7 8 9 10] => 4.0
```

The highlighted parts in the preceding code show the current window is used to calculate the subset average.

Now that we know what rolling averages are, we can move on and implement them in our program:

```
(defn roll-buffer [buffer num buffer-size]
  (let [buffer (conj buffer num)]
    (if (> (count buffer) buffer-size)
      (pop buffer)
      buffer)))

(defn avg [numbers]
```

```
      (float (/ (reduce + numbers)
                (count numbers))))

  (defn make-running-avg [buffer-size]
    (let [buffer (atom clojure.lang.PersistentQueue/EMPTY)]
      (fn [n]
        (swap! buffer roll-buffer n buffer-size)
        (avg @buffer))))

  (def running-avg (make-running-avg 5))
```

The `roll-buffer` function is a utility function that takes a queue, a number, and a buffer size as arguments. It adds that number to the queue, popping the oldest element if the queue goes over the buffer limit, thus causing its contents to *roll* over.

Next, we have a function for calculating the average of a collection of numbers. We cast the result to float if there's an uneven division.

Finally, the higher-order `make-running-avg` function returns a stateful, single argument function that closes over an empty persistent queue. This queue is used to keep track of the current subset of data.

We then create an instance of this function by calling it with a buffer size of 5 and save it to the `running-avg` var. Each time we call this new function with a number, it will add it to the queue using the `roll-buffer` function and then finally return the average of the items in the queue.

The code we have written to manage the thread pool will be reused as is, so all that is left to do is update our periodic function:

```
(defn worker []
  (let [price (share-price "XYZ")]
    (->> (str "Price: " price) (text! price-label))
    (->> (str "Running average: " (running-avg price))
         (text! running-avg-label))))

(defn -main [& args]
  (show! main-frame)
  (.addShutdownHook (Runtime/getRuntime)
                    (Thread. #(shutdown @pool)))
  (init-scheduler 1)
  (run-every @pool 500
             #(invoke-now (worker))))
```

Since our function isn't a one-liner anymore, we abstract it away in its own function, called worker. As before, it updates the price label, but we have also extended it to use the running-avg function that we created earlier.

We're ready to run the program once more:

```
lein trampoline run -m stock-market-monitor.core
```

You should see a window like the one that's shown in the following screenshot:

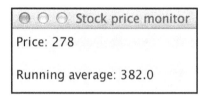

You should see that, in addition to displaying the current share price for XYZ, the program also keeps track and refreshes the running average of the stream of prices.

Identifying problems with our current approach

Aside from the lines of code responsible for building the user interface, our program is roughly 48 lines long.

The core of the program resides in the share-price and avg functions, which are responsible for querying the price service and calculating the average of a list of *n* numbers, respectively. They represent only six lines of code. There is a lot of *incidental complexity* in this small program.

Incidental complexity is complexity that's caused by code that is not essential to the problem at hand. In this example, we have two sources of such complexity: the thread pool and the rolling buffer function (we are disregarding UI-specific code for this discussion). They add a great deal of cognitive load to someone reading and maintaining the code.

The thread pool is external to our problem. It is only concerned with the semantics of how to run tasks asynchronously. The rolling buffer function specifies a detailed implementation of a queue and how to use it to represent the concept.

Ideally, we should be able to abstract over these details and focus on the core of our problem; **Compositional Event Systems** (CES) allow us to do just that.

Removing incidental complexity with RxClojure

In Chapter 2, *A Look at Reactive Extensions*, we learned about the basic building blocks of RxClojure, an open source CES framework. In this section, we'll use this knowledge to remove the incidental complexity from our program. This will give us a clear, declarative way to display both prices and rolling averages.

The UI code we've written so far remains unchanged, but we need to make sure that RxClojure is declared in the dependencies section of our project.clj file:

```
[io.reactivex/rxclojure "1.0.0"]
```

Then, we must ensure that we have the following library:

```
(ns stock-market-monitor.core
  (:require [rx.lang.clojure.core :as rx]
            [seesaw.core :refer :all])
  (:import (java.util.concurrent TimeUnit)
           (rx Observable)))
```

The way we will approach the problem this time is also different. Let's take a look at the first requirement: it requires that we display the current price of a company's share on the stock market.

Every time we query the price service, we get a possibly different price for the company in question. As we saw in Chapter 2, *A Look at Reactive Extensions*, modeling this as an observable sequence is easy, so we'll start with that. We'll create a function that gives us back a stock price observable for the given company:

```
(defn make-price-obs [company-code]
  (rx/return (share-price company-code)))
```

This is an observable that yields a single value and terminates. It's equivalent to the following marble diagram:

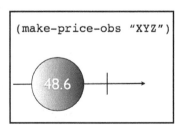

Part of the first requirement is that we query the service on a predefined time interval every 500 milliseconds, in this case. This hints at an observable we have encountered before, aptly named *interval*. To get the polling behavior we want, we need to combine the interval and the price observables.

As you probably recall, `flatmap` is the tool for the job here:

```
(rx/flatmap (fn [_] (make-price-obs "XYZ"))
            (Observable/interval 500 TimeUnit/MILLISECONDS))
```

The preceding snippet creates an observable that will yield the latest stock price for XYZ every 500 milliseconds indefinitely. It corresponds to the following diagram:

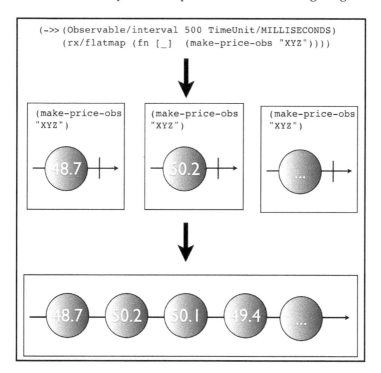

In fact, we can simply subscribe to this new observable and test it out. Modify your main function so that it looks like the following snippet and run the program:

```
(defn -main [& args]
  (show! main-frame)
  (let [price-obs (rx/flatmap (fn [_] (make-price-obs "XYZ"))
                              (Observable/interval 500
TimeUnit/MILLISECONDS))]
    (rx/subscribe price-obs
```

```
(fn [price]
  (text! price-label (str "Price: " price))))))
```

This is very cool! We replicated the behavior of our first program with only a few lines of code. The best part is that we did not have to worry about thread pools or scheduling actions. By thinking about the problem in terms of observable sequences, as well as combining existing and new observables, we were able to declaratively express what we want the program to do.

This already provides great benefits in maintainability and readability. However, we are still missing the other half of our program: rolling averages.

Observable rolling averages

It might not be immediately obvious how we can model rolling averages as observables. What we need to keep in mind is that pretty much anything we can think of as a sequence of values, we can probably model as an observable sequence.

Rolling averages are no different. Let's forget for a moment that the prices are coming from a network call wrapped in an observable. Let's imagine we have all of the values we care about in a Clojure vector:

```
(def values (range 10))
```

What we need is a way to process these values in partitions or buffers—of size 5—in such a way that only a single value is dropped at each interaction. In Clojure, we can use the `partition` function for this purpose:

```
(doseq [buffer (partition 5 1 values)]
  (prn buffer))

(0 1 2 3 4)
(1 2 3 4 5)
(2 3 4 5 6)
(3 4 5 6 7)
(4 5 6 7 8)
...
```

The second argument to the `partition` function is called a *step* and it is the offset of how many items should be skipped before starting a new partition. Here, we set it to 1 to create the sliding window effect we need.

The big question then is: can we somehow leverage `partition` when working with observable sequences?

It turns out that RxJava has a transformer called `buffer` just for this purpose. The previous example can be rewritten as follows:

```
(-> (rx/seq->o (vec (range 10)))
    (.buffer 5 1)
    (rx/subscribe
     (fn [price]
       (prn (str "Value: " price)))))
```

 As mentioned previously, not all of RxJava's API is exposed through RxClojure, so here, we need to use interop to access the `buffer` method from the observable sequence.

As before, the second argument to `buffer` is the offset, but it's called `skip` in the RxJava documentation. If you run this at the REPL, you'll see the following output:

```
"Value: [0, 1, 2, 3, 4]"
"Value: [1, 2, 3, 4, 5]"
"Value: [2, 3, 4, 5, 6]"
"Value: [3, 4, 5, 6, 7]"
"Value: [4, 5, 6, 7, 8]"
...
```

This is exactly what we want. The only difference is that the buffer method waits until it has enough elements—five, in this case—before proceeding.

Now, we can go back to our program and incorporate this idea with our main function. Here is what it looks like:

```
(defn -main [& args]
  (show! main-frame)
  (let [price-obs (-> (rx/flatmap make-price-obs
                                  (Observable/interval 500
  TimeUnit/MILLISECONDS))
                      (.publish))
        sliding-buffer-obs (.buffer price-obs 5 1)]
    (rx/subscribe price-obs
                  (fn [price]
                    (text! price-label (str "Price: " price))))
    (rx/subscribe sliding-buffer-obs
                  (fn [buffer]
                    (text! running-avg-label (str "Running average: " (avg
  buffer)))))
    (.connect price-obs)))
```

The preceding snippet works by creating two observables. The first one, `price-obs`, we created before. The new sliding buffer observable is created using the `buffer` transformer on `price-obs`.

Now, we can independently subscribe to each one in order to update the price and rolling average labels. Running the program will display the same screen we saw previously:

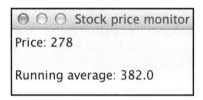

You might have noticed two method calls we hadn't seen before: `publish` and `connect`.

The `publish` method returns a connectable observable. This means that the observable won't start emitting values until its `connect` method has been called. We do this here because we want to make sure that all of the subscribers receive all of the values that were emitted by the original observable.

In conclusion, without much additional code, we implemented all of the requirements in a concise, declarative manner that is easy to maintain and follow. We have also made the previous roll-buffer function completely unnecessary.

The full source code for the CES version of the program is given here for reference:

```
(ns stock-market-monitor.05frp-price-monitor-rolling-avg
  (:require [rx.lang.clojure.core :as rx]
            [seesaw.core :refer :all])
  (:import (java.util.concurrent TimeUnit)
           (rx Observable)))

(native!)

(def main-frame (frame :title "Stock price monitor"
                       :width 200 :height 100
                       :on-close :exit))

(def price-label       (label "Price: -"))
(def running-avg-label (label "Running average: -"))

(config! main-frame :content
         (border-panel
           :north  price-label
           :center running-avg-label
```

```
                     :border 5))

(defn share-price [company-code]
  (Thread/sleep 200)
  (rand-int 1000))

(defn avg [numbers]
  (float (/ (reduce + numbers)
            (count numbers))))

(defn make-price-obs [_]
  (rx/return (share-price "XYZ")))

(defn -main [& args]
  (show! main-frame)
  (let [price-obs (-> (rx/flatmap make-price-obs
                                   (Observable/interval 500
TimeUnit/MILLISECONDS))
                       (.publish))
        sliding-buffer-obs (.buffer price-obs 5 1)]
    (rx/subscribe price-obs
                  (fn [price]
                    (text! price-label (str "Price: " price))))
    (rx/subscribe sliding-buffer-obs
                  (fn [buffer]
                    (text! running-avg-label (str "Running average: " (avg
buffer)))))
    (.connect price-obs)))
```

Note how, in this version of the program, we didn't have to use a shutdown hook. This is because RxClojure creates daemon threads, which are automatically terminated once the application exits.

Summary

In this chapter, we simulated a real-world application with our stock market program. We wrote it in a somewhat traditional way using thread pools and a custom queue implementation. We then refactored it into a CES style using RxClojure's observable sequences.

The resulting program is shorter, simpler, and easier to read once you get familiar with the core concepts of RxClojure and RxJava.

In the next chapter, we will be introduced to `core.async`, in preparation for implementing our own basic CES framework.

4
Introduction to core.async

Long gone are the days when programs were required to do only one thing at a time. Being able to perform several tasks concurrently is at the core of the vast majority of modern business applications. This is where asynchronous programming comes in.

Asynchronous programming and, more generally, concurrency is about doing more with your hardware resources than you previously could. It means fetching data from the network or a database connection without having to wait for the result or, perhaps, reading an Excel spreadsheet into memory while the user can still operate the graphical interface. In general, it improves a system's responsiveness.

In this chapter, we will look at how different platforms handle this style of programming. More specifically, we will cover the following topics:

- An introduction to the background of `core.async` and its API
- Solidifying our understanding of `core.async` by re-implementing the stock market application in terms of its abstractions
- Understanding how `core.async` deals with error handling and backpressure
- A brief tour of transducers

Asynchronous programming and concurrency

Different platforms have different programming models. For instance, JavaScript applications are single-threaded and have an event loop. When making a network call, it is common to register a callback that will be invoked at a later stage, when that network call completes either successfully or with an error.

In contrast, when we're on a JVM, we can take full advantage of multithreading to achieve concurrency. It is simple to spawn new threads via one of the many concurrency primitives provided by Clojure, such as futures.

However, asynchronous programming becomes cumbersome. Clojure futures don't provide a native way for us to be notified of their completion at a later stage. In addition, retrieving values from a not-yet-completed `future` is a blocking operation. This can be seen clearly in the following snippet:

```
(defn do-something-important []
  (let [f (future (do (prn "Calculating...")
                      (Thread/sleep 10000)))]
    (prn "Perhaps the future has done its job?")
    (prn @f)
    (prn "You will only see this in about 10 seconds..."))))

(do-something-important)
```

The second call to print dereferences `future`, causing the main thread to block since it hasn't finished yet. This is why you only see that the last print after the thread in which `future` is running has finished. Callbacks can, of course, be simulated by spawning a separate thread to monitor the first one, but this solution is clunky at best.

An exception to the lack of callbacks is GUI programming in Clojure. Much like JavaScript, Clojure Swing applications also possess an event loop and can respond to user input and invoke listeners (callbacks) to handle them.

Another option is rewriting the previous example with a custom callback that is passed into `future`:

```
(defn do-something-important [callback]
  (let [f (future (let [answer 42]
                    (Thread/sleep 10000)
                    (callback answer)))]
    (prn "Perhaps the future has done its job?")
    (prn "You should see this almost immediately and then in 10 secs...")
    f))

(do-something-important (fn [answer]
                          (prn "Future is done. Answer is " answer)))
```

This time, the order of the outputs should make more sense. However, if we return `future` from this function, we have no way to give it another callback. We have lost the ability to perform an action when `future` ends and are back to having to dereference it, thus blocking the main thread again—exactly what we wanted to avoid.

Java 8 introduced a new class, `CompletableFuture`, which allows registering a callback to be invoked once `future` completes. If that's an option for you, you can use interop to make Clojure leverage the new class.

As you might have realized, CES is closely related to asynchronous programming: the stock market application we built in the previous chapter is an example of such a program. The main—or UI—thread is never blocked by the observables fetching data from the network. Additionally, we were also able to register callbacks when subscribing to them.

In many asynchronous applications, however, callbacks are not the best way to go. Heavy use of callbacks can lead to what is known as callback hell. Clojure provides a more powerful and elegant solution.

In the next few sections, we will explore `core.async`, a Clojure library for asynchronous programming, and how it relates to Reactive Programming.

The core.async library

If you've ever done any amount of JavaScript programming, you have probably experienced callback hell. If you haven't, the following code should give you a good idea about what it is:

```
http.get('api/users/find?name=' + name, function(user){
  http.get('api/orders?userId=' + user.id, function(orders){
    orders.forEach(function(order){
      container.append(order);
    });
  });
});
```

This style of programming can easily get out of hand. Instead of writing more natural, sequential steps to achieve a task, that logic is instead scattered across multiple callbacks, increasing the developer's cognitive load.

In response to this, the JavaScript community released several promises libraries that are meant to solve this issue. We can think of promises as empty boxes we can pass into and return from our functions. At some point in future, another process might put a value inside this box.

As an example, the preceding snippet can be written with promises, like so:

```
http.get('api/users/find?name=' + name)
  .then(function(user){
    return http.get('api/orders?userId=' + user.id);
  })
  .then(function(orders){
    orders.forEach(function(order){
      container.append(order);
    });
  });
```

The preceding snippet shows how using promises can flatten your callback pyramid, but they don't eliminate callbacks. The `then` function is a public function of the promises API. It is definitely a step in the right direction, as the code is composable and easier to read.

As we tend to think in sequences of steps, however, we would like to write the following:

```
user   = http.get('api/users/find?name=' + name);
orders = http.get('api/orders?userId=' + user.id);
orders.forEach(function(order){
  container.append(order);
});
```

Even though the code looks synchronous, the behavior should be no different from the previous examples. This is exactly what `core.async` lets us do in both Clojure and ClojureScript.

The Communicating Sequential Processes paper

The `core.async` library is built on an old idea. The foundation upon which it lies was first described by Tony Hoare of Quicksort fame in his 1978 paper *Communicating Sequential Processes (CSP)*[1]. CSP has since been extended and implemented in several languages, the latest of which being Google's **Go** programming language[2].

It is beyond the scope of this book to go into the details of this seminal paper, so what follows is a simplified description of the main ideas.

In CSP, work is modeled using two main abstractions: channels and processes. CSP is also message-driven and, as such, it completely decouples the producer from the consumer of the message. It is useful to think of channels as blocking queues.

A simplistic approach that demonstrates these basic abstractions is as follows:

```
(import 'java.util.concurrent.ArrayBlockingQueue)

(defn producer [c]
  (prn "Taking a nap")
  (Thread/sleep 5000)
  (prn "Now putting a name in queue...")
  (.put c "Leo"))

(defn consumer [c]
  (prn "Attempting to take value from queue now...")
  (prn (str "Got it. Hello " (.take c) "!")))

(def chan (ArrayBlockingQueue. 10))

(future (consumer chan))
(future (producer chan))
```

Running this code in the REPL should show us an output similar to the following:

```
"Attempting to take value from queue now..."
"Taking a nap"
;; then 5 seconds later
"Now putting a name in queue..."
"Got it. Hello Leo!"
```

So that we don't block our program, we start both the consumer and the producer in their own threads, using `future`. Since the consumer was started first, we will most likely see its output immediately. However, as soon as it attempts to take a value from the channel—or queue—it will block. It will wait for a value to become available and will only proceed after the producer is done taking its nap—clearly a very important task.

Now, let's compare it with a solution by using `core.async`. First, create a new Leiningen project and add a dependency to it:

```
[org.clojure/core.async "0.4.474"]
```

Now, type the following into the REPL or in your core namespace:

```
(ns core-async-playground.core
  (:require [clojure.core.async :refer [go chan <! >! timeout <!!]]))

(defn prn-with-thread-id [s]
  (prn (str s " - Thread id: " (.getId (Thread/currentThread)))))

(defn producer [c]
```

```
    (go (prn-with-thread-id "Taking a nap ")
        (<! (timeout 5000))
        (prn-with-thread-id "Now putting a name in que queue...")
        (>! c "Leo"))))

(defn consumer [c]
  (go (prn-with-thread-id "Attempting to take value from queue now...")
      (prn-with-thread-id (str "Got it. Hello " (<! c) "!")))))

(def c (chan))

(consumer c)
(producer c)
```

This time, we are using a helper function, `prn-with-thread-id`, which appends the current thread ID to the output string. I will explain why shortly, but apart from that, the output will be equivalent to the previous one:

```
"Attempting to take value from queue now... - Thread id: 43"
"Taking a nap  - Thread id: 44"
"Now putting a name in que queue... - Thread id: 48"
"Got it. Hello Leo! - Thread id: 48"
```

Structurally, both solutions look fairly similar, but since we are using quite a few new functions here, let's break it down:

- `chan` is a function that creates a `core.async` channel. As mentioned previously, it can be thought of as a concurrent blocking queue and is the main abstraction in the library. By default, `chan` creates an unbuffered channel, but `core.async` provides many more useful channel constructors, a few of which we'll be using later.
- `timeout` is another such channel constructor. It gives us a *channel* that will *wait* for a given amount of time before returning nil to the taking process, closing itself immediately afterward. This is the `core.async` equivalent of **thread/sleep**.
- The `>!` and `<!` functions are used to put and take values from a channel, respectively. The caveat is that they have to be used inside a `go` block, as we will explain later.

- `go` is a macro that takes a body of expressions—that form a `go` block—and creates lightweight processes. This is where the magic happens. Inside a `go` block, any calls to `>!` and `<!` that would ordinarily block, waiting for values to be available in channels, are instead parked. Parking is a special type of blocking that's used internally in the state machine of `core.async`. A blog post by Huey Petersen covers this state machine in depth (see `http://hueypetersen.com/posts/2013/08/02/the-state-machines-of-core-async/`).

The `go` blocks are the very reason I chose to print the thread IDs in our example. If we look closely, we'll realize that the last two statements were executed in the same thread. However, this isn't true 100% of the time, as concurrency is inherently non-deterministic. This is the fundamental difference between `core.async` and solutions that are using threads/futures.

Threads can be expensive. On the JVM, their default stack size is 512 kilobytes, which can be configured via the `-Xss` JVM startup option. When developing a highly concurrent system, creating thousands of threads can quickly drain the resources of the machine the application is running on.

`core.async` acknowledges this limitation and gives us lightweight processes. Internally, they do share a thread pool, but instead of wastefully creating a thread per go block, threads are recycled and reused when a put/take operation is waiting for a value to become available.

> At the time of writing, the thread pool used by `core.async` defaults to the number of available processors x 2, + 42. So, a machine with eight processors will have a pool with 58 threads.

Therefore, it is common for `core.async` applications to have dozens of thousands of lightweight processes. They are extremely cheap to create.

Since this is a book on Reactive Programming, the question that might be in your head now is: can we build reactive applications using `core.async`? The short answer is yes, we can! To prove it, we will revisit our stock market application and rewrite it using `core.async`.

Rewriting the stock market application with core.async

By using an example we are familiar with, we are able to focus on the differences between all of the approaches we have discussed so far, without getting sidetracked with new, specific domain rules.

Before we dive into the implementation, let's quickly get an overview of how our solution should work.

Just as in our previous implementations, we have a service from which we can query share prices. Where our approach differs, however, is a direct consequence of how core.async channels work.

On a given schedule, we would like to write the current price to a core.async channel. This might appear as follows:

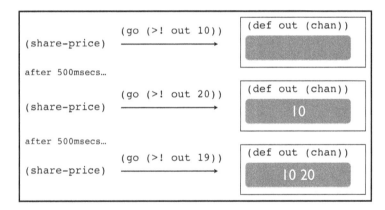

This process will continuously put prices in the out channel. We need to do two things with each price: display it and display the calculated sliding window. Since we like our functions to be decoupled, we will use two go blocks—one for each task:

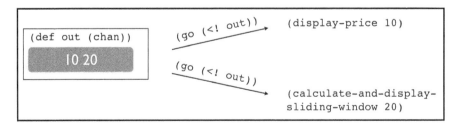

Hold on. There seems to be something off with our approach. Once we take a price from the output channel, it is not available to be taken by other go blocks any longer. So, instead of calculating the sliding window starting with 10, our function ends up getting the second value, 20. With this approach, we will end up with a sliding window that calculates a sliding window with roughly every other item, depending on how consistent the interleaving between the go blocks is.

Clearly, this is not what we want, but it helps us think about the problem a little more. The semantics of core.async prevent us from reading a value from a channel more than once. Most of the time, this behavior is just fine, especially if you think of them as queues. So, how can we provide the same value to both functions?

To solve this problem, we will take advantage of another channel constructor provided by core.async, called broadcast. As the name implies, broadcast returns a channel, which, when written to, writes its value into the channels passed to it as arguments. Effectively, this changes our high-level picture to something like the following:

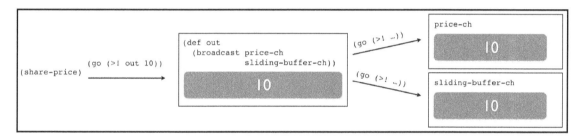

In summary, we will have a go loop writing prices to this broadcast channel, which will then forward its values to the two channels from which we will be operating: prices and the sliding window.

With this general idea in place, we are ready to dive into the code.

Implementing the application code

We already have a project depending on core.async, which we created in the previous section, so we'll be working off that. Let's start by adding an extra dependency on seesaw to our project.clj file:

```
:dependencies [[org.clojure/clojure "1.9.0"]
               [org.clojure/core.async "0.4.474"]
               [seesaw "1.5.0"]]
```

Next, we need to create a file called `stock_market.clj` in the `src` directory and add the following namespace declaration:

```
(ns core-async-playground.stock-market
  (:require [clojure.core.async
             :refer [go chan <! >! timeout go-loop map>] :as async])
  (:require [clojure.core.async.lab :refer [broadcast]])
  (:use [seesaw.core]))
```

This might be a good point to restart your REPL if you haven't done so. Don't worry about any functions we haven't seen yet. We'll get a feel for them in this section.

The GUI code remains largely unchanged, so no explanation should be necessary for the following snippet:

```
(native!)

(def main-frame (frame :title "Stock price monitor"
                       :width 200 :height 100
                       :on-close :exit))

(def price-label       (label "Price: -"))
(def running-avg-label (label "Running average (5): -"))

(config! main-frame :content
         (border-panel
          :north  price-label
          :center running-avg-label
          :border 5))

(defn share-price [company-code]
  (Thread/sleep 200)
  (rand-int 1000))

(defn avg [numbers]
  (float (/ (reduce + numbers)
            (count numbers))))

(defn roll-buffer [buffer val buffer-size]
  (let [buffer (conj buffer val)]
    (if (> (count buffer) buffer-size)
      (pop buffer)
      buffer)))
```

```
(defn make-sliding-buffer [buffer-size]
  (let [buffer (atom clojure.lang.PersistentQueue/EMPTY)]
    (fn [n]
      (swap! buffer roll-buffer n buffer-size))))

(def sliding-buffer (make-sliding-buffer 5))
```

The only difference is that we now have a `sliding-buffer` function that returns a window of data. This is in contrast to our original application, where the `rolling-avg` function was responsible for both creating the window and calculating the average. This new design is more general, as it makes this function easier to reuse. The sliding logic is the same, however.

Next, we have our main application logic by using `core.async`:

```
(defn broadcast-at-interval [msecs task & ports]
  (go-loop [out (apply broadcast ports)]
    (<! (timeout msecs))
    (>! out (task))
    (recur out)))

(defn -main [& args]
  (show! main-frame)
  (let [prices-ch        (chan)
        sliding-buffer-ch (map> sliding-buffer (chan))]
    (broadcast-at-interval 500 #(share-price "XYZ") prices-ch sliding-
buffer-ch)
    (go-loop []
      (when-let [price (<! prices-ch)]
        (text! price-label (str "Price: " price))
        (recur)))
    (go-loop []
      (when-let [buffer (<! sliding-buffer-ch)]
        (text! running-avg-label (str "Running average: " (avg buffer)))
        (recur)))))
```

Let's walk through the code.

The first function, `broadcast-at-interval`, is responsible for creating the broadcasting channel. It receives a variable number of arguments: a number of milliseconds describing the interval, the function representing the task to be executed, and a sequence of one or more output channels. These channels are used to create the broadcasting channel to which the go loop will be writing prices.

Next, we have our main function. The `let` block is where the interesting bits are. As we discussed in our high-level diagrams, we need two output channels: one for prices and one for the sliding window. They are both created in the following code:

```
...
  (let [prices-ch         (chan)
        sliding-buffer-ch (map> sliding-buffer (chan))]
...
```

`prices-ch` should be self-explanatory; however, `sliding-buffer-ch` is using a function we haven't encountered before: `map>`. This is yet another useful channel constructor in `core.async`. It takes two arguments: a function and a target channel. It returns a channel that applies this function to each value before writing it to the target channel. An example will help illustrate how it works:

```
(def c (map> sliding-buffer (chan 10)))
(go (doseq [n (range 10)]
      (>! c n)))
(go (doseq [n (range 10)]
      (prn  (vec (<! c)))))
;; [0]
;; [0 1]
;; [0 1 2]
;; [0 1 2 3]
;; [0 1 2 3 4]
;; [1 2 3 4 5]
;; [2 3 4 5 6]
;; [3 4 5 6 7]
;; [4 5 6 7 8]
;; [5 6 7 8 9]
```

That is, we write a price to the channel and get a sliding window on the other end. Finally, we create the two go blocks containing the side effects. They loop indefinitely, getting values from both channels and updating the user interface.

You can see it in action by running the program from the Terminal:

```
$ lein run -m core-async-playground.stock-market
```

Error handling

Back in `Chapter 2`, *A Look at Reactive Extensions*, we learned how Reactive Extensions treats errors and exceptions. It provides a rich set of combinators to deal with exceptional cases and is straightforward to use.

Despite being a pleasure to work with, `core.async` doesn't ship with much support for exception handling. In fact, if we write our code with only the happy path in mind, we don't even know an error occurred!

Let's have a look at an example:

```
(defn get-data []
  (throw (Exception. "Bad things happen!")))

(defn process []
  (let [result (chan)]
    ;; do some processing...
    (go (>! result (get-data)))
    result))
```

In the preceding snippet, we introduced two functions:

- `get-data` simulates a function that fetches data from the network or an in-memory cache. In this case, it simply throws an exception.
- `process` is a function that depends on `get-data` to do something interesting and puts the result into a channel, which is returned at the end.

Let's watch what happens when we put this together:

```
(go (let [result  (<! (->> (process)
                           (map> #(* % %))
                           (map> #(prn %))))]
      (prn "result is: " result)))
```

Nothing happens. Zero, zip, zilch, nada.

This is precisely the problem with error handling in `core.async`: by default, our exceptions are swallowed by the go block as it runs on a separate thread. We are left in this state where we don't really know what happened.

Not all is lost, however. David Nolen outlined a pattern for dealing with such asynchronous exceptions on his blog[3]. It only requires a few extra lines of code.

We start by defining a helper function and macro—this would probably live in a utility namespace that we would require anywhere we use `core.async`:

```
(defn throw-err [e]
  (when (instance? Throwable e) (throw e))
  e)
```

```
(defmacro <? [ch]
  `(throw-err (async/<! ~ch)))
```

The `throw-err` function receives a value and, if it's a subclass of `Throwable`, it is thrown. Otherwise, it is simply returned.

The macro `<?` is essentially a drop-in replacement for `<!`. In fact, it uses `<!` to get the value out of the channel, but passes it to `throw-err` first.

With these utilities in place, we need to make a couple of changes. First, we are going to make some changes to our `process` function:

```
(defn process []
  (let [result (chan)]
    ;; do some processing...
    (go (>! result (try (get-data)
                        (catch Exception e
                          e))))
    result))
```

The only change is that we wrapped `get-data` in a `try/catch` block. Look closely at the `catch` block: it simply returns the exception.

This is important, as we need to ensure that the exception gets put into the channel.

Next, we update our consumer code:

```
(go (try (let [result  (<? (->> (process)
                                (map> #(* % %))
                                (map> #(prn %))))]
           (prn "result is: " result))
         (catch Exception e
           (prn "Oops, an error happened! We better do something about
 it here!"))))
    ;; "Oops, an error happened! We better do something about it here!"
```

This time, we use `<?` in place of `<!`. This makes sense, as it will rethrow any exceptions found in the channel. As a result, we can now use a simple `try/catch` block to regain control over our exceptions.

Backpressure

The main mechanism by which core.async allows for coordinating backpressure is buffering. core.async doesn't allow unbounded buffers as this can be a source of bugs and a resource hog.

Instead, we are required to think hard about our application's unique needs and choose an appropriate buffering strategy.

Fixed buffer

This is the simplest form of buffering. It is fixed to a chosen number, n, allowing producers to put items in the channel without having to wait for consumers:

```
(def result (chan (async/buffer 5)))
(go-loop []
  (<! (async/timeout 1000))
  (when-let [x (<! result)]
    (prn "Got value: " x)
    (recur)))
(go  (doseq [n (range 5)]
       (>! result n))
     (prn "Done putting values!")
     (async/close! result))
;; "Done putting values!"
;; "Got value: " 0
;; "Got value: " 1
;; "Got value: " 2
;; "Got value: " 3
;; "Got value: " 4
```

In the preceding example, we created a buffer of size 5 and started a go loop to consume values from it. The go loop uses a timeout channel to delay each loop cycle.

Then, we started another go block that puts numbers from 0 to 4 into the result channel and prints to the console once it's done.

By then, the first timeout will have expired and we will see the values printed to the REPL.

Now, let's watch what happens if the buffer isn't large enough:

```
(def result (chan (async/buffer 2)))
(go-loop []
  (<! (async/timeout 1000))
  (when-let [x (<! result)]
```

```
      (prn "Got value: " x)
      (recur)))
(go  (doseq [n (range 5)]
        (>! result n))
     (prn "Done putting values!")
     (async/close! result))
;; "Got value: " 0
;; "Got value: " 1
;; "Got value: " 2
;; "Done putting values!"
;; "Got value: " 3
;; "Got value: " 4
```

This time, our buffer size is 2, but everything else is the same. As you can see, the go loop finishes much later, as it attempted to put another value in the result channel and was blocked/parked, since its buffer was full.

As with most things, this might be OK, but if we are not willing to block a fast producer just because we can't consume its items fast enough, we must look for another option.

Dropping buffer

A dropping buffer also has a fixed size. However, instead of blocking producers when it is full, it simply ignores any new items, as shown here:

```
(def result (chan (async/dropping-buffer 2)))
(go-loop []
  (<! (async/timeout 1000))
  (when-let [x (<! result)]
    (prn "Got value: " x)
    (recur)))
(go  (doseq [n (range 5)]
        (>! result n))
     (prn "Done putting values!")
     (async/close! result))
;; "Done putting values!"
;; "Got value: " 0
;; "Got value: " 1
```

As before, we still have a buffer of size two, but this time, the producer ends quickly without ever getting blocked. The dropping-buffer simply ignored all items over its limit.

Sliding buffer

A drawback of dropping buffers is that we might not be processing the latest items at a given time. For the times where processing the latest information is a must, we can use a sliding buffer:

```
(def result (chan (async/sliding-buffer 2)))
(go-loop []
  (<! (async/timeout 1000))
  (when-let [x (<! result)]
    (prn "Got value: " x)
    (recur)))
(go  (doseq [n (range 5)]
       (>! result n))
     (prn "Done putting values!")
     (async/close! result))
;; "Done putting values!"
;; "Got value: " 3
;; "Got value: " 4
```

As before, we only get two values, but they are the latest ones that have been produced by the go loop.

When the limit of the sliding buffer is overrun, core.async drops the oldest items to make room for the newest ones. I end up using this buffering strategy most of the time.

Transducers

Before we finish up with our core.async portion of this book, we should mention what came up in Clojure 1.7, as well as how this affects core.async.

One of the big changes in this release was the introduction of transducers. We will not cover the nuts and bolts of it here, but rather focus on what it means at a high-level with examples using both Clojure sequences and core.async channels.

If you would like to know more, I recommend Carin Meier's *Green Eggs and Transducers* blog post[4]. It's a great place to start.

Additionally, the official Clojure documentation site on the subject is another useful resource[5].

Let's get started by creating a new Leiningen project:

```
$ lein new core-async-transducers
```

Now, open your `project.clj` file and make sure you have the right dependencies:

```
...
   :dependencies [[org.clojure/clojure "1.9.0"]
                  [org.clojure/core.async "0.4.474"]]
...
```

Next, fire up a REPL session in the project root and require `core.async`, which we will be using shortly:

```
$ lein repl
user> (require '[clojure.core.async :refer [go chan map< filter< into
>! <! go-loop close! pipe] :as async])
```

We will start with a familiar example:

```
(->> (range 10)
     (map inc)            ;; creates a new sequence
     (filter even?)       ;; creates a new sequence
     (prn "result is "))
;; "result is " (2 4 6 8 10)
```

The preceding snippet is straightforward and highlights an interesting property of what happens when we apply combinators to Clojure sequences: each combinator creates an intermediate sequence.

In the previous example, we ended up with three in total: the one created by `range`, the one created by `map`, and finally, the one created by `filter`. Most of the time, this won't really be an issue, but for large sequences, this means a lot of unnecessary allocation.

Starting in Clojure 1.7, the previous example can be written like so:

```
(def xform
  (comp (map inc)
        (filter even?)))   ;; no intermediate sequence created
(->> (range 10)
     (sequence xform)
     (prn "result is "))
;; "result is " (2 4 6 8 10)
```

The Clojure documentation describes transducers as composable algorithmic transformations. Let's see why that is.

In the new version, a whole range of the core sequence combinators, such as `map` and `filter`, have gained extra arity: if you don't pass it a collection, it instead returns a transducer.

In the previous example, `(map inc)` returns a transducer that knows how to apply the `inc` function to elements of a sequence. Similarly, `(filter even?)` returns a transducer that will eventually filter elements of a sequence. Neither of them do anything yet—they simply return functions.

This is interesting because transducers are composable. We can build larger and more complex transducers by using simple function composition:

```
(def xform
  (comp (map inc)
        (filter even?)))
```

Once we have our transducer ready, we can apply it to a collection in a few different ways. For this example, we chose `sequence`, as it will return a lazy sequence of the applications of the given transducer to the input sequence:

```
(->> (range 10)
     (sequence xform)
     (prn "result is "))
;; "result is " (2 4 6 8 10)
```

As we highlighted previously, this code does not create intermediate sequences; transducers extract the very core of the algorithmic transformation at hand and abstract it away from having to deal with sequences directly.

Transducers and core.async

Now, we might be asking ourselves, *What do transducers have to do with* `core.async`?

It turns out that once we're able to extract the core of these transformations and put them together using simple function composition, there is nothing stopping us from using transducers with data structures other than sequences!

Let's revisit our first example using standard `core.async` functions:

```
(def result (chan 10))

(def transformed
  (->> result
       (map< inc)        ;; creates a new channel
       (filter< even?)   ;; creates a new channel
       (into [])))

(go
```

```
    (prn "result is " (<! transformed)))

(go
  (doseq [n (range 10)]
    (>! result n))
  (close! result))

;; "result is " [2 4 6 8 10]
```

This code should look familiar by now: it's the `core.async` equivalent of the sequence-only version that was shown earlier. As before, we have unnecessary allocations here as well, except that this time we're allocating channels.

With the new support for transducers, `core.async` can take advantage of the same transformation that we defined earlier:

```
(def result (chan 10))

(def xform
    (comp (map inc)
          (filter even?)))  ;; no intermediate channels created

(def transformed (->> (pipe result (chan 10 xform))
                      (into [])))

(go
 (prn "result is " (<! transformed)))

(go
 (doseq [n (range 10)]
  (>! result n))
 (close! result))

;; "result is " [2 4 6 8 10]
```

The code remains largely unchanged, except we now use the same `xform` transformation defined earlier when creating a new channel. It's important to note that we did not have to use `core.async` combinators—in fact, a lot of these combinators have been deprecated and will be removed in future versions of `core.async`.

The `map` and `filter` functions that are used to define `xform` are the same ones we used previously, that is, they are core Clojure functions.

This is the next big advantage of using transducers: by removing the underlying data structure from the equation via transducers, libraries such as `core.async` can reuse Clojure's core combinators to prevent unnecessary allocation and code duplication.

It's not too far-fetched to imagine that other frameworks, such as RxClojure, could take advantage of transducers as well. All of them would be able to use the same core function across substantially different data structures and contexts: sequences, channels, and observables.

> The concept of extracting the essence of computations, disregarding their underlying data structures, is an exciting topic and has been seen before in the Haskell Community, although they deal with lists specifically[6].
>
> Two papers worth mentioning on the subject are *Stream Fusion* by Duncan Coutts, Roman Leshchinskiy, and Don Stewart[7], and *Transforming programs to eliminate trees* by Philip Wadler[8]. There are some overlaps, so the reader might find these interesting.

Summary

By now, I hope I have proved to you that you can write reactive applications using `core.async`. It's an extremely powerful and flexible concurrency model with a rich API. If you can design your solution in terms of queues, it is more than likely that `core.async` is the tool you want to reach for.

This version of the stock market application is shorter and simpler than the version that uses only the standard Java API we developed earlier in this book in Chapter 3, *Asynchronous Programming and Networking*. For instance, we didn't have to worry about thread pools. On the other hand, it feels like it is a little more complex than the version we implemented using Reactive Extensions in Chapter 3, *Asynchronous Programming and Networking*.

This is because `core.async` operates at a lower level of abstraction when compared to other frameworks. This became especially obvious in our application, as we had to worry about creating broadcasting channels, go loops, and so on—all of which can be considered incidental complexity, and not directly related to the problem at hand.

`core.async` does, however, provide an excellent foundation for building our own CES abstractions. This is what we will be exploring in the next chapter, when we create our own framework using `core.async` as a foundation.

Further reading

Here is a list of information you may refer to regarding what was covered in this chapter:

1. *Communicating Sequential Processes*, Tony Hoare: `http://www.cs.ucf.edu/courses/cop4020/sum2009/CSP-hoare.pdf`

2. The Go Programming Language: `https://golang.org/`

3. *Asynchronous Error Handling*, David Nolen: `http://swannodette.github.io/2013/08/31/asynchronous-error-handling`

4. *Green Eggs and Transducers*, Carin Meier: `http://gigasquidsoftware.com/blog/2014/09/06/green-eggs-and-transducers/`

5. Transducers, Clojure: `https://clojure.org/reference/transducers`

6. The Haskel programming language: `https://www.haskell.org/`

7. *Stream Fusion*, Duncan Coutts, Roman Leshchinskiy, and Don Stewart: `https://www.cs.tufts.edu/~nr/cs257/archive/duncan-coutts/stream-fusion.pdf`

8. *Transforming programs to eliminate trees*, Philip Wadler: `http://homepages.inf.ed.ac.uk/wadler/papers/deforest/deforest.ps`

5
Creating Your Own CES Framework with core.async

In the previous chapter, it was alluded to that `core.async` operates at a lower level of abstraction when compared to other frameworks, such as RxClojure or RxJava. This is because, most of the time, we have to think carefully about the channels we are creating, as well as what types and sizes of buffers to use, whether we need pub/sub functionality, and so on.

Not all applications require such level of control, however. Now that we are familiar with the motivations and main abstractions of `core.async`, we can embark on writing a minimal CES framework, using `core.async` as the underlying foundation.

By doing so, we avoid having to think about thread pool management, as the framework takes care of that for us.

In this chapter, we will cover the following topics:

- Building a CES framework using `core.async` as its underlying concurrency strategy
- Building an application that uses our CES framework
- Understanding the trade-offs in terms of the different approaches that have been presented so far

A minimal CES framework

Before we get started on the details, we should define what *minimal* means.

Let's start with the two main abstractions our framework will provide: behaviors and event streams.

If you can recall from `Chapter 1`, *What is Reactive Programming?*, behaviors represent continuous, time-varying values such as time or mouse position behavior. Event streams, on the other hand, represent discrete occurrences at a point in time, *T*, such as a key press.

Next, we should think about what kinds of operations we would like to support. Behaviors are fairly simple, so at the very least we need to do the following:

1. Create new behaviors
2. Retrieve the current value of a behavior
3. Convert a behavior into an event stream

Event streams have more interesting logic at play and we should at least support these operations:

- Push/deliver a value down the stream
- Create a stream from a given interval
- Transform the stream with the `map` and `filter` operations
- Combine streams with `flatmap`
- Subscribe to a stream

This is a small subset, but big enough to demonstrate the overall architecture of a CES framework. Once we're done, we'll use it to build a simple example.

Clojure or ClojureScript?

Here, we'll shift gears and add another requirement to our little library: it should work both in Clojure and ClojureScript. At first, this might sound like a tough requirement. However, remember that `core.async`—the foundation of our framework—works both on the JVM and in JavaScript. This means that we have a lot less work to do to make it happen.

Clojure 1.7 introduced reader conditionals, which allow us to write portable `.cljc` files that can be loaded by multiple Clojure platforms[1]. `.cljc` allows us to write code that is portable between Clojure and ClojureScript by placing annotations that its preprocessor can understand[2].

Let's get started by creating a new Leiningen project. We'll call our framework respondent—one of the many synonyms for the word reactive:

```
$ lein new respondent
```

We need to make a few changes to the `project.clj` file so that it includes the dependencies and configurations we'll be using. First, make sure that the project dependencies look like the following:

```
:dependencies [[org.clojure/clojure "1.9.0"]
               [org.clojure/core.async "0.4.474"]
               [org.clojure/clojurescript "1.10.339"]]
```

Go ahead and delete the following files, which were created by the Leiningen template, as we won't be using them:

```
$ rm src/respondent/core.clj
$ rm test/respondent/core_test.clj
```

Then, create a new `core.cljc` file under `src/respondent/` and add the following namespace declaration:

```
(ns respondent.core
  (:refer-clojure :exclude [filter map deliver])
  #?@(:clj [(:import [clojure.lang IDeref])
            (:require [clojure.core.async :as async
                       :refer [go go-loop chan <! >! timeout
                               map> filter> close! mult tap untap]])]
      :cljs [(:require [cljs.core.async :as async
                        :refer [chan <! >! timeout map> filter>
                                close! mult tap untap]])
             (:require-macros [cljs.core.async.macros :refer
                               [go go-loop]])]))
```

Here, we start seeing `cljc` annotations. `cljc` is simply a text preprocessor, so when it is processing a file using `clj` rules, it will keep the `s-expressions` preceded by the `:clj` annotation in the output file, while removing the ones prefixed by `:cljs`. The reverse process happens when using `cljs` rules.

This is necessary because macros need to be compiled on the JVM, so they have to be included separately using the `:require-macros` namespace option when using ClojureScript. Don't worry about the `core.async` functions we haven't encountered before; they will be explained as we use them to build our framework.

Also, note how we are excluding functions from the Clojure standard API, as we wish to use the same names and don't want any undesired naming collisions.

This section has set us up with a new project and the configurations that are needed for our framework. Now, we're ready to start implementing it.

Designing the public API

One of the requirements for behaviors that we agreed on is the ability to turn a given behavior into an event stream. A common way of doing this is by sampling a behavior at a specific interval. If we take the *mouse position* behavior as an example, by sampling it every x seconds we get an event stream, which will emit the current mouse position at discrete points in time.

This leads to the following protocol:

```
(defprotocol IBehavior
  (sample [b interval]
    "Turns this Behavior into an EventStream from the sampled values at the
given interval"))
```

It has a single function, `sample`, which we described in the preceding code. There are more things that we need to do with behavior, but for now, this will suffice.

Our next main abstraction is `EventStream`, which, based on the requirements we saw previously, leads to the following protocol:

```
(defprotocol IEventStream
  (map       [s f]
    "Returns a new stream containing the result of applying f
    to the values in s")
  (filter    [s pred]
    "Returns a new stream containing the items from s
    for which pred returns true")
  (flatmap   [s f]
    "Takes a function f from values in s to a new EventStream.
    Returns an EventStream containing values from all underlying streams
combined.")
  (deliver   [s value]
    "Delivers a value to the stream s")
  (completed? [s]
    "Returns true if this stream has stopped emitting values. False
otherwise."))
```

This gives us a few basic functions so that we can transform and query an event stream. It does leave out the ability to subscribe to a stream. Don't worry—I didn't forget it!

Although it is common to subscribe to an event stream, the protocol itself doesn't mandate it, and this is because the operation fits best in its own protocol:

```
(defprotocol IObservable
  (subscribe [obs f] "Register a callback to be invoked when the underlying
source changes.
   Returns a token the subscriber can use to cancel the subscription."))
```

As far as subscriptions go, it is useful to have a way of unsubscribing from a stream. This can be implemented in a couple of ways, but the docstring of the preceding function hints at a specific one: a token that can be used to unsubscribe from a stream. This leads to our last protocol:

```
(defprotocol IToken
  (dispose [tk]
    "Called when the subscriber isn't interested in receiving more items"))
```

Implementing tokens

The token type is the simplest in the whole framework, as it has got a single function with a straightforward implementation:

```
(deftype Token [ch]
  IToken
  (dispose [_]
    (close! ch)))
```

It simply closes whatever channel it is given, stopping events from flowing through subscriptions.

Implementing event streams

The event stream implementation, on the other hand, is the most complex in our framework. We'll tackle it gradually, implementing it and experimenting as we go.

First, let's look at our main constructor function, event-stream:

```
(defn event-stream
  "Creates and returns a new event stream. You can optionally provide an
existing
  core.async channel as the source for the new stream"
```

```
([]
   (event-stream (chan)))
([ch]
   (let [multiple  (mult ch)
         completed (atom false)]
      (EventStream. ch multiple completed))))
```

The docstring should be sufficient to understand the public API. What might not be clear, however, is what all the constructor arguments mean. From left to right, the arguments to EventStream are as follows:

- ch: This is the core.async channel backing this stream.
- multiple: This is a way to broadcast information from one channel to many other channels. It's a core.async concept that we will be explaining shortly.
- completed: This is a Boolean flag that indicates whether this event stream has completed and will not emit any new values.

From the implementation, you can see that multiple is created from the channel backing the stream. multiple works kind of like a broadcast. Consider the following example:

```
(def in (chan))
(def multiple (mult in))

(def out-1 (chan))
(tap multiple out-1)

(def out-2 (chan))
(tap multiple out-2)
(go (>! in "Single put!"))

(go (prn "Got from out-1 " (<! out-1)))
(go (prn "Got from out-2 " (<! out-2)))
```

In the previous snippet, we created an input channel, in, and a mult of it called multiple. Then, we created two output channels, out-1 and out-2, which are both followed by a call to tap. This essentially means that whatever values are written to in will be taken by multiple and written to any channels that are tapped into it, as the following output shows:

```
"Got from out-1 " "Single put!"
"Got from out-2 " "Single put!"
```

This will make understanding the EventStream implementation easier.

Next, let's take a look at what a minimal implementation of the `EventStream` looks like. Make sure that the implementation goes before the constructor function, as described earlier:

```
(declare event-stream)

(deftype EventStream [channel multiple completed]
  IEventStream
  (map [_ f]
    (let [out (map> f (chan))]
      (tap multiple out)
      (event-stream out)))

  (deliver [_ value]
    (if (= value ::complete)
      (do (reset! completed true)
          (go (>! channel value)
              (close! channel)))
      (go (>! channel value))))


  IObservable
  (subscribe [this f]
    (let [out (chan)]
      (tap multiple out)
      (go-loop []
        (let [value (<! out)]
          (when (and value (not= value ::complete))
            (f value)
            (recur))))
      (Token. out))))
```

For now, we have chosen to implement only the `map` and `deliver` functions from the `IEventStream` protocol. This allows us to deliver values to the stream, as well as to transform those values.

However, this would not be very useful if we could not retrieve the values that have been delivered. This is why we also implement the `subscribe` function from the `IObservable` protocol.

In a nutshell, `map` needs to take a value from the input stream, apply a function to it, and send it to the newly created stream. We do this by creating an output channel that taps into the current `multiple`. We then use this channel to back the new event stream.

The `deliver` function simply puts the value into the backing channel. If the value is the namespace keyword, `::complete`, we update the `completed` atom and close the backing channel. This ensures that the stream will not emit any other values.

Finally, we have the `subscribe` function. The way subscribers are notified is by using an output channel that's been tapped to backing `multiple`. We loop indefinitely, calling the subscribing function whenever a new value is emitted.

We finish by returning a token, which will close the output channel once disposed of, causing the `go-loop` to stop.

Let's make sure that all of this makes sense by experimenting with a couple of examples in the REPL:

```
(def es1 (event-stream))
(subscribe es1 #(prn "first event stream emitted: " %))
(deliver es1 10)
;; "first event stream emitted: " 10


(def es2 (map es1 #(* 2 %)))
(subscribe es2 #(prn "second event stream emitted: " %))

(deliver es1 20)
;; "first event stream emitted: " 20
;; "second event stream emitted: " 40
```

Excellent! We have a minimal, working implementation of our `IEventStream` protocol!

The next function we'll implement is `filter`, and it is very similar to `map`:

```
(filter [_ pred]
  (let [out (filter> pred (chan))]
    (tap multiple out)
    (event-stream out)))
```

The only difference is that we use the `filter>` function. `pred` should be a Boolean function:

```
(def es1 (event-stream))
(def es2 (filter es1 even?))
(subscribe es1 #(prn "first event stream emitted: " %))
(subscribe es2 #(prn "second event stream emitted: " %))

(deliver es1 2)
(deliver es1 3)
(deliver es1 4)
```

```
;; "first event stream emitted: " 2
;; "second event stream emitted: " 2
;; "first event stream emitted: " 3
;; "first event stream emitted: " 4
;; "second event stream emitted: " 4
```

As we can see, es2 only emits a new value if, and only if, that value is an even number.

If you are following along, typing the examples step by step, you will need to restart your REPL whenever we add new functions to any deftype definition. This is because deftype generates and compiles a Java class when evaluated. As such, simply reloading the namespace won't be enough.

Alternatively, you can use a tool such as tools.namespace, which addresses some of these REPL reloading limitations[3].

Moving down our list, we now have flatmap:

```
(flatmap [_ f]
    (let [es (event-stream)
          out (chan)]
      (tap multiple out)
      (go-loop []
        (when-let [a (<! out)]
          (let [mb (f a)]
            (subscribe mb (fn [b]
                            (deliver es b)))
            (recur))))
      es))
```

We've encountered this operator before, when surveying Reactive Extensions.

In the docstring, for flatmap implementation, we put the following sentence:

"Takes a function f from values in s to a new EventStream.

Returns an EventStream containing values from all underlying streams combined."

This means flatmap needs to combine all the possible event streams into a single output event stream. As before, we tap a new channel to the multiple stream, but then we loop over the output channel, applying f to each output value.

However, as we saw, f itself returns a new event stream, so we simply subscribe to it. Whenever the function registered in the subscription gets called, we deliver that value to the output event stream, effectively combining all streams into a single stream.

Consider the following example:

```
(defn range-es [n]
  (let [es (event-stream (chan n))]
    (doseq [n (range n)]
      (deliver es n))
    es))

(def es1 (event-stream))
(def es2 (flatmap es1 range-es))
(subscribe es1 #(prn "first event stream emitted: " %))
(subscribe es2 #(prn "second event stream emitted: " %))

(deliver es1 2)
;; "first event stream emitted: " 2
;; "second event stream emitted: " 0
;; "second event stream emitted: " 1

(deliver es1 3)
;; "first event stream emitted: " 3
;; "second event stream emitted: " 0
;; "second event stream emitted: " 1
;; "second event stream emitted: " 2
```

We have a function, range-es, that receives a number, n, and returns an event stream that emits numbers from 0 to n. As before, we have a starting stream, es1, and a transformed stream that's been created with flatmap, es2.

We can see from the preceding output that the stream created by range-es gets flattened into es2, allowing us to receive all values by simply subscribing to it once.

This leaves us with a single function from IEventStream left to implement:

```
(completed? [_] @completed)
```

completed? simply returns the current value of the completed atom. We are now ready to implement behaviors.

Implementing behaviors

If you recall, the `IBehavior` protocol has a single function, called `sample`, whose docstring states: *Turns this Behavior into an EventStream from the sampled values at the given interval.*

To implement `sample`, we will first create a useful helper function that we will call `from-interval`:

```
(defn from-interval
  "Creates and returns a new event stream which emits values at the given
interval.
  If no other arguments are given, the values start at 0 and increment by
one at each delivery.

  If given seed and succ it emits seed and applies succ to seed to get
the next value. It then applies succ to the previous result and so on."
  ([msecs]
    (from-interval msecs 0 inc))
  ([msecs seed succ]
    (let [es (event-stream)]
      (go-loop [timeout-ch (timeout msecs)
                value seed]
        (when-not (completed? es)
          (<! timeout-ch)
          (timeout msecs)
          (deliver es value)
          (recur (succ value))))
      es)))
```

The docstring function should be clear enough at this stage, but we would like to ensure that we understand its behavior correctly by trying it at the REPL:

```
(def es1 (from-interval 500))
(def es1-token (subscribe es1 #(prn "Got: " %)))
;; "Got: " 0
;; "Got: " 1
;; "Got: " 2
;; "Got: " 3
;; ...
(dispose es1-token)
```

As expected, `es1` emits integers starting at zero at 500 millisecond intervals. By default, it would emit numbers indefinitely; therefore, we keep a reference to the token that's returned by calling `subscribe`.

This way, we can dispose of it whenever we're done, causing `es-1` to complete and stop emitting items.

Next, we can finally implement the `Behavior` type:

```
(deftype Behavior [f]
  IBehavior
  (sample [_ interval]
    (from-interval interval (f) (fn [& args] (f))))
  IDeref
  (#?(:clj deref :cljs -deref) [_]
    (f)))

(defmacro behavior [& body]
  `(Behavior. #(do ~@body)))
```

A behavior is created by passing it a function. You can think of this function as a generator that's responsible for generating the next value in this event stream.

This generator function will be called whenever we (1) `deref` the `Behavior` or (2) at the interval given to `sample`.

The `behavior` macro is there for convenience and allows us to create a new `Behavior` without wrapping the body in a function ourselves:

```
(def time-behavior (behavior (System/nanoTime)))

@time-behavior
;; 201003153977194

@time-behavior
;; 201005133457949
```

In the preceding example, we defined `time-behavior` as something that always contains the current system time. We can, then, turn this behavior into a stream of discrete events by using the `sample` function:

```
(def time-stream (sample time-behavior 1500))
(def token      (subscribe time-stream #(prn "Time is " %)))
;; "Time is " 201668521217402
;; "Time is " 201670030219351
;; ...
(dispose token)
```

 Always remember to keep a reference to the subscription token when dealing with infinite streams such as the ones created by `sample` and `from-interval`, otherwise, you might incur undesired memory leaks.

Congratulations! We have a working, minimal CES framework using `core.async`!

We didn't prove that it works with ClojureScript, however, which was one of the main requirements early on. That's okay. We will be tackling that soon by developing a simple ClojureScript application that makes use of our new framework.

To do this, we need to deploy the framework to our local Maven repository. From the project root, type the following `lein` command:

```
$ lein install
Created respondent/target/respondent-0.1.0-SNAPSHOT.jar
Wrote respondent/pom.xml
Installed jar and pom into local rep.
```

Exercises

The following sections have a few exercises for you.

Exercise 5.1

Extend our current `EventStream` implementation to include a function called `take`. It works much like Clojure's core `take` function for sequences: it will take n items from the underlying event stream, after which, it will stop emitting items.

A sample interaction, which takes the first five items emitted from the original event stream, is shown here:

```
(def es1 (from-interval 500))
(def take-es (take es1 5))

(subscribe take-es #(prn "Take values: " %))

;; "Take values: " 0
;; "Take values: " 1
;; "Take values: " 2
;; "Take values: " 3
;; "Take values: " 4
```

 Keeping some state might be useful here. Atoms can help. Additionally, try to think of a way to dispose of any unwanted subscriptions that are required by the solution.

Exercise 5.2

In this exercise, we will add a function called `zip`, which zips together items that are emitted from two different event streams into a vector.

A sample interaction with the `zip` function is as follows:

```
(def es1 (from-interval 500))
(def es2 (map (from-interval 500) #(* % 2)))
(def zipped (zip es1 es2))

(def token (subscribe zipped #(prn "Zipped values: " %)))

;; "Zipped values: " [0 0]
;; "Zipped values: " [1 2]
;; "Zipped values: " [2 4]
;; "Zipped values: " [3 6]
;; "Zipped values: " [4 8]

(dispose token)
```

For this exercise, we need a way to know when we have enough items to emit from both event streams. Managing this internal state can be tricky at first. Clojure's `ref` types and, in particular, `dosync`, can be of use.

A respondent application

This chapter would not be complete if we didn't go through the whole development life cycle of deploying and using the new framework in a new application. This is the purpose of this section.

The application we will build is extremely simple. All it does is track the position of the mouse using the reactive primitives we built into `respondent`.

To that end, we will be using the excellent Lein template, `figwheel`, which was created by Bruce Hauman to help developers get started with ClojureScript[4].

Let's get started:

```
lein new figwheel respondent-app
```

Next, let's modify the project file to include the following dependencies:

```
[respondent/respondent "0.1.0-SNAPSHOT"]
[prismatic/dommy "1.1.0"]
```

The first dependency is self-explanatory. It's simply our own framework. `dommy` is a DOM manipulation library for ClojureScript. We'll briefly use it when building our web page.

Next, edit the `resources/public/index.html` file to match the following:

```
<!doctype html>
<html lang="en">
<head>
    <meta charset="utf-8">

    <title>Example: tracking mouse position</title>
    <!--[if lt IE 9]>
    <script
src="http://html5shiv.googlecode.com/svn/trunk/html5.js"></script>
    <![endif]-->
</head>

<body>
    <div id="test">
        <h1>Mouse (x,y) coordinates:</h1>
    </div>
    <div id="mouse-xy">
      (0,0)
    </div>
    <script src="js/compiled/respondent_app.js"></script> </body> </html>
```

In the preceding snippet, we created a new `div` element, which will contain the mouse's position. It defaults to `(0,0)`.

The last piece of the puzzle is modifying `src/respondent_app/core.cljs` to match the following:

```
(ns respondent-app.core
  (:require [respondent.core :as r]
            [dommy.core :as dommy]))


(def mouse-pos-stream (r/event-stream))
(def mouse-pos-selector (dommy/sel1 :#mouse-xy))
(set! (.-onmousemove js/document)
      (fn [e]
        (r/deliver mouse-pos-stream [(.-pageX e) (.-pageY e)])))
```

```
(r/subscribe mouse-pos-stream
            (fn [[x y]]
              (dommy/set-text! mouse-pos-selector
                               (str "(" x "," y ")")))))
```

This is our main application logic. It creates an event stream to which we deliver the current mouse position from the `onmousemove` event of the browser window.

Later, we simply subscribe to it and use `dommy` to select and set the text of the `div` element we added previously.

We are now ready to use the app! Let's start a `figwheel` server:

```
$ lein figwheel
```

This should take a few seconds. Navigate to `http://localhost:3449/index.html` and drag the mouse around to see its current position.

Congratulations on successfully developing, deploying, and using your own CES framework!

CES versus core.async

At this stage, you might be wondering when you should choose one approach over the other. After all, as demonstrated at the beginning of this chapter, we could use `core.async` to do everything we have done using `respondent`.

It all comes down to using the right level of abstraction for the task at hand.

`core.async` gives us many low-level primitives that are extremely useful when working with processes, which need to talk to each other. The `core.async` channels work as concurrent blocking queues and are an excellent synchronization mechanism in these scenarios.

However, it makes other solutions harder to implement: for instance, channels are single-take by default, so if we have multiple consumers interested in the values that have been put inside a channel, we have to implement the distribution ourselves using tools such as `mult` and `tap`.

CES frameworks, on the other hand, operate at a higher level of abstraction and work with multiple subscribers by default.

Additionally, `core.async` relies on side effects, as can be seen by the use of functions such as `>!` inside `go` blocks. Frameworks such as RxClojure promote stream transformations with the use of pure functions.

This is not to say there aren't side effects in CES frameworks. There most definitely are. However, as a consumer of the library, this is mostly hidden from our eyes, allowing us to think of most of our code as simple sequence transformations.

In conclusion, different application domains will benefit more or less from either approach—sometimes, they can benefit from both. We should think hard about our application domain and analyze the types of solutions and idioms developers are most likely to design. This will point us in the direction of better abstraction for whatever application we are developing at a given time.

Summary

In this chapter, we developed our very own CES framework. By developing our own framework, we have solidified our understanding of both CES and how to effectively use `core.async`.

The idea that `core.async` could be used as the foundation of a CES framework isn't mine, however. James Reeves[5]—the creator of the **Compojure**[6] routing library and many other useful Clojure libraries—also saw the same potential and set off to write **Reagi**[7], a CES library built on top of `core.async`, similar in spirit to the one we developed in this chapter.

He has put a lot more effort into it, making it a more robust option for a pure Clojure framework. We'll be looking at it in the next chapter.

Further reading

Here is a list of information you can refer to regarding what we have covered in this chapter:

1. Reader conditionals: `https://clojure.org/reference/reader#_reader_conditionals`
2. Reader conditionals: `https://dev.clojure.org/display/design/Reader+Conditionals`
3. Tools namespace plugin: `https://github.com/clojure/tools.namespace`
4. Figwheel: `https://github.com/bhauman/lein-figwheel`
5. James Reeves: `https://github.com/weavejester`
6. Compojure: `https://github.com/weavejester/compojure`
7. Reagi: `https://github.com/weavejester/reagi`

6
Building a Simple ClojureScript Game with Reagi

In the previous chapter, we learned about how a framework for **Compositional Event Systems** (**CES**) works by building our own framework, which we called **respondent**. It gave us great insight into the main abstractions involved in such a piece of software, as well as a good overview of `core.async`, Clojure's library for asynchronous programming and the foundation of our framework.

Respondent is but a toy framework, however. We paid little attention to cross-cutting concerns, such as memory efficiency and exception handling. This is okay, as we use it as a vehicle for learning more about handling and composing event systems with `core.async`. Additionally, its design is intentionally similar to Reagi's design[1].

In this chapter, we will cover the following topics:

- Reagi, a CES framework built on top of `core.async`
- Using Reagi to build the rudiments of a ClojureScript game, which will teach us how to handle user input in a clean and maintainable way
- Comparing Reagi to other CES frameworks and getting a feel for when to use each one

Setting up the project

Have you ever played Asteroids[2]? If you haven't, Asteroids is an arcade space shooter that was first released by Atari in 1979. In Asteroids, you are the pilot of a ship flying through space. As you do so, you get surrounded by asteroids and flying saucers that you have to shoot and destroy.

Developing the whole game in one chapter is too ambitious and would distract us from the subject of this book. We will limit ourselves to making sure that we have a ship on the screen that we can fly around, as well as the ability to shoot space bullets into the void. By the end of this chapter, we will have something that looks like what is shown in the following screenshot:

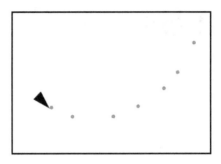

To get started, we will create a new ClojureScript project using the same Leiningen template we used in the previous chapter, figwheel[3]:

```
lein new figwheel reagi-game
```

Next, add the following dependencies to your project file:

```
[org.clojure/clojurescript "1.10.238"]
[reagi "0.10.1"]
[rm-hull/monet "0.1.12"]
```

The last dependency, monet, is a ClojureScript library that you can use to work with HTML5 Canvas[4]. It is a high-level wrapper on top of the Canvas API and makes interacting with it a lot simpler.

Before we continue, it's probably a good idea to make sure that our setup is working properly. Change into the project directory, start a Clojure REPL, and then start the embedded web server:

```
cd reagi-game/
lein figwheel
```

This will compile the ClojureScript source files into JavaScript and start the sample web server. In your browser, navigate to http://localhost:3449/index.html. If you see something like the following, we are good to go:

```
Figwheel template

Checkout your developer console.
```

As we will be working with HTML5 Canvas, we need an actual canvas to render to. Let's update our HTML document to include that. It's located under `resources/public/index.html`:

```html
<!DOCTYPE html>
<html lang="en">
  <head>
    <meta charset="utf-8">
     <meta name="viewport" content="width=device-width, initial-scale=1">
    <link rel="icon"
href="https://clojurescript.org/images/cljs-logo-icon-32.png">
       <!--[if lt IE 9]>
          <script
src="https://oss.maxcdn.com/html5shiv/3.7.3/html5shiv.min.js"></script>
          <![endif]-->
  </head>

  <body>
    <canvas id="canvas" width="800" height="600"></canvas>
    <script src="js/compiled/reagi_game.js"
type="text/javascript"></script>
  </body>
</html>
```

We have added a `canvas` DOM element to our document. All rendering will happen in this context.

Game entities

Our game will have only two entities – one representing the spaceship and the other representing bullets. To better organize the code, we will put all entity-related code in its own file, `src/reagi_game/entities.cljs`. This file will also contain some of the rendering logic, so we'll need to require `monet`:

```clojure
(ns reagi-game.entities
  (:require [monet.canvas :as canvas]
            [monet.geometry :as geom]))
```

Next, we'll add a few helper functions so that we avoid repeating ourselves too much:

```
(defn shape-x [shape]
  (-> shape :pos deref :x))

(defn shape-y [shape]
  (-> shape :pos deref :y))

(defn shape-angle [shape]
  @(:angle shape))


(defn shape-data [x y angle]
  {:pos   (atom {:x x :y y})
   :angle (atom angle)})
```

The first three functions are simply a shorter way of getting data out of our shape data structure. The `shape-data` function creates a structure. Note that we are using atoms, one of Clojure's reference types, to represent a shape's position and angle.

This way, we can safely pass our shape data into Monet's rendering functions and still be able to update it in a consistent way.

Next up is our ship constructor function. This is where the bulk of the interaction with `monet` happens:

```
(defn ship-entity [ship]
  (canvas/entity {:x (shape-x ship)
                  :y (shape-y ship)
                  :angle (shape-angle ship)}
                 (fn [value]
                   (-> value
                       (assoc :x     (shape-x ship))
                       (assoc :y     (shape-y ship))
                       (assoc :angle (shape-angle ship))))
                 (fn [ctx {:keys [x y angle]}]
                   (-> ctx
                       canvas/save
                       (canvas/translate x y)
                       (canvas/rotate angle)
                       (canvas/begin-path)
                       (canvas/move-to 50 0)
                       (canvas/line-to 0 -15)
                       (canvas/line-to 0 15)
                       (canvas/fill)
                       canvas/restore))))
```

There's quite a bit going on, so let's break it down.

`canvas/entity` is a `monet` constructor and expects you to provide three arguments that describe our ship: its initial *x*, *y* coordinates and angle, an update function that gets called in the draw loop, and a draw function that is responsible for actually drawing the shape onto the screen after each update.

The update function is fairly straightforward:

```
(fn [value]
  (-> value
      (assoc :x     (shape-x ship))
      (assoc :y     (shape-y ship))
      (assoc :angle (shape-angle ship))))
```

We simply update its attributes to the current values from the ship's atoms.

The next function, which is responsible for drawing, interacts with Monet's API more heavily:

```
(fn [ctx val]
  (-> ctx
      canvas/save
      (canvas/translate (:x val) (:y val))
      (canvas/rotate (:angle val))
      (canvas/begin-path)
      (canvas/move-to 50 0)
      (canvas/line-to 0 -15)
      (canvas/line-to 0 15)
      (canvas/fill)
      canvas/restore))
```

We start by saving the current context so that we can restore things such as drawing style and canvas positioning later. Next, we translate the canvas to the ship's *x*, *y* coordinates and rotate it according to its angle. We then start drawing our shape, a triangle, and finish by restoring our saved context.

The next function also creates an entity, that is, our bullet:

```
(declare move-forward!)

(defn make-bullet-entity [monet-canvas key shape]
  (canvas/entity {:x (shape-x shape)
                  :y (shape-y shape)
                  :angle (shape-angle shape)}
                 (fn [value]
                   (when-not
```

```
              (geom/contained?
                {:x 0 :y 0
                 :w (.-width (:canvas monet-canvas))
                 :h (.-height (:canvas monet-canvas))}
                {:x (shape-x shape)
                 :y (shape-y shape)
                 :r 5})
          (canvas/remove-entity monet-canvas key))
      (move-forward! shape)
      (assoc value :x (shape-x shape)
                   :y (shape-y shape)
                   :angle (shape-angle shape)))
  (fn [ctx {:keys [x y angle]}]
    (-> ctx
        canvas/save
        (canvas/translate x y)
        (canvas/rotate angle)
        (canvas/fill-style "red")
        (canvas/circle {:x 10 :y 0 :r 5})
        canvas/restore)))
```

As before, let's inspect the update and drawing functions. We'll start with the update:

```
(fn [value]
  (when (not
          (geom/contained?
            {:x 0 :y 0
             :w (.-width (:canvas monet-canvas))
             :h (.-height (:canvas monet-canvas))}
            {:x (shape-x shape)
             :y (shape-y shape)
             :r 5}))
    (canvas/remove-entity monet-canvas key))
  (move-forward! shape)
  (-> value
      (assoc :x     (shape-x shape))
      (assoc :y     (shape-y shape))
      (assoc :angle (shape-angle shape))))
```

Bullets have a little more logic in their update function. As you fire them from the ship, you might create hundreds of these entities, so it's good practice to get rid of them as soon as they go off the visible canvas area. That's the first thing the function does: it uses geom/contained? to check whether the entity is within the dimensions of the canvas, removing it when it isn't.

Different from the ship, however, bullets don't need user input in order to move. Once fired, they move on their own. That's why the next thing we do is call `move-forward!`. We haven't implemented this function yet, so we had to declare it beforehand. We'll get to it later.

Once the bullet's coordinates and angle have been updated, we simply return the new entity.

The draw function is a bit simpler than the ship's version, mostly due to its shape being simpler; it's just a red circle:

```
(fn [ctx val]
  (-> ctx
      canvas/save
      (canvas/translate (:x val) (:y val))
      (canvas/rotate (:angle val))
      (canvas/fill-style "red")
      (canvas/circle {:x 10 :y 0 :r 5})
      canvas/restore))
```

Now, we'll move on to the functions that are responsible for updating our shape's coordinates and angle, starting with `move!`:

```
(def speed 200)

(defn calculate-x [angle]
  (* speed (/ (* (Math/cos angle)
                 Math/PI)
              180)))

(defn calculate-y [angle]
  (* speed (/ (* (Math/sin angle)
                 Math/PI)
              180)))

(defn move! [shape f]
  (let [pos (:pos shape)]
    (swap! pos (fn [xy]
                 (-> xy
                     (update-in [:x]
                                #(f % (calculate-x
                                        (shape-angle shape)))))
                     (update-in [:y]
                                #(f % (calculate-y
                                        (shape-angle shape)))))))))))))
```

To keep things simple, both the ship and bullets use the same speed value to calculate their positioning, which is defined as 200 here.

move! takes two arguments: the shape map and a function, f. This function will either be the + (plus) or the – (minus) function, depending on whether we're moving forward or backward, respectively. Next, it updates the shape's *x, y* coordinates using some basic trigonometry.

If you're wondering why we are passing the plus and minus functions as arguments, it's all about not repeating ourselves, as the following two functions show:

```
(defn move-forward! [shape]
  (move! shape +))

(defn move-backward! [shape]
  (move! shape -))
```

With movement taken care of, the next step is to write the rotation functions:

```
(defn rotate! [shape f]
  (swap! (:angle shape) #(f % (/ (/ Math/PI 3) 20))))

(defn rotate-right! [shape]
  (rotate! shape +))

(defn rotate-left! [shape]
  (rotate! shape -))
```

So far, we've got ship movement covered! But what good is our ship if we can't fire bullets? Let's make sure we have that covered as well:

```
(defn fire! [monet-canvas ship]
  (let [entity-key (keyword (gensym "bullet"))
        data (shape-data (shape-x ship)
                         (shape-y ship)
                         (shape-angle ship))
        bullet (make-bullet-entity monet-canvas
                                   entity-key
                                   data)]
    (canvas/add-entity monet-canvas entity-key bullet)))
```

The fire! function takes two arguments – a reference to the game canvas and the ship. It then creates a new bullet by calling make-bullet-entity and adds it to the canvas.

Note how we use Clojure's gensym function to create a unique key for the new entity. We use this key to remove an entity from the game.

This concludes the code for the `entities` namespace.

> `gensym` is quite heavily used in writing hygienic macros, as you can be sure that the generated symbols will not clash with any local bindings belonging to the code using the macro. Macros are beyond the scope of this book, but you might find this series of macro exercises useful in the learning process[5].

Putting it all together

We're now ready to assemble our game. Go ahead and open the core namespace file, `src/reagi_game/core.cljs`, and add the following code:

```
(ns reagi-game.core
  (:require [monet.canvas :as canvas]
            [reagi.core :as r]
            [reagi-game.entities :as entities
             :refer [move-forward! move-backward! rotate-left! rotate-
right! fire!]]))
```

The following snippet sets up various data structures and references that we'll need to develop the game:

```
(def canvas-dom (.getElementById js/document "canvas"))

(def monet-canvas (canvas/init canvas-dom "2d"))

(def ship
      (entities/shape-data (/ (.-width (:canvas monet-canvas)) 2)
                           (/ (.-height (:canvas monet-canvas)) 2)
                           0))

(def ship-entity (entities/ship-entity ship))

(canvas/add-entity monet-canvas :ship-entity ship-entity)
(canvas/draw-loop monet-canvas)
```

We start by creating `monet-canvas` from a reference to our `canvas` DOM element. We then create our ship data, placing it at the center of the canvas, and add the entity to `monet-canvas`. Finally, we start `draw-loop`, which will handle our animations using the browser's native capabilities – internally, it calls `window.requestAnimationFrame()`, if available, but it falls back to `window.setTimemout()` otherwise.

If you were to try the application now, this would be enough to draw the ship on the middle of the screen, but nothing else would happen as we haven't started handling user input yet.

As far as user input goes, we're concerned with a few actions:

- Ship movement, that is, rotation, forward, and backward
- Firing the ship's gun
- Pausing the game

To account for these actions, we'll define some constants that represent the ASCII codes of the keys involved:

```
(def UP     38)
(def RIGHT  39)
(def DOWN   40)
(def LEFT   37)
(def FIRE   32) ;; space
(def PAUSE  80) ;; lower-case P
```

This should look sensible, as we are using the keys that are traditionally used for these types of actions.

Modeling user input as event streams

One of the things that we discussed in the previous chapters is that, if you can think of events as a list of things that haven't happened yet, you can probably model it as an event stream. In our case, this list is composed of the keys that the player presses during the game, and can be visualized like so:

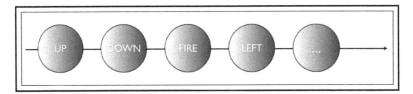

There is a catch, though. Most games need to handle simultaneously pressed keys.

Say you're flying the spaceship forward. You don't want to have to stop it in order to rotate it to the left and then continue moving forward. What you want is to press left at the same time you're pressing up and have the ship respond accordingly.

This hints at the fact that we need to be able to tell whether the player is currently pressing multiple keys. Traditionally, this is done in JavaScript by keeping track of which keys are being held down in a map-like object, using flags. Something similar to the following snippet is used:

```
var keysPressed = {};

document.addEventListener('keydown', function(e) {
    keysPressed[e.keyCode] = true;
}, false);
document.addEventListener('keyup', function(e) {
    keysPressed[e.keyCode] = false;
}, false);
```

Then, later in the game loop, you would check whether there are multiple keys being pressed, like so:

```
function gameLoop() {
    if (keyPressed[UP] && keyPressed[LEFT]) {
        // update ship position
    }
    // ...
}
```

While this code works, it relies on mutating the `keysPressed` object, which isn't ideal.

Additionally, with a setup similar to the preceding one, the `keysPressed` object is global to the application, as it is needed both in the `keyup`/`keydown` event handlers, as well as in the game loop itself.

In functional programming, we strive to eliminate or reduce the amount of global mutable state in order to write readable, maintainable code that is less error-prone. We will apply these principles here.

As seen in the preceding JavaScript example, we can register callbacks so that we're notified whenever a `keyup` or `keydown` event happens. This is useful, as we can easily turn them into event streams:

```
(defn keydown-stream []
  (let [out (r/events)]
    (set! (.-onkeydown js/document)
          #(r/deliver out [::down (.-keyCode %)]))
    out))

(defn keyup-stream []
  (let [out (r/events)]
```

```
(set! (.-onkeyup    js/document)
      #(r/deliver out [::up (.-keyCode %)])))
out))
```

Both `keydown-stream` and `keyup-stream` return a new stream to which they deliver events whenever they happen. Each event is tagged with a keyword so that we can easily identify its type.

We would like to handle both types of events simultaneously and, as such, we need a way to combine these two streams in a single one.

There are many ways in which we can combine streams, for example, using operators such as `zip` and `flatmap`. For this instance, however, we are interested in the `merge` operator. `merge` creates a new stream that emits values from both streams as they arrive:

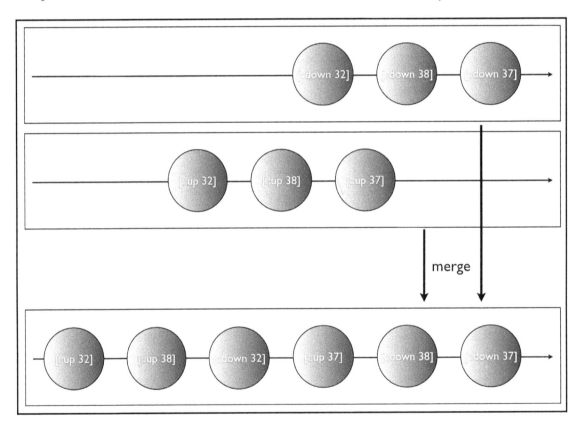

This gives us enough so that we can start creating our stream of active keys. Based on what we have discussed so far, our stream looks something like the following at the moment:

```
(def active-keys-stream
  (->> (r/merge (keydown-stream) (keyup-stream))
       ...
       ))
```

To keep track of which keys are currently being pressed, we will use a ClojureScript set. This way, we don't have to worry about setting flags to true or false – we can simply perform standard set operations and add/remove keys from the data structure.

The next thing we need is a way to accumulate the pressed keys into this set as new events are emitted from the merged stream.

In functional programming, whenever we wish to accumulate or aggregate a type of data over a sequence of values, we use reduce.

Most—if not all—CES frameworks have this function built in. RxJava calls it scan. Reagi, on the other hand, calls it reduce, making it intuitive to functional programmers in general.

That is the function we will use to finish the implementation of active-keys-stream:

```
(def active-keys-stream
  (->> (r/merge (keydown-stream) (keyup-stream))
       (r/reduce (fn [acc [event-type key-code]]
         (condp = event-type
            ::down (conj acc key-code)
            ::up (disj acc key-code)
            acc))
        #{})
       (r/sample 25)))
```

r/reduce takes three arguments: a reducing function, an optional initial/seed value, and the stream to reduce over.

Our seed value is an empty set as, initially, the user hasn't pressed any keys yet. Then, our reducing function checks the event type, removing or adding the key from/to the set as appropriate.

As a result, what we have is a stream like the one represented as follows:

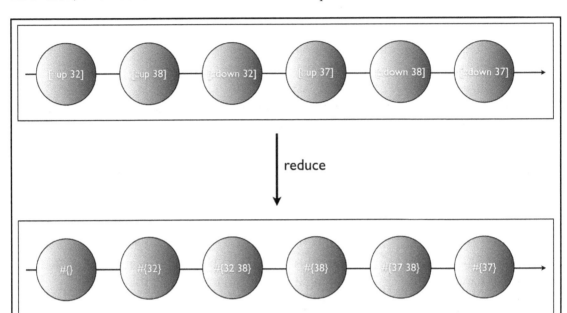

Working with the active keys stream

The groundwork we've done so far will make sure that we can easily handle game events in a clean and maintainable way. The main idea behind having a stream representing the game keys is that now we can partition it much like we would a normal list.

For instance, if we're interested in all events where the key being pressed is UP, we would run the following code:

```
(->> active-keys-stream
     (r/filter (partial some #{UP}))
     (r/map (fn [_] (.log js/console "Pressed up...")))))
```

Similarly, for events involving the FIRE key, we could do the following:

```
(->> active-keys-stream
     (r/filter (partial some #{FIRE}))
     (r/map (fn [_] (.log js/console "Pressed fire...")))))
```

This works because, in Clojure, sets can be used as predicates. We can quickly verify this at the REPL:

```
user> (def numbers #{12 13 14})
#'user/numbers
user> (some #{12} numbers)
12
user> (some #{15} numbers)
nil
```

By representing the events as a stream, we can easily operate on them using familiar sequence functions, such as map and filter.

Writing code like this, however, is a little repetitive. The two previous examples are pretty much saying something along these lines: filter all events matching a given predicate pred and then map the f function over them. We can abstract this pattern in a function we'll call filter-map:

```
(defn filter-map [pred f & args]
  (->> active-keys-stream
       (r/filter (partial some pred))
       (r/map (fn [_] (apply f args)))))
```

With this helper function in place, it becomes easy to handle our game actions:

```
(filter-map #{FIRE}  fire! monet-canvas ship)
(filter-map #{UP}    move-forward!  ship)
(filter-map #{DOWN}  move-backward! ship)
(filter-map #{RIGHT} rotate-right!  ship)
(filter-map #{LEFT}  rotate-left!   ship)
```

The only thing missing now is taking care of pausing the animations when the player presses the PAUSE key. We follow the same logic as before, but with a slight change:

```
(defn pause! [_]
  (if @(:updating? monet-canvas)
    (canvas/stop-updating monet-canvas)
    (canvas/start-updating monet-canvas)))

(->> active-keys-stream
     (r/filter (partial some #{PAUSE}))
     (r/throttle 100)
     (r/map pause!))
```

Monet makes a flag available that tells us whether it is currently updating the animation state. We use that as a cheap mechanism to *pause* the game.

Note that `active-keys-stream` pushes events as they happen. Therefore, if a user is holding a button down for any amount of time, we will get multiple events for that key. As such, we would probably get multiple occurrences of the PAUSE key in a very short amount of time. This would cause the game to frantically stop/start. To prevent this from happening, we throttle the filtered stream and ignore all PAUSE events that happen in a window shorter than 100 milliseconds.

To make sure that we didn't miss anything, this is what our `src/reagi_game/core.cljs` file should look like, in full:

```clojure
(ns reagi-game.core
  (:require [monet.canvas :as canvas]
            [reagi.core :as r]
            [reagi-game.entities :as entities
             :refer [move-forward! move-backward! rotate-left! rotate-
right! fire!]]))

(def canvas-dom (.getElementById js/document "canvas"))

(def monet-canvas (canvas/init canvas-dom "2d"))

(def ship (entities/shape-data (/ (.-width (:canvas monet-canvas)) 2)
                               (/ (.-height (:canvas monet-canvas)) 2)
                               0))

(def ship-entity (entities/ship-entity ship))

(canvas/add-entity monet-canvas :ship-entity ship-entity)
(canvas/draw-loop monet-canvas)

(def UP    38)
(def RIGHT 39)
(def DOWN  40)
(def LEFT  37)
(def FIRE  32) ;; space
(def PAUSE 80) ;; lower-case P

(defn keydown-stream []
  (let [out (r/events)]
    (set! (.-onkeydown js/document) #(r/deliver out [::down (.-keyCode
%)]))
    out))

(defn keyup-stream []
  (let [out (r/events)]
    (set! (.-onkeyup  js/document) #(r/deliver out [::up (.-keyCode %)]))
    out))
```

```
(def active-keys-stream
  (->> (r/merge (keydown-stream) (keyup-stream))
       (r/reduce (fn [acc [event-type key-code]]
           (condp = event-type
               ::down (conj acc key-code)
               ::up (disj acc key-code)
               acc))
           #{})
       (r/sample 25)))

(defn filter-map [pred f & args]
  (->> active-keys-stream
       (r/filter (partial some pred))
       (r/map (fn [_] (apply f args)))))

(filter-map #{FIRE}  fire! monet-canvas ship)
(filter-map #{UP}     move-forward!   ship)
(filter-map #{DOWN}  move-backward! ship)
(filter-map #{RIGHT} rotate-right!  ship)
(filter-map #{LEFT}  rotate-left!   ship)

(defn pause! [_]
  (if @(:updating? monet-canvas)
    (canvas/stop-updating monet-canvas)
    (canvas/start-updating monet-canvas)))

(->> active-keys-stream
     (r/filter (partial some #{PAUSE}))
     (r/throttle 100)
     (r/map pause!))

(defn start-game []
  (->> active-keys-stream
       (r/filter (partial some #{PAUSE}))
       (r/throttle 100)
       (r/map pause!)))

(defn on-js-reload []
  (start-game))
```

This completes the code, and we're now ready to have a look at the results. If you still have `figwheel` running, go to `http://localhost:3449/index.html`. If not, start it:

```
lein figwheel
```

You are now ready to fly around in your spaceship! Don't forget to shoot some bullets as well!

Reagi and other CES frameworks

Back in `Chapter 5`, *Creating Your Own CES Framework with core.async*, we looked at an overview of the main differences between `core.async` and CES. Another question that might have arisen in this chapter is this—how do we decide which CES framework to use?

The answer is less clear than before and often depends on the specifics of the tool being looked at. We have learned about two such tools so far: **Reactive Extensions (Rx)** encompassing RxJS, RxJava, and RxClojure) and Reagi.

Reactive Extensions is a much more mature framework. Its first version for the .NET platform was released in 2011 and the ideas in it have since evolved substantially.

Additionally, ports for other platforms, such as RxJava, are being heavily used in production by big names such as Netflix.

A drawback of Rx is that if you would like to use it both in the browser and on the server, you have to use two separate frameworks, RxJS and RxJava, respectively. While they do share the same API, they are different code bases, which can incur bugs that might have been solved in one port but not yet in another.

For Clojure developers, it also means relying more on interoperability to interact with the full API of Rx.

Reagi, on the other hand, is a new player in this space, but builds on the solid foundation that was laid out by `core.async`. It is fully developed in Clojure and solves the in-browser/on-server issue by compiling to both Clojure and ClojureScript.

Reagi also allows for seamless integration with `core.async` via functions such as `port` and `subscribe`, which allow channels to be created from event streams.

Moreover, the use of `core.async` in ClojureScript applications is becoming ubiquitous, so, chances, are you already have it as a dependency. This makes Reagi an attractive option for the times when we need a higher level of abstraction than the one provided by `core.async`.

Summary

In this chapter, we learned about how we can use the techniques from Reactive Programming we have about learned so far to write code that is cleaner and easier to maintain. To do so, we insisted on thinking about asynchronous events simply as lists and saw how that way of thinking lends itself quite easily to being modeled as an event stream. All our game has to do, then, is operate on these streams using familiar sequence processing functions.

We also learned about the basics of Reagi, a framework for CES, similar to the one we created in Chapter 5, *Creating Your Own CES Framework with core.async,* but that is more feature-rich and robust.

In the next chapter, we will take a break from CES and look at how a more traditional reactive approach based on data flows can be useful.

Further reading

Here is a list of information you can refer to regarding what has been covered in this chapter:

1. Clojure library Reagi: https://github.com/weavejester/reagi
2. Asteroids game: https://en.wikipedia.org/wiki/Asteroids_(video_game)
3. Leiningen template – Figwheel: https://github.com/bhauman/lein-figwheel
4. Clojure library, Monet: https://github.com/rm-hull/monet
5. Clojure macros workshop: https://github.com/leonardoborges/clojure-macros-workshop

7

The UI as a Function

So far, we have taken a journey through managing complexity by efficiently handling and modeling asynchronous workflows in terms of streams of data. In particular, Chapter 4, *Introduction to core.async*, and Chapter 5, *Creating Your Own CES Framework with core.async*, explored what's involved in libraries that provide primitives and combinators for **Compositional Event Systems** (**CES**). We also built a simple ClojureScript application that made use of our framework.

One thing you might have noticed is that none of the examples so far have dealt with what happens to the data once we are ready to present it to our users. It's still an open question that we, as application developers, need to answer.

In this chapter, we will look at one way to handle Reactive User Interfaces in web applications using React[1], a modern JavaScript framework developed by Facebook, as well as the following topics:

- How React renders user interfaces efficiently
- An introduction to Om, a ClojureScript interface for React
- How Om leverages persistent data structures for performance
- Developing two fully working ClojureScript applications with Om, including the use of core.async for inter-component communication

The problem with complex web UIs

With the rise of single-page web applications, it became a must to be able to manage the growth and complexity of a JavaScript code base. The same applies to ClojureScript.

In an effort to manage this complexity, a plethora of JavaScript MVC frameworks have emerged, such as AngularJS, Backbone.js, Ember.js, and KnockoutJS, to name a few.

They are very different, but share a few common features:

- Giving single-page applications more structure by providing models, views, controllers, templates, and so on
- Providing client-side routing
- Employing two-way data binding

In this chapter, we'll be focusing on the last goal.

Two-way data binding is absolutely crucial if we are to develop even a moderately complex single-page web application. Here's how it works.

Suppose we're developing a phone book application. More than likely, we will have a model—or entity, map, or what have you—that represents a contact. The contact model might have attributes such as name, phone number, and email address.

Of course, this application would not be all that useful if users couldn't update contact information, so we will need a form that displays the current details for contact and lets you update the contact's information.

The contact model might have been loaded via an AJAX request, and they might have used explicit DOM manipulation code to display the form. This would look something like the following pseudocode:

```
function editContact(contactId) {
  contactService.get(contactId, function(data) {
    contactForm.setName(data.name);
    contactForm.setPhone(data.phone);
    contactForm.setEmail(data.email);
  })
}
```

But what happens when the user updates someone's information? We need to store it somehow. Upon clicking on save, a function such as the following would do the trick, assuming you're using jQuery:

```
$("save-button").click(function(){
  contactService.update(contactForm.serialize(), function(){
    flashMessage.set("Contact Updated.")
  })
```

This seemingly harmless code poses a big problem. The contact model for this particular person is now out of date. If we were still developing web applications the old way, where we reload the page at every update, this wouldn't be a problem. However, the whole point of single-page web applications is to be responsive, so it keeps a lot of state on the client, and it is important to keep our models synced with our views.

This is where two-way data binding comes in. An example from AngularJS would look like the following:

```
// JS
// in the Controller
$scope.contact = {
  name: 'Leonardo Borges',
  phone '+61 xxx xxx xxx',
  email: 'leonardoborges.rj@gmail.com'
}


<!-- HTML -->
<!-- in the View -->
<form>
  <input type="text" name="contactName"  ng-model="contact.name"/>
  <input type="text" name="contactPhone" ng-model="contact.phone"/>
  <input type="text" name="contactEmail" ng-model="contact.email"/>
</form>
```

Angular isn't the target of this chapter, so I won't dig into the details. All we need to know from this example is that `$scope` is how we tell Angular to make our contact model available to our views. In the view, the custom attribute `ng-model` tells Angular to look up that property in the scope. This establishes a two-way relationship in such a way that when your model data changes in the scope, Angular refreshes the UI. Similarly, if the user edits the form, Angular updates the model, keeping everything in sync.

There are, however, two main problems with this approach:

- It can be slow. The way Angular and friends implement two-way data binding is, roughly speaking, by attaching event handlers and watchers to view both custom attributes and model attributes. For complex-enough user interfaces, you will start noticing that the UI becomes slower to render, diminishing user experience.
- It relies heavily on mutation. As functional programmers, we strive to limit side effects to a minimum.

The slowness that comes with this and similar approaches is two-fold. First, AngularJS and friends have to **watch** all of the properties of every model in the scope to track updates. Once the framework determines that data has changed in the model, it then looks up parts of the UI, which depend on information such as the fragments by using `ng-model`, and then it re-renders them.

Secondly, the DOM is the slowest part of most single-page web applications. If we think about it for a moment, these frameworks are triggering dozens or perhaps hundreds of DOM event handlers to keep the data in sync, each of which ends up updating a node—or several in the DOM.

Don't take my word for it, though. I ran a simple benchmark to compare a pure calculation versus locating a DOM element and updating its value to the result of the said calculation. Here are the results—I've used JSPerf to run the benchmark, and these results are for Chrome 37.0.2062.94 on macOS X Mavericks[2]:

```
document.getElementsByName("sum")[0].value = 1 + 2
// Operations per second: 2,090,202

1 + 2
// Operations per second: 780,538,120
```

Updating the DOM is orders of magnitude slower than performing a simple calculation. It seems logical that we would want to do this in the most efficient manner possible.

However, if we don't keep our data in sync, we're back to square one. There should be a way by which we can drastically reduce the amount of rendering being done, while retaining the convenience of two-way data binding. Can we have our cake and eat it too?

Enter React.js

As we'll see in this chapter, the answer to the question posed in the previous section is a resounding yes and, as you might have guessed, it involves React.js.

But what makes it special?

It's wise to start with what React is not. It is not an MVC framework and, as such, it is not a replacement for the likes of AngularJS, Backbone.js, and so on. React focuses solely on the *V* in *MVC*, and presents a refreshingly different way to think about user interfaces. We must take a slight detour in order to explore how it does that.

Lessons from functional programming

As functional programmers, we don't need to be convinced of the benefits of immutability. We bought into this premise long ago. However, were we not be able to use immutability efficiently, it would not have become commonplace in functional programming languages.

We owe it to the huge amount of research that went into *Purely Functional Data Structures,* first by Okasaki in his book of the same title[3] and then improved by others.

Without it, our programs would be ballooning, both in space and runtime complexity.

The general idea is that given a data structure, the only way to update it is by creating a copy of it with the desired delta applied:

```
(conj [1 2 3] 4) ;; [1 2 3 4]
```

In the following diagram, we have a simplistic view of how `conj` operates. On the left, you have the underlying data structure, representing the vector we wish to update. On the right, we have the newly created vector, which, as we can see, shares some structure with the previous vector, as well as containing our new item:

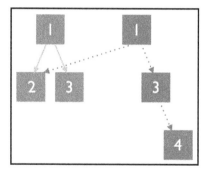

In reality, the underlying data structure is a tree and the representation was simplified for the purposes of this book. I highly recommend referring to Okasaki's book should the reader want more details on how purely functional data structures work.

Additionally, these functions are considered pure. That is, it relates every input to a single output and does nothing else. This is, in fact, remarkably similar to how React handles user interfaces.

If we think of a UI as a visual representation of a data structure, which reflects the current state of our application, we can, without too much effort, think of UI updates as simple functions whose input is the application state and the output is a DOM representation.

You'll have noticed I didn't say the output is rendering to the DOM—that would make the function impure, as rendering is clearly a side effect. It would also make it just as slow as the alternatives.

This DOM representation is essentially a tree of DOM nodes that model how your UI should look, and nothing else.

React calls this representation a **virtual DOM**, and roughly speaking, instead of watching individual bits and pieces of the application state that trigger a DOM re-render upon change, React turns your UI into a function to which you give the whole application state.

When you give this function the newly updated state, React renders that state to the virtual DOM. Remember that the virtual DOM is simply a data structure, so the rendering is extremely fast. Once it's done, React does one of two things:

- It commits the virtual DOM to the actual DOM if this is the first render.
- Otherwise, it compares the new virtual DOM with the current virtual DOM, cached from the previous render of the application. It then uses an efficient diff algorithm to compute the minimum set of changes required to update the real DOM. Finally, it commits this delta to the DOM.

Without digging into the nuts and bolts of React, this is essentially how it is implemented and the reason it is faster than the alternatives. Conceptually, we could imagine that React hits the refresh button in our browser whenever your application state changes.

Another great benefit is that by thinking of your UI as a function from application state to a virtual DOM, we recover some of the reasoning we're able to do when working with immutable data structures in functional languages.

In the upcoming sections, we will understand why this is a big win for us Clojure developers.

ClojureScript and Om

Why have I spent six pages talking about JavaScript and React in a Clojure book? I promise I'm not trying to waste your precious time; we simply needed some context to understand what's to come.

Om[4] is a ClojureScript interface to React.js that was developed by the prolific and amazing individual, David Nolen, from Cognitect. Yes, he has also developed `core.logic`, `core.match`, and the ClojureScript compiler. That's how prolific. But I digress.

When Facebook released React, David immediately saw the potential and, more importantly, how to take advantage of the assumptions we are able to make when programming in Clojure, the most important of which is that data structures don't change.

React provides several component life cycle functions that allow developers to control various properties and behaviors. One, in particular, `shouldComponentUpdate`, is used to decide whether a component needs to be re-rendered.

React has a big challenge here. JavaScript is inherently mutable, so it is extremely hard when comparing virtual DOM trees to identify which nodes have changed in an efficient way. React employs a few heuristics to avoid $O(n^3)$ worst-case performance and is able to do it in $O(n)$ most of the time. Since heuristics aren't perfect, we can choose to provide our own implementation of `shouldComponentUpdate` and take advantage of the knowledge we possess when rendering a component.

ClojureScript, on the other hand, uses immutable data structures. As such, Om provides the simplest and most efficient implementation possible for `shouldComponentUpdate`: a simple reference equality check.

Because we're always dealing with immutable data structures, to find out whether two trees are the same, all we need to do is compare whether their roots are the same. If they are, we're done. Otherwise, descend and repeat the process. This is guaranteed to yield $O(log\ n)$ runtime complexity and allows Om to always render the UI from the root efficiently.

Of course, performance isn't the only thing that's good about Om—we will now explore what makes an Om application.

Since the first edition, a new version of Om called Om Next was introduced. Om Next borrows ideas from Facebook's Relay[5], Netflix's Falcor[6], and Cognitect's Datomic[7]. We will mention how these technologies influenced Om Next in the following subsections. Unless otherwise stated, we will use the term Om to mean Om Next.

Building a simple Contacts application with Om

This chapter has been very text heavy so far. It's time we get our hands dirty and build a simple Om application. Since we talked about contacts before, that's what we will start with.

The main driver behind React and Om is the ability to build highly reusable, self-contained components and, as such, even in a simple Contacts application, we will have multiple components working in concert to achieve a common goal.

This is what our users should be able to do in the application:

- Display a list of contacts currently in storage
- Display the details of a given contact
- Edit the details of a specific contact

Once we're done, it will look like the following:

As mentioned previously, Om/React will eventually render the DOM based on our application state. We'll be using data that's in memory to keep the example simple. Here's what our application's initial data will look like:

```
(def init-data
  {:list/contacts [{:name  "James Hetfield"
                    :email "james@metallica.com"
                    :phone "+1 XXX XXX XXX"}
                   {:name  "Adam Darski"
                    :email "the.nergal@behemoth.pl"
                    :phone "+48 XXX XXX XXX"}]})
```

The data should be mostly self-explanatory. We have a map containing all contacts.

Setting up the Contacts project

Once again, we will use a `figwheel` template to help us get started. Type the following into the Terminal to create a base project using this template:

```
lein new figwheel contacts
cd contacts
```

Next, let's open the `project.clj` file and make sure that we have the same versions for the various different dependencies the template pulls in. This is just so that we don't have any surprises with incompatible versions:

```
...
   :dependencies [[org.clojure/clojure "1.9.0"]
                  [org.clojure/clojurescript "1.10.238"]
                  [org.clojure/core.async "0.4.474"]
                  [org.omcljs/om "1.0.0-beta4"]]
...
```

To validate the new project skeleton, still in the Terminal, type the following to auto-compile your ClojureScript source files:

```
lein figwheel
```

Now, if we navigate to `http://localhost:3449/index.html` in the browser, we should see the default template `Hello World`.

Application components

The next thing we'll do is open the `src/contacts/core.cljs` file, which is where our application code will go, and make sure it looks like the following so that we have a clean slate with the appropriate namespace declaration:

```
(ns contacts.core
  (:require [om.next :as om]
            [contacts.parser :as parser]
            [contacts.ui :as ui]))

(enable-console-print!)

(def init-data
  {:list/contacts [{:name  "James Hetfield"
                    :email "james@metallica.com"
                    :phone "+1 XXX XXX XXX"}
                   {:name  "Adam Darski"
```

```
                      :email "the.nergal@behemoth.pl"
                      :phone "+48 XXX XXX XXX"}]})

(def reconciler
  (om/reconciler
    {:state init-data
     :parser parser/parser}))

(defn mount-root-view! []
  (om/add-root! reconciler ui/RootView (.getElementById js/document
"app")))

(mount-root-view!)

(defn on-js-reload []
  (mount-root-view!))
```

Every Om application starts with a root component, created by the om/add-root! function. It takes three arguments, as follows:

- reconciler, which manages application state
- A component to render
- A place to mount the component

In this instance, the component will mount on a DOM element whose ID is app. This element was given to us by the figwheel template and is located in the resources/public/index.html file.

Of course, this code won't compile yet, as we don't have reconciler and ui/RootView. Let's solve that and create them.

Managing application state

In Om, changes in application state are managed by reconciler. It accepts changes to state, merges them to the current state, finds components that need to be rendered, and schedules rendering.

As we saw in the previous section, we passed two keys to reconciler. The first key, :state, allowed us to pass the initial state. The second key, :parser, needs more explanation as it is a new feature that was introduced in Om.

Instead of mixing state control logic with the component template, Om moves state management to parser abstraction. Components request data (read) from the parser. They do not mutate the application state; instead, they request application state changes (mutations) from the parser.

In our project, we will keep the parser code in the `parser.cljs` file:

```
(ns contacts.parser
  (:require [om.next :as om])
  (:refer-clojure :exclude [read]))
```

The parser is created from two functions, which are responsible for reading and mutations:

```
(def parser (om/parser {:read read :mutate mutate}))
```

Often, you will have many readers and mutators. Using Clojure's `defmethod` simplifies design:

```
(defmulti read om/dispatch)
(defmulti mutate om/dispatch)

(defn get-contacts [state key]
  (let [st @state]
    (into [] (map #(get-in st %)) (get st key))))

(defmethod read :list/contacts
  [{:keys [state] :as env} key params]
  {:value (get-contacts state key)})
```

The `read` function takes three arguments. The first argument, `env`, contains component's context for reading. Using `env` we can access component's state. The second argument, `key`, is the key from the state being read. The third argument, `params`, allow us to customize the reader.

We have the `get-contacts` convenience function to read a list of contacts from state. `read` functions must return a hash map containing a `:value` key with data. In our case, we return a vector with contacts saved in the state. The data will look like this:

```
[{:name James Hetfield, :email james@metallica.com, :phone +1 XXX XXX XXX}
 {:name Adam Darski, :email the.nergal@behemoth.pl, :phone +48 XXX XXX XXX}]
```

We now know how components can read data, but how do they alter state? This is done using mutating functions:

```
(defmethod mutate 'list/toggle-select-contact
  [{:keys [state]} _ {:keys [name id]}]
  {:action
```

```
(fn []
  (swap! state update-in
         [:contact/by-name name :show-details]
         #(not %)))})
```

This function will update the person's details, adding information about whether this person is selected or not, and the need to show or hide information about this person.

Om components

We will keep our components in the `ui.cljs` file:

```
(ns contacts.ui
  (:require [om.next :as om :refer-macros [defui]]
            [om.dom :as dom]))

(defui RootView
  static om/IQuery
  (query [this]
    (let [subquery (om/get-query Contact)]
      `[{:list/contacts ~subquery}]))
  Object
  (render [this]
    (let [{:keys [list/contacts]} (om/props this)]
      (dom/div nil
               (apply dom/div nil
                      [(dom/h2 nil "Contacts")
                       (list-view contacts)]))))))
```

This snippet introduces a number of new features and terminology, so it deserves a few paragraphs.

When describing `om/add-root!`, we saw that its second argument must be an Om component. The `defui` macro creates one. The Om component uses a single function, `render`, which gets called when the application state changes and components need to be displayed. The `render` function must return an Om/React component or something React knows how to render, such as a DOM representation of the component. Om components are pure JavaScript objects.

The `dom` namespace contains thin wrappers around React's DOM classes. It's essentially the data structure representing what the application will look like. Its first argument is a hash map representing HTML attributes. Components in the `RootView` component do not need any attributes, so we pass `nil` to them. We will see examples of passing hash maps into the `Contact` component in the following subsections.

This time, we give, as the second argument to `dom/div`, a hash map representing HTML attributes. Next, we will look at two examples of how we can create Om components inside another Om component. We simply pass them as the second argument to `dom/div`.

Query expressions

Let's have a look at the following code snippet:

```
static om/IQuery
(query [this]
  (let [subquery (om/get-query Contact)]
    `[{:list/contacts ~subquery}]))
```

In Om components, we declare what data we want to read and use. We do this by implementing the `om/IQuery` protocol. It should return a query expression for data we want. Queries are written with a variant of the Datomic pull syntax[8]. We use `static` because we want the method attached to class (and not instance). This way, `reconciler` can use the query without instantiating any components at all. The query expression is a vector that enumerates state for reads and mutations, allowing us to get the desired data for components.

In `RootView`, we want `:list/contacts`, which contains the list of our contacts. Components can access this data using `om/props`, as we saw in `RootView`. Each `Contact` in our contacts list is another component that we will implement shortly.

Filling in the blanks

Moving down the `RootView` component, we saw `list-view`. To create an Om component, we must first produce a factory from the component class. The function returned by `om/factory` has the same signature as pure React components, with the exception that the first argument is usually an immutable data structure. In `RootView`, we pass the `contacts` list that we got from the query expression:

```
(defui ListView
  Object
  (render [this]
    (let [list (om/props this)]
      (apply dom/ul nil
             (map contact list)))))

(def list-view (om/factory ListView))
```

Finally, we can implement the `Contact` component, which is responsible for displaying information about each contact, such as name, phone, and email address:

```
(defui Contact
  static om/Ident
  (ident [this {:keys [name]}]
    [:contact/by-name name])
  static om/IQuery
  (query [this]
    '[:name :phone :email])
  Object
  (render [this]
    (let [{:keys [phone name email show-details] :as props} (om/props
this)]
      (dom/li nil
            (dom/label nil (str name " (" phone ") (" email ")"))
            (dom/button
              #js {:style #js {:marginLeft "10px"}
                   :onClick
                   (fn [e]
                     (om/transact! this
                                   `[(list/toggle-select-contact
~props)])))}
              "Show details")
            (if show-details
              (dom/div nil
                     (dom/div #js {:className "input-div"}
                            (dom/label #js {:className "label"}
"Email")
                            (dom/input #js {:value email :onChange
(set-value this name :email)}))
                     (dom/div #js {:className "input-div"}
                            (dom/label #js {:className "label"}
"Phone")
                            (dom/input #js {:value phone :onChange
(set-value this name :phone)})))))))))

(def contact (om/factory Contact {:keyfn :name}))
```

If you are not familiar with the `#js {...}` syntax, it's simply a reader macro that expands to (`clj->js {...}`) in order to convert a ClojureScript hash map into a JavaScript object. The only thing to watch for is that it is not recursive, as evidenced by the nested use of `#js`.

We use a query expression to get the name, phone, and email of each person. The component uses dom/button to handle clicks. It calls the list/toggle-select-contact mutator from parser.cljs. :onClick and :style are passed here as the first argument—a hash map to Om component. Once the mutator sets show-details for the person, we display the dom/input that allows the user to change their email and phone.

We use the convenience function set-value to handle the input change that calls another mutator, list/edit-contact, from parsers.cljs. This mutator simply finds a person by name and updates the required key, that is, either a phone number or email address, with the value passed:

```
(defn set-value [component name key]
  (fn [e]
    (om/transact! component `[(list/edit-contact ~{:name name :key key
:value (.. e -target -value)})])))

(defmethod mutate 'list/edit-contact
  [{:keys [state]} _ {:keys [name key value]}]
  {:action
   (fn []
     (swap! state update-in
            [:contact/by-name name key] (fn [_] value)))})
```

 If you're not familiar with the .. syntax, it's simply a convenience macro for Java and JavaScript interoperability. The previous example expands to (. (. e -target) -value). This and other interoperability operators are described in the Java interop page of the Clojure website[9].

dom/div and dom/label elements set CSS classes.

Open resources/public/css/styles.css and add the following CSS declarations:

```
.input-div {
    margin: 5px 0;
}
.label {
    display: inline-block;
    min-width: 60px;
}
```

Identity

In the `Contact` component, we saw the `om/Ident` declaration. Om uses identity to normalize data and prevent duplication. If we query a component with `om/get-query`, we will see that each component has got metadata attached to it:

```
(-> Contact om/get-query meta)
;; {:component contacts.ui/Contact}
```

To normalize data, we need to tell Om which unique key to use to for normalization. `om/Ident` uses component properties and returns a unique key. In our case, we use the `name` property and return `[:contact/by-name name]`. We return a unique identifier, which we then use to normalize data. It also helps Om to identify which components rely on the same data and need to be updated together.

At the beginning of this chapter, we mentioned that Om borrows ideas from Relay and Falcor. Normalization is an example of that.

This is it. Make sure your code is still compiling—or if you haven't yet, start `figwheel` by typing the following into the Terminal:

```
lein figwheel
```

Then, open up `http://localhost:3449/index.html` in your browser once more and take our Contacts app for a spin! Note, in particular, how the application state is always in sync while you edit the `contact` attributes.

If there are any issues at this stage, make sure that the files that you have to match the companion code for this book.

Intercomponent communication

In our previous example, the components we built communicated with each other exclusively through the application state, both for reading and transacting data. While this approach works, it is not always the best, except for very simple use cases. In this section, we will learn an alternate way of performing this communication—by using `core.async` channels.

The application we will build is a super-simple virtual agile board. If you've heard of it, it's similar to Trello[10]. If you haven't, fear not—it's essentially a task management web application in which you have cards that represent tasks. You then move these tasks between columns such as `Backlog`, `In Progress`, and `Done`.

By the end of this section, the application will look like the following:

Backlog	In Progress	Done
Expenses Submit last client's expense report	Groceries shopping Almond milk, mixed nuts, eggs...	

We'll limit ourselves to a single feature—moving cards between columns by dragging and dropping them. Let's get started.

Creating an agile board with Om

We're already familiar with the `figwheel` Leiningen template, and since there is no reason to change it, that's what we will use to create our project, which I called `om-pm`—short for **Om Project Management**:

```
lein new figwheel om-pm
cd om-pm
```

As we did previously, we should ensure that we have the right dependencies in our `project.clj` file:

```
:dependencies [[org.clojure/clojure "1.9.0"]
               [org.clojure/clojurescript "1.10.238"]
               [org.omcljs/om "1.0.0-beta4"]
               [org.clojure/core.async "0.4.474"]]
```

Now, let's validate that we are in good shape by making sure that the project compiles properly:

```
lein figwheel
```

Next, open the `src/cljs/om_pm/core.cljs` file and add the namespaces that we will be using to build the application:

```
(ns om-pm.core
  (:require [goog.dom :as gdom]
            [om.dom :as dom]
            [om.next :as om :refer-macros [defui]]
            [cljs.core.async :refer [put! chan <!]]
            [om-pm.parser :as parser]
            [om-pm.util :refer [set-transfer-data! get-transfer-data!]])
  (:require-macros [cljs.core.async.macros :refer [go-loop]]))
```

The main difference this time is that we require `core.async` functions and macros. We don't have an `om-pm.util` namespace yet, but we'll get to that at the end.

The board state

It's time we started thinking about what our application state will look like. Our entities in this application are the **card**, which represents a task and has the attributes id, name, and description, and the **column**. To keep things simple, we will work with only three columns: Backlog, In Progress, and Done:

```
(def init-data
  {:card/by-id {1 {:db/id 1 :card/name "Expenses" :card/description "Submit
last client's expense report"}
               2 {:db/id 2 :card/name "Groceries shopping"
:card/description "Almond milk, mixed nuts, eggs..."}}
   :column/list    [[:column/by-id 1]
                    [:column/by-id 2]
                    [:column/by-id 3]]
   :column/by-id {1 {:db/id 1
                     :column/title "Backlog"
                     :column/cards [[:card/by-id 1] [:card/by-id 2]]}
                  2 {:db/id 2
                     :column/title "In Progress"
                     :column/cards []}
                  3 {:db/id 3
                     :column/title "Done"
                     :column/cards []}}})
```

We have two interesting keys—:`card/by-id` and :`column/by-id`. The first one is a hash with cards, together with their details, keyed by IDs. The second one contains the details about our columns. We should notice that the `Backlog` column has a :`colums/cards` key that references the currently assigned cards. The :`column/list` key contains IDs of columns. By keying **cards** and **columns** by `id`, we can reference them easily in our application state. This provides normalization to our data and, as we will see, helps to retrieve data in Om.

Components overview

There are many ways to slice up an Om application into components, and in this section, we will present one way as we walk through each component's implementation.

The approach we will follow is similar to our previous application, in that from this point on, we present the components bottom-up.

Before we see our first component, however, we should start with Om's own `root` component and `reconciler`:

```
(def reconciler
 (om/reconciler
 {:state (atom init-data)
 :parser parser/parser}))

(defn start []
 (om/add-root!
 reconciler
 RootView
 (gdom/getElement "app")))

(start)

(defn on-js-reload []
  (start))
```

This gives us a hint as to what our next component will be, that is, `RootView`:

```
(defui RootView
  static om/IQuery
  (query [this]
    [{:column/list (om/get-query Column)}])
  Object
  (initLocalState [_]
    {:transfer-chan (chan)})
  (componentDidMount [this nextprops nextstate]
```

```
(let [transfer-chan (om/get-state this :transfer-chan)]
  (go-loop []
          (let [transfer-data (<! transfer-chan)]
            (om/transact! this `[(card/move ~transfer-data)])
            (recur)))))
(render [this]
  (let [{:keys [:column/list]} (om/props this)
        {:keys [transfer-chan]} (om/get-state this)]
    (dom/div nil
            (column-view list transfer-chan)))))
```

Life cycle and component local state

The previous component is fairly different from the ones we have seen so far. More specifically, it uses `initLocalState` and `componentDidMount`. These are React's component life cycle methods[11]. Before we explain what these life cycle methods are good for, we need to discuss our high-level design.

The `RootView` component is our application's main entry point and obtains `:column/list` using `om/IQuery`. As in our earlier Contacts application, it then instantiates the remaining components with the data they need.

Different from the Contacts example, however, it creates a `core.async` channel—`transfer-chan`—which works as a message bus. The idea is that when we drag a card from one column and drop it onto another, one of our components will put a transfer event in this channel and let something else—most likely a `go` block—perform the actual move operation.

This is done in the following snippet, which was taken from the component shown earlier:

```
(initLocalState
  {:transfer-chan (chan)})
```

This creates what Om calls the component local state. It uses a different life cycle protocol, `initLocalState`, which is guaranteed to be called only once. After all, we need a single channel for this component. It should return a map representing the local state.

Now that we have the channel, we need to install `go-loop` so that we can handle messages that are sent to it. For this purpose, we are using a different protocol:

```
(componentDidMount [this nextprops nextstate]
  (let [transfer-chan (om/get-state this :transfer-chan)]
    (go-loop []
            (let [transfer-data (<! transfer-chan)]
```

```
(om/transact! this `[(card/move ~transfer-data)])
(recur)))))
```

As in the previous protocol, `componentDidMount` is also guaranteed to be called once in the component life cycle. It is called when component mounted into the DOM and is the perfect place to install `go-loop` into our channel.

 When creating `core.async` channels in Om applications, it is important to avoid creating them inside life cycle functions that are called multiple times. Besides non-deterministic behavior, this is a source of memory leaks.

We get hold of it from the component local state by using the `om/get-state` function. Once we get a message, we transact the state using the mutator function `card/move`. We will see what it looks like very shortly.

Remaining components

Next, we will build multiple `column-view` components, one per column. Each of them receives the list of cards from the application state as their shared state. We will use that to retrieve the card details from the IDs we store in each column.

We also pass `transfer-chan` to each column, since all of the columns need a reference to it:

```
(defui Column
       static om/Ident
       (ident [this {:keys [db/id]}]
              [:column/by-id id])
       static om/IQuery
       (query [this]
              [:db/id :column/title {:column/cards [:db/id :card/name
:card/description]}])
       Object
       (render [this]
               (let [{:keys [db/id column/title column/cards transfer-chan]
:as data} (om/props this)]
                    (dom/div #js {:className "column"
                                  :onDragOver #(.preventDefault %)
                                  :onDrop #(handle-drop % transfer-chan id)}
                       (dom/div #js {:className "column-title"} title)
                       (if cards
                         (map #(card-view % id) cards)))))))
```

```
(def column* (om/factory Column ))

(defn column [props transfer-chan]
  (column* (assoc props :transfer-chan transfer-chan)))

(defn column-view [columns transfer-chan]
  (apply dom/div nil
         (map #(column % transfer-chan) columns)))
```

We build `column-view` by mapping data for each factory column and passing the transfer channel as a property.

The `om/IQuery` protocol looks a bit different than what we have seen before. On top of asking about the column data, such as `id` and `title`, we want to obtain **cards** information, including card ID, name, and description.

The component view code should look fairly familiar at this point. We add CSS classes for each column and its title. We put the styles in `resources/public/css/style.css`:

```
.column {
    width: 30%;
    float: left;
    border: 1px solid;
    padding: 10px;
}

.column-title {
    font-weight: bold;
    margin-bottom: 10px;
}

.card {
    border: 1px solid;
    margin: 10px 0;
    padding: 5px;
}
```

Each column responds to drag and drop behavior. The `onDrop` JavaScript event is fired by the browser when a user drops a draggable DOM element onto this component. `handle-drop` takes care of this, like so:

```
(defn- handle-drop [e transfer-chan destination-column-id]
  (.preventDefault e)
  (let [data {:card-id (js/parseInt (get-transfer-data! e "cardId"))
              :source-column-id (get-transfer-data! e "sourceColumnId")
              :destination-column-id destination-column-id}]
    (put! transfer-chan data)))
```

This function creates the transfer data—a map with the keys :card-id, :source-column-id, and :destination-column-id—which is everything we need to move the cards between columns. Finally, we put! it into the transfer channel.

Next, we build a number or card-view component:

```
(defn- card-view [{:keys [db/id card/name card/description]} column-id]
  (dom/div #js {:key id
                :className  "card"
                :draggable  true
                :onDragStart (fn [e]
                               (set-transfer-data! e "cardId" id)
                               (set-transfer-data! e "sourceColumnId"
  column-id))}
           (dom/div nil name)
           (dom/div nil description)))
```

We make it draggable and install an event handler on the onDragStart event, which will be triggered when the user starts dragging the card.

This event handler sets the transfer data, which we use from handle-drop.

We have glossed over the fact that these components use a few utility functions. That's OK, as we will now define them in a new namespace.

Utility functions

Go ahead and create a new file under src/cljs/om_pm/ called util.cljs and add the following code:

```
(ns om-pm.util)

(defn set-transfer-data! [e key value]
  (.setData (-> e .-nativeEvent .-dataTransfer)
            key value))

(defn get-transfer-data! [e key]
  (-> (-> e .-nativeEvent .-dataTransfer)
      (.getData key)))
```

These functions use JavaScript interoperability to interact with HTML's DataTransfer object[12]. This is how browsers share data related to drag and drop events.

The drag and drop events manipulate/mutate the cards. Next, we will see the parser.cljs file.

Application's parser

Let's have a look at the following code:

```clojure
(ns om-pm.parser
  (:require [om.next :as om])
  (:refer-clojure :exclude [read]))

(defmulti read om/dispatch)

(defmethod read :default
  [{:keys [state query]} k _]
  (let [st @state]
    {:value (om/db->tree query (k st) st)}))

(defmulti mutate om/dispatch)

(defmethod mutate 'card/move
  [{:keys [state]} _ {:keys [card-id source-column-id destination-column-
id]}]
  {:action
   (fn []
     (swap! state update-in
            [:column/by-id (int source-column-id) :column/cards]
            (fn [existing-cards]
              (vec (remove (fn [[_ id]] (= card-id id)) existing-cards))))
     (swap! state update-in
            [:column/by-id (int destination-column-id) :column/cards]
            (fn [existing-cards]
              (conj existing-cards [:card/by-id card-id]))))})

(def parser (om/parser {:read read :mutate mutate}))
```

We use multimethods for reading and mutating our data. We provide one `:default read` method. What is interesting in this implementation is the use of the `om/db->tree` function. In the previous Contacts application, we built the UI data manually. This time, we are using Om's utility function to do this for us.

The following has been taken from the functions documentation:

> "Given a query, some data in the default database format, and the entire application state in the default database format, return the tree where all ident links have been replaced with their original node values."

This shows the power of Om. We structure our initial data using IDs to normalize our database format. Each UI component provides queries for particular data that we need. By using normalized data, Om can build unique data for each UI component.

Now, let's simply save the file and make sure that the code compiles properly. We can finally open `http://localhost:3449/index.html` in the browser and play around with the product of our work!

Exercises

In this exercise, we will modify the `om-pm` project we created in the previous section. The objective is to add keyboard shortcuts so that power users can operate the agile board more efficiently.

The shortcuts to be supported are as follows:

- **The** `up`, `down`, `left`, **and** `right` **arrow keys**: These allow the user to navigate through the cards, highlighting the current one
- **The** n **and** p **keys**: These are used to move the current card to the next (right) or previous (left) column, respectively

The key insight here is to create a new `core.async` channel, which will contain keypress events. These events will then trigger the actions that were outlined previously. We can use the Google Closure library to listen for events. Just add the following `require` to the application namespace:

```
(:require [goog.events :as events])
```

Then, use the following function to create a channel from DOM events:

```
(defn listen [el type]
  (let [c (chan)]
    (events/listen el type #(put! c %))
    c))
```

The actual logic of moving the cards around based on keyboard shortcuts can be implemented in a number of ways, so don't forget to compare your solution with the answers provided in this book's companion code.

Summary

In this chapter, we looked at a different approach on how to handle reactive web interfaces via Om and React. In turn, these frameworks make this possible and painless by applying functional programming principles such as immutability and persistent data structures for efficient rendering.

We also learned to think the Om way by structuring our applications as a series of functions, which receive state and output a DOM representation of state changes.

Additionally, we saw that by structuring application state transitions through `core.async` channels, we separate the presentation logic from the code, which will actually perform the work, making our components even easier to reason about.

In the next chapter, we will turn to an often overlooked yet useful tool for creating reactive applications—**Futures**.

Further reading

Here is a list of information you can refer to regarding what we have covered in this chapter:

1. Facebook, React: `http://facebook.github.io/react/`
2. JSPerf, benchmark: `http://jsperf.com/purefunctions-vs-dom`
3. *Purely Functional Data Structures*, Chris Osaki: `http://www.amazon.com/Purely-Functional-Structures-Chris-Okasaki/dp/0521663504/ref=sr_1_1?ie=UTF8&qid=1409550695&sr=8-1&keywords=purely+functional+data+structures`
4. ClojureScript, Om: `https://github.com/omcljs/om`
5. Facebook, Relay: `https://facebook.github.io/relay/`
6. Netflix, Falcor: `http://netflix.github.io/falcor/`
7. Cognitect, Datomic: `https://www.datomic.com/`
8. Datomic, pull: `https://docs.datomic.com/on-prem/pull.html`
9. Clojure, Java interop: `http://clojure.org/java_interop`
10. Trello: `https://trello.com/`
11. React, life cycle: `https://reactjs.org/docs/state-and-lifecycle.html`
12. `DataTransfer`: `https://developer.mozilla.org/en-US/docs/Web/API/DataTransfer`

A New Approach to Futures

8

In general, applications waste a lot of time waiting for things to happen. Maybe we are waiting for an expensive computation—say, calculating the 1,000[th] Fibonacci number. Perhaps we are waiting for some information to be written to the database. We could also be waiting for a network call to return, bringing us the latest recommendations from our favorite online store.

Regardless of what we're waiting for, we should never block clients of our application. This is crucial to achieving the responsiveness we desire when building reactive systems. And the first step toward reactive applications is to break out of synchronous processing.

In an age where processing cores are abundant—my MacBook Pro has eight processor cores—blocking APIs severely underutilizes the resources we have at our disposal.

After seeing a few examples of applications of functional programming, it is appropriate to step back a little and appreciate that not all classes of problems that deal with concurrent, asynchronous computations require the machinery of frameworks such as RxJava or `core.async`.

In this chapter, we will look at another abstraction that helps us develop concurrent, asynchronous applications: **futures**. We will learn about the following topics:

- The problems and limitations with Clojure's implementation of futures
- An alternative to Clojure's futures that provides asynchronous, composable semantics
- How to optimize concurrency in the face of blocking IO

Clojure futures

The first step toward fixing this issue—that is, to prevent a potentially long-running task from blocking our application—is to create new threads, which do the work and wait for it to complete. This way, we keep the application's main thread free to serve more clients.

Working directly with threads, however, is tedious and error-prone, so Clojure's core library includes futures, which are extremely simple to use:

```
(def f (clojure.core/future
         (println "doing some expensive work...")
         (Thread/sleep 5000)
         (println "done")
         10))
(println "You'll see me before the future finishes")
;; doing some expensive work...
;; You'll see me before the future finishes
;; done
```

In the preceding snippet, we invoked the `clojure.core/future` macro with a body simulating an expensive computation. In this example, it simply sleeps for five seconds before returning the value `10`. As the output demonstrates, this does not block the main thread, which is free to serve more clients, pick work items from a queue, or what have you.

Of course, the most interesting computations, such as the expensive ones, return results we care about. This is where the first limitation of Clojure futures becomes apparent. If we attempt to retrieve the result of a future—by derefing it—before it has completed, the calling thread will be blocked until the future returns a value. Try running the following, slightly modified, version of the previous snippet:

```
(def f (clojure.core/future
         (println "doing some expensive work...")
         (Thread/sleep 5000)
         (println "done")
         10))
(println "You'll see me before the future finishes")
@f
(println "I could be doing something else. Instead I had to wait")


;; doing some expensive work...
;; You'll see me before the future finishes
;; 5 SECONDS LATER
;; done
;; I could be doing something else. Instead, I had to wait
```

The only difference now is that we immediately try to `deref` the future after we create it. Since the future isn't done, we sit there waiting for 5 seconds until it returns its value. Only then is our program allowed to continue.

In general, this poses a problem when building modular systems. Often, a long-running operation like the one described earlier would be initiated within a specific module or function and handed over to the next logical step for further processing.

Clojure futures don't allow us to schedule a function to be executed when the future finishes in order to perform such further processing. This is an important feature of building reactive systems.

Fetching data in parallel

To understand the issues outlined in the previous section better, let's build a more complex example that fetches data about one of my favorite movies, *The Lord of the Rings*.

The idea is that, given the movie, we wish to retrieve its actors and, for each actor, retrieve the movies they have been a part of. We would also like to find out more information about each actor, such as their spouses.

Additionally, we will match each actor's movies against the list of top five movies to highlight them as such. Finally, the result will be printed to the screen.

From the problem statement, we can identify the following two main characteristics we will need to account for:

- Some of these tasks need to be performed in parallel
- They establish dependencies on each other

To get started, let's create a new Leiningen project:

```
lein new clj-futures-playground
```

Next, open the core namespace file in `src/clj_futures_playground/core.clj` and add the data we will be working with:

```
(ns clj-futures-playground.core
  (:require [clojure.pprint :refer [pprint]]))

(def movie
  {:name "Lord of The Rings: The Fellowship of The Ring"
   :cast ["Cate Blanchett"
          "Elijah Wood"
          "Liv Tyler"
          "Orlando Bloom"]})

(def actor-movies
```

```
    [{:name "Cate Blanchett"
      :movies ["Lord of The Rings: The Fellowship of The Ring"
               "Lord of The Rings: The Return of The King"
               "The Curious Case of Benjamin Button"]}

     {:name "Elijah Wood"
      :movies ["Eternal Sunshine of the Spotless Mind"
               "Green Street Hooligans"
               "The Hobbit: An Unexpected Journey"]}

     {:name "Liv Tyler"
      :movies ["Lord of The Rings: The Fellowship of The Ring"
               "Lord of The Rings: The Return of The King"
               "Armageddon"]}

     {:name "Orlando Bloom"
      :movies ["Lord of The Rings: The Fellowship of The Ring"
               "Lord of The Rings: The Return of The King"
               "Pirates of the Caribbean: The Curse of the Black Pearl"]}])

(def actor-spouse
  [{:name "Cate Blanchett"    :spouse "Andrew Upton"}
   {:name "Elijah Wood"       :spouse "Unknown"}
   {:name "Liv Tyler"         :spouse "Royston Langdon"}
   {:name "Orlando Bloom"     :spouse "Miranda Kerr"}])
(def top-5-movies
  ["Lord of The Rings: The Fellowship of The Ring"
   "The Matrix"
   "The Matrix Reloaded"
   "Pirates of the Caribbean: The Curse of the Black Pearl"
   "Terminator"])
```

The namespace declaration is simple and only requires the pprint function, which will help us print our result in an easy-to-read format. With all the data in place, we can create the functions that will simulate remote services that are responsible for fetching the relevant data:

```
(defn cast-by-movie [name]
  (future (do (Thread/sleep 5000)
              (:cast movie))))

(defn movies-by-actor [name]
  (do (Thread/sleep 2000)
      (->> actor-movies
           (filter #(= name (:name %)))
           first)))

(defn spouse-of [name]
```

```
    (do (Thread/sleep 2000)
        (->> actor-spouse
             (filter #(= name (:name %)))
             first)))

(defn top-5 []
  (future (do (Thread/sleep 5000)
              top-5-movies)))
```

Each `service` function sleeps the current thread by a given amount of time to simulate a slow network. The `cast-by-movie` and `top 5` functions each return a future, indicating that we wish to fetch this data on a different thread. The remaining functions simply return the actual data. They will also be executed in a different thread, as we will see shortly.

The next thing we need is a function to aggregate all fetched data, match spouses to actors, and highlight movies in the `top-5` list. We'll call it the `aggregate-actor-data` function:

```
(defn aggregate-actor-data [spouses movies top-5]
  (map (fn [{:keys [name spouse]} {:keys [movies]}]
         {:name    name
          :spouse spouse
          :movies (map (fn [m]
                         (if (some #{m} top-5)
                           (str m " - (top 5)")
                           m))
                       movies)})
       spouses
       movies))
```

The preceding function is fairly straightforward. It simply zips spouses and movies together, building a map of keys, that is, :name, :spouse, and :movies. It further transforms `movies` to append the *Top 5* suffix to the ones in the `top-5` list.

The last piece of the puzzle is the `-main` function, which allows us to run the program from the command line:

```
(defn -main [& args]
  (time (let [cast (cast-by-movie "Lord of The Rings: The Fellowship of The Ring")
              movies (pmap movies-by-actor @cast)
              spouses (pmap spouse-of @cast)
              top-5 (top-5)]
          (prn "Fetching data...")
          (pprint (aggregate-actor-data spouses movies @top-5))
(shutdown-agents))))
```

There are a number of things worth highlighting in the preceding snippet.

1. First, we wrapped the whole body in a call to `time`, a simple benchmarking function that comes with Clojure. This was just so we know how long the program took to fetch all data—this information will become relevant later.

2. Then, we set up a number of `let` bindings. The first, `cast`, is the result of calling `cast-by-movie`, which returns a future.

3. The next binding, `movies`, used a function we haven't seen before: `pmap`.

4. The `pmap` function works like `map`, except that the function is mapped over the items in the list in parallel. The `pmap` function uses futures under the covers, and that is the reason `movies-by-actor` doesn't return a future—it leaves that for `pmap` to handle.

> The `pmap` function is actually meant for CPU-bound operations, but is used here to keep the code simple. In the face of blocking IO, `pmap` wouldn't perform optimally. We will talk more about blocking IO later in this chapter.
>
> We got the list of actors by derefing the `cast` binding, which, as we saw in the previous section, blocks the current thread waiting for the asynchronous fetch to finish. Once all of the results are ready, we simply call the `aggregate-actor-data` function.

5. Lastly, we called the `shutdown-agents` function, which shuts down the **thread pool** backing futures in Clojure. This was necessary for our program to terminate properly, otherwise, it would simply hang in the Terminal.

To run the program, type the following into the Terminal, under the project's root directory:

```
lein run -m clj-futures-playground.core
"Fetching data..."
({:name "Cate Blanchett",
  :spouse "Andrew Upton",
  :movies
  ("Lord of The Rings: The Fellowship of The Ring - (top 5)"
   "Lord of The Rings: The Return of The King"
   "The Curious Case of Benjamin Button")}
 {:name "Elijah Wood",
  :spouse "Unknown",
  :movies
  ("Eternal Sunshine of the Spotless Mind"
   "Green Street Hooligans"
   "The Hobbit: An Unexpected Journey")}
```

```
    {:name "Liv Tyler",
     :spouse "Royston Langdon",
     :movies
     ("Lord of The Rings: The Fellowship of The Ring - (top 5)"
      "Lord of The Rings: The Return of The King"
      "Armageddon")}
    {:name "Orlando Bloom",
     :spouse "Miranda Kerr",
     :movies
     ("Lord of The Rings: The Fellowship of The Ring - (top 5)"
      "Lord of The Rings: The Return of The King"
      "Pirates of the Caribbean: The Curse of the Black Pearl - (top
  5)")})
    "Elapsed time: 10120.267 msecs"
```

You would have noticed that the program takes a while to print the first message. Additionally, because futures block when they are derefed, the program doesn't start fetching the list of top five movies until it has completely finished fetching the cast of *The Lord of the Rings*.

Let's have a look at why that is so:

```
(time (let [cast     (cast-by-movie "Lord of The Rings: The Fellowship of
The Ring")
            ;; the following line blocks
            movies  (pmap movies-by-actor @cast)
            spouses (pmap spouse-of @cast)
            top-5   (top-5)]
```

The highlighted section in the preceding snippet shows where the program blocks, are waiting for cast-by-movie to finish. As we stated previously, Clojure futures don't give us a way to run a piece of code when the future finishes—such as a callback—forcing us to block too soon.

This prevents top-5—a completely independent parallel data fetch—from running before we retrieve the movie's cast.

Of course, this is a contrived example, and we could solve this particular annoyance by calling top-5 before anything else. The problem is that the solution isn't always crystal clear and, ideally, we should not have to worry about the order of execution.

As we will see in the next section, there is a better way to do this.

Imminent – a composable futures library for Clojure

The author of the first edition of this book, Leonardo Borges, created an open source library that aims to fix the previous issues with Clojure futures. The result of this work is called **imminent** (see `https://github.com/leonardoborges/imminent`).

The fundamental difference is that imminent futures are asynchronous by default and provide a number of combinators that allow us to declaratively write our programs without us having to worry about its order of execution.

The best way to demonstrate how the library works is to rewrite the previous movies example in it. We will do this in two broad steps.

First, we will individually examine the bits of imminent's API that will be part of our final solution. Then, we'll put it all together in a working application.

Let's start by creating a new project:

```
lein new imminent-playground
```

Next, add a dependency on imminent to your `project.clj`:

```
:dependencies [[org.clojure/clojure "1.9.0"]
               [com.leonardoborges/imminent "0.1.1"]]
```

Then, create a new file, `src/imminent_playground/repl.clj`, and add imminent's core namespace:

```
(ns imminent-playground.repl
  (:require [imminent.core :as i]))

(def  repl-out *out*)
(defn prn-to-repl [& args]
  (binding [*out* repl-out]
    (apply prn args)))
```

The preceding snippet also creates a helper function that comes in useful when we're dealing with multiple threads in the REPL. This will be explained in detail later, but for now, just take this as being a reliable way to print to the REPL across multiple threads.

Feel free to type this in the REPL as we go along. Otherwise, you can acquire the namespace file from a running REPL, like so:

```
(require 'imminent-playground.repl)
```

All of the examples in this chapter will be in this file.

Creating futures

Creating a future in imminent isn't much different from creating a future in Clojure. It's as simple as this:

```
(def age (i/future 31))

;; #<Future@2ea0ca7d: #<Success@3e4dec75: 31>>
```

What looks very different, however, is the return value. A key decision in imminent's API is to represent the value of a computation as either a `Success` or a `Failure` type. `Success`, as in the preceding example, wraps the result of the computation. `Failure`, as you might have guessed, will wrap any exceptions that happened in the future:

```
(def failed-computation    (i/future (throw (Exception. "Error"))))
;; #<Future@63cd0d58: #<Failure@2b273f98: #<Exception java.lang.Exception:
Error>>>

(def failed-computation-1 (i/failed-future :invalid-data))
;; #<Future@a03588f: #<Failure@61ab196b: :invalid-data>>
```

As you can see, you're not limited to exceptions only. We can use the `failed-future` function to create a future that completes immediately with the given reason, which, in the second example, is simply a keyword.

The next question we might ask is, *How do we get the result out of a future?* As with Clojure futures, we can `deref` it, as follows:

```
@age              ;; #<Success@3e4dec75: 31>
(deref @age)      ;; 31
(i/dderef age)    ;; 31
```

The idiom of using a double-deref is common, so imminent provides the convenience shown, `dderef`, which is equivalent to calling `deref` twice.

However, what's different from Clojure futures is that this is a non-blocking operation, so if the future hasn't completed yet, you'll get the following:

```
@(i/future (do (Thread/sleep 500)
               "hello"))
;; :imminent.future/unresolved
```

The initial state of a future is `unresolved`, so unless you are absolutely certain a future has completed, derefing might not be the best way to work with the result of a computation. This is where combinators come in handy.

Combinators and event handlers

Let's say we would like to double the value in the age future. As we do with lists, we can simply map a function over the future to do just this:

```
(def double-age (i/map age #(* % 2)))
;; #<Future@659684cb: #<Success@7ce85f87: 62>>
```

 While `i/future` schedules its body for execution on a separate thread, it's worth noting that future combinators such as `map`, `filter`, and so on, do not create a new thread immediately. Instead, they schedule a function to be executed asynchronously in the thread pool once the original future completes.

Another way to do something with the value of a future is to use the `on-success` event handler that gets called with the wrapped value of the future if it is successful:

```
(i/on-success age #(prn-to-repl (str "Age is: " %)))
;; "Age is: 31"
```

Similarly, an `on-failure` handler exists, which does the same for `Failure` types. While we're on the subject of failures, imminent futures understand the context in which they are being executed and, if the current future yields `Failure`, it simply short-circuits the computation:

```
(-> failed-computation
    (i/map #(* % 2)))
;; #<Future@7f74297a: #<Failure@2b273f98: #<Exception java.lang.Exception:
Error>>>
```

In the preceding example, we don't get a new error, but rather the original exception contained in `failed-computation`. The function that was passed to `map` never runs.

The decision to wrap the result of a future in a type such as `Success` or `Failure` might seem arbitrary, but it is actually quite the opposite. Both types implement the `IReturn`, `IFuture`, `IAwaitable`, and `IPromise` protocols. All of these come with a set of useful functions, one of which is `map`:

```
(i/map (i/success "hello")
       #(str % " world"))
```

```
;; #<Success@714eea92: "hello world">

(i/map (i/failure "error")
       #(str % " world"))
;; #<Failure@6d685b65: "error">
```

We get a similar behavior here as we did previously—mapping a function over a failure simply short-circuits the whole computation. If you do, however, wish to map over the failure, you can use map's counterpart, `map-failure`, which behaves similarly to `map` but is its inverse:

```
(i/map-failure (i/success "hello")
               #(str % " world"))
;; #<Success@779af3f4: "hello">

(i/map-failure (i/failure "Error")
               #(str "We failed: " %))
;; #<Failure@52a02597: "We failed: Error">
```

This plays well with the last event handler imminent provides—`on-complete`:

```
(i/on-complete age
               (fn [result]
                 (i/map result #(prn-to-repl "success: " %))
                 (i/map-failure result #(prn-to-repl "error: " %))))

;; "success: " 31
```

Contrary to `on-success` and `on-failure`, `on-complete` calls the provided function with the result type wrapper, so it is a convenient way to handle both cases in a single function.

Coming back to combinators, sometimes we will need to map a function over a future that itself returns a future:

```
(defn range-future [n]
  (i/const-future (range n)))

(def age-range (i/map age range-future))

;; #<Future@3d24069e: #<Success@82e8e6e: #<Future@2888dbf4:
#<Success@312084f6: (0 1 2...)>>>>
```

The `range-future` function returns a successful future that yields a range of *n*. The `const-future` function is analogous to `failed-future`, except it immediately completes the future with a `Success` type.

However, we end up with a nested future, which is almost never what you want. That's OK. This is precisely the scenario in which you would use another combinator, `flatmap`.

You can think of it as `mapcat` for futures—it flattens the computation for us:

```
(def age-range (i/flatmap age range-future))

;; #<Future@601c1dfc: #<Success@55f4bcaf: (0 1 2 ...)>>
```

Another very useful combinator is used to bring together multiple computations that are to be used in a single function—`sequence`:

```
(def name (i/future (do (Thread/sleep 500)
                        "Leo")))
(def genres (i/future (do (Thread/sleep 500)
                          ["Heavy Metal" "Black Metal" "Death Metal" "Rock
'n Roll"])))

(->  (i/sequence [name age genres])
     (i/on-success
      (fn [[name age genres]]
        (prn-to-repl (format "%s is %s years old and enjoys %s"
                             name
                             age
                             (clojure.string/join "," genres))))))

;; "Leo is 31 years old and enjoys Heavy Metal,Black Metal,Death Metal,Rock
'n Roll"
```

Essentially, `sequence` creates a new future, which will complete only when all other futures in the vector have completed or any one of them has failed.

This is a nice segue into the last combinator we will look at—`map-future`—which we would use in place of `pmap`. This was used in the movies example:

```
(defn calculate-double [n]
  (i/const-future (* n 2)))

(-> (i/map-future calculate-double [1 2 3 4])
    i/await
    i/dderef)

;; [2 4 6 8]
```

In the preceding example, `calculate-double` is a function that returns a future with the value n doubled. The `map-future` function then maps `calculate-double` over the list, effectively performing the calculations in parallel. Finally, `map-future` sequences all futures together, returning a single future, which yields the result of all computations.

Because we are performing a number of parallel computations and don't really know when they will finish, we call `await` on the future, which is a way to block the current thread until its result is ready. In general, you would use the combinators and event handlers instead, but for this example, using `await` is acceptable.

Imminent's API provides many more combinators that help us write asynchronous programs in a declarative way. This section gave us a taste of what is possible with the API and is enough to allow us to write the movies example using imminent futures.

The movies example revisited

Still within our `imminent-playground` project, open the `src/imminent_playground/core.clj` file and add the appropriate definitions:

```
(ns imminent-playground.core
  (:require [clojure.pprint :refer [pprint]]
            [imminent.core :as i]))

(def movie ...)

(def actor-movies ...)

(def actor-spouse ...)

(def top-5-movies ...)
```

We will be using the same data as in the previous program, which is represented in the preceding snippet by the use of ellipses. Simply copy the relevant declarations over.

The `service` functions will need small tweaks in this new version:

```
(defn cast-by-movie [name]
  (i/future (do (Thread/sleep 5000)
                (:cast  movie))))

(defn movies-by-actor [name]
  (i/future (do (Thread/sleep 2000)
                (->> actor-movies
                     (filter #(= name (:name %)))
```

```
                        first))))

(defn spouse-of [name]
  (i/future (do (Thread/sleep 2000)
                (->> actor-spouse
                     (filter #(= name (:name %)))
                     first))))

(defn top-5 []
  (i/future (do (Thread/sleep 5000)
                top-5-movies)))

(defn aggregate-actor-data [spouses movies top-5]
    ...)
```

The main difference is that all of them now return an imminent future. The aggregate-actor-data function is also the same as before.

This brings us to the -main function, which was rewritten to use imminent combinators:

```
(defn -main [& args]
  (time (let [cast    (cast-by-movie "Lord of The Rings: The Fellowship of
The Ring")
              movies  (i/flatmap cast #(i/map-future movies-by-actor %))
              spouses (i/flatmap cast #(i/map-future spouse-of %))
              result  (i/sequence [spouses movies (top-5)])]
          (prn "Fetching data...")
          (pprint (apply aggregate-actor-data
                         (i/dderef (i/await result))))))))
```

This function starts much like its previous version, and even the first binding, cast, looks familiar. Next, we have movies, which is obtained by fetching an actor's movies in parallel. This in itself returns a future, so we flatmap it over the cast future to obtain our final result:

```
movies  (i/flatmap cast #(i/map-future movies-by-actor %))
```

spouses works in exactly the same way as movies, which brings us to result. This is where we would like to bring all asynchronous computations together. Therefore, we use the sequence combinator:

```
result  (i/sequence [spouses movies (top-5)])
```

Finally, we decide to block on the `result` future—by using `await` so that we can print the final result:

```
(pprint (apply aggregate-actor-data
                (i/dderef (i/await result))))
```

We run the program in the same way as before, so simply type the following into the command line, under the project's root directory:

```
lein run -m imminent-playground.core
"Fetching data..."
({:name "Cate Blanchett",
  :spouse "Andrew Upton",
  :movies
  ("Lord of The Rings: The Fellowship of The Ring - (top 5)"
   "Lord of The Rings: The Return of The King"
   "The Curious Case of Benjamin Button")}
...
"Elapsed time: 7088.398 msecs"
```

The resultant output was trimmed, as it is exactly the same as before, but two things are different and deserve attention:

- The first output, `Fetching data...`, is printed to the screen a lot faster than in the example where we used Clojure futures
- The overall time it took to fetch everything is shorter, clocking in at just over seven seconds

This highlights the asynchronous nature of imminent futures and combinators. The only time we had to wait is when we explicitly called `await` at the end of the program.

More specifically, the performance boost comes from the following section in the code:

```
(let [...
      result  (i/sequence [spouses movies (top-5)])]
  ...)
```

Because none of the previous bindings block the current thread, we never have to wait to kick off `top-5` in parallel, shaving off roughly three seconds from the overall execution time. We didn't have to explicitly think about the order of execution—the combinators simply did the right thing.

Finally, one last difference is that we didn't have to explicitly call `shutdown-agents` like before. The reason for this is that imminent uses a different type of thread pool: `ForkJoinPool`[1].

This pool has a number of advantages, each with its own trade-off, over the other thread pools, and one characteristic is that we don't need to explicitly shut it down—all of its threads create daemon threads.

When the JVM shuts down, it hangs, waiting for all non-daemon threads to finish. Only then does it exit. That's why using Clojure futures would cause the JVM to hang if we had not called `shutdown-agents`.

All of the threads that were created by `ForkJoinPool` are set as daemon threads by default: when the JVM attempts to shut down, and if the only threads running are daemon ones, they are abandoned and the JVM exits gracefully.

Combinators such as `map` and `flatmap`, as well as the `sequence` and `map-future` functions, aren't exclusive to futures. They have many more fundamental principles by which they abide, making them useful in a range of domains. Understanding these principles isn't necessary for following the contents of this book. Should you want to know more about these principles, please refer to the `Appendix`, *The Algebra of Library Design*.

Futures and blocking IO

The choice of using `ForkJoinPool` for imminent is deliberate. `ForkJoinPool`, which was added in Java 7, is extremely smart. When created, you give it a desired level of parallelism, which defaults to the number of available processors.

`ForkJoinPool` then attempts to honor this desired parallelism by dynamically shrinking and expanding the pool as required. When a task is submitted to this pool, it doesn't necessarily create a new thread if it doesn't have to. This allows the pool to serve an extremely large number of tasks with a much smaller number of actual threads.

However, it cannot guarantee such optimizations in the face of blocking IO, as it can't know whether the thread is blocking, waiting for an external resource. Nevertheless, `ForkJoinPool` provides a mechanism by which threads can notify the pool when they might block.

Imminent takes advantage of this mechanism by implementing the `ManagedBlocker` interface [2], and provides another way to create futures, as demonstrated here:

```
(-> (immi/blocking-future
     (Thread/sleep 100)
     10)
    (immi/await))
```

```
;; #<Future@4c8ac77a: #<Success@45525276: 10>>

(-> (immi/blocking-future-call
      (fn []
        (Thread/sleep 100)
        10))
    (immi/await))
;; #<Future@37162438: #<Success@5a13697f: 10>>
```

`blocking-future` and `blocking-future-call` have the same semantics as their counterparts, `future` and `future-call`, but should be used when the task to be performed is of a blocking nature (that is, not CPU-bound). This allows `ForkJoinPool` to better utilize its resources, making it a powerful and flexible solution.

Summary

In this chapter, we learned that Clojure futures leave a lot to be desired. More specifically, Clojure futures don't provide a way to express dependencies between results. It doesn't mean, however, that we should dismiss futures altogether.

They are still a useful abstraction and with the right semantics for asynchronous computations and a rich set of combinators, such as the ones provided by imminent, they can be an ally in building reactive applications that are performant and responsive. Sometimes, this is all we need.

For the times where we need to model data that varies over time, we turn to richer frameworks that were inspired by **Functional Reactive Programming (FRP)** and **Compositional Event Systems (CES)**, such as RxJava, or **Communicating Sequential Processes (CSP)**, such as `core.async`. As they have a lot more to offer, much of this book has been dedicated to these approaches. In the next chapter, we will go back to discussing FRP/CES by way of a case study.

Further reading

Here is a list of information you may refer to regarding what was covered in this chapter:

1. Java, `ForkJoinPool`: http://docs.oracle.com/javase/7/docs/api/java/util/concurrent/ForkJoinPool.html
2. Java, `ManagedBlocker`: http://docs.oracle.com/javase/7/docs/api/java/util/concurrent/ForkJoinPool.ManagedBlocker.html

9
A Reactive API to Amazon Web Services

Throughout this book, you have learned about a number of tools and techniques to aid you in building reactive applications: futures with `imminent`, Observables with RxClojure/RxJava, channels with `core.async`, and even Reactive User Interfaces with Om and React.

In the process, you also became acquainted with the concepts of **Functional Reactive Programming** (**FRP**) and **Compositional Event Systems** (**CES**), and what makes them different.

In this chapter, we will bring a few of these different tools and concepts together by developing an application based on a real-world use case from a client that I worked with in Sydney, Australia.

This chapter will cover the following topics:

- The problem of infrastructure automation that we tried to solve
- A brief look at some of Amazon's AWS services
- Building an AWS dashboard by using the concepts that you have learned so far

Amazon Services use case

The client (which we will call BubbleCorp from now on) had a problem that is all too common and well known in big enterprises: one massive, a monolithic application that had many unrelated business features.

Aside from making the monolithic applications move and evolve slow, as individual components can't evolve independently, such an application makes deployment incredibly difficult, due to its environmental constraints: all of the infrastructure needs to be available in order for the application to work at all.

As a result, developing new features and bug fixes involves having only a handful of development environments, each shared across dozens of developers. This makes for a wasteful amount of coordination between teams just so that they won't step on each other's toes, further slowing down the whole life cycle.

The long-term solution to this problem is to break down the big application into smaller components, which can then be deployed and worked on independently; however, as good as this sounds, it's a laborious and lengthy process.

As a first step, BubbleCorp decided that the best improvement they could make in the short term was to give developers the ability to work on the application independent of one another, which meant creating a new environment as well.

Given the infrastructure constraints, running the application on a single developer machine was impossible. Instead, they turned to infrastructure automation; they wanted a tool that would, with the press of a button, spin up a completely new environment.

This new environment would be preconfigured with the proper application servers, database instances, DNS entries, and everything else needed to run the application. This way, the developers would only need to deploy their code and test their changes, without having to worry about the application setup.

Infrastructure automation

Amazon Web Services (AWS) is the most mature and comprehensive cloud computing platform available today, and as such it was a natural choice for BubbleCorp in terms of infrastructure hosting.

If you haven't used AWS previously, don't worry; we'll only focus on a few of its services, as follows:

- **Elastic Compute Cloud** (**EC2**): A service that provides users with the ability to rent virtual computers to run their applications in.
- **Relational Database Service** (**RDS**): This can be thought of as a specialized version of EC2 that provides managed database services.
- **CloudFormation**: With CloudFormation, users have the ability to specify the infrastructure templates, called **stacks**, of several different AWS resources (such as EC2, AWS, and many others), as well as how they interact with each other. Once it has been written, the infrastructure template can be sent to AWS to be executed.

For BubbleCorp, the idea was to write the infrastructure templates, which once submitted would result in a completely new, isolated environment containing all of the data and components required to run its app. At any given time, there would be dozens of these environments running, with developers working on them.

As decent a plan as this sounds, big corporations usually have an added burden: cost centers. Unfortunately, BubbleCorp couldn't simply allow developers to log in to the AWS Console (where we can manage AWS resources) and spin up environments at will. They needed a way to, among other things, add cost center metadata to the environment, in order to handle their internal billing process.

This brings us to the application that we will be focusing on for the remainder of this chapter.

AWS resources dashboard

My team and I were tasked with building a web-based dashboard for AWS. This dashboard would allow developers to log in using their BubbleCorp credentials, and, once authenticated, create new CloudFormation environments, as well as visualize the status of each individual resource within a CloudFormation stack.

The application itself is fairly involved, so we will focus on a subset of it: interfacing with the necessary AWS services, in order to gather information about the status of each individual resource in a given CloudFormation stack.

Once it has been finished, this is what our simplified dashboard will look like:

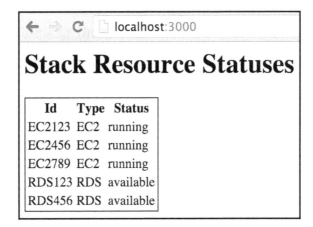

It will display the ID, the type, and the current status of each resource. This might not seem like much right now, but given that all of this information is coming from different, independent web services, it would be far too easy to end up with unnecessarily complex code.

We will be using ClojureScript for this, and therefore, the JavaScript version of the AWS SDK[1].

Before we get started, let's take a look at each of the AWS APIs that we will be interacting with.

In reality, we will not be interacting with the real AWS services, but rather, a stub server provided for download from the book's GitHub repository. This will make following the chapter easier, as you won't need to create an account or generate an API access key to interact with AWS. Additionally, creating resources incurs costs, and the last thing that I want is for you to be charged hundreds of dollars at the end of the month because someone accidentally left resources running for longer than they should (trust me, this has happened before).

CloudFormation

The first service that we will look at is CloudFormation. This makes sense, as the APIs found there will give us a starting point for finding information about the resources in a given stack.

The describeStacks endpoint

The `describeStacks` endpoint is responsible for listing all of the stacks associated with a particular AWS account. For a given stack, the response will look as follows:

```
{"Stacks"
  [{"StackId"
    "arn:aws:cloudformation:ap-
southeast-2:337944750480:stack/DevStack-62031/1",
    "StackStatus" "CREATE_IN_PROGRESS",
    "StackName" "DevStack-62031",
    "Parameters" [{"ParameterKey" "DevDB", "ParameterValue" nil}]}]}
```

Unfortunately, this doesn't say anything about which resources belong to the stack. It does, however, give us the stack name, which we can use to look up resources in the next service.

The describeStackResources endpoint

The `describeStackResources` endpoint receives many arguments, but the one that we're interested in is the stack name, which, once provided, returns the following:

```
{"StackResources"
  [{"PhysicalResourceId" "EC2123",
    "ResourceType" "AWS::EC2::Instance"},
   {"PhysicalResourceId" "EC2456",
    "ResourceType" "AWS::EC2::Instance"}
   {"PhysicalResourceId" "EC2789",
    "ResourceType" "AWS::EC2::Instance"}
   {"PhysicalResourceId" "RDS123",
    "ResourceType" "AWS::RDS::DBInstance"}
   {"PhysicalResourceId" "RDS456",
    "ResourceType" "AWS::RDS::DBInstance"}]}
```

We seem to be getting somewhere now. This stack has several resources: three EC2 instances and two RDS instances. Not too bad for only two API calls.

However, as we mentioned previously, our dashboard needs to show the status of each of the resources. With the list of resource IDs at hand, we need to look at other services that could give us detailed information about each resource.

Elastic Compute Cloud Service

The next service that we will look at is specific to EC2. As you will see, the responses of the different services aren't as consistent as we would like them to be.

The describeInstances endpoint

The `describeInstances` endpoint sounds promising. Based on the documentation, it seems that we can give it a list of instance IDs, and it will give us back the following response:

```
{"Reservations"
  [{"Instances"
    [{"InstanceId" "EC2123",
      "Tags"
      [{"Key" "StackType", "Value" "Dev"}
       {"Key" "junkTag", "Value" "should not be included"}
       {"Key" "aws:cloudformation:logical-id", "Value" "theDude"}],
      "State" {"Name" "running"}}
     {"InstanceId" "EC2456",
      "Tags"
      [{"Key" "StackType", "Value" "Dev"}
       {"Key" "junkTag", "Value" "should not be included"}
       {"Key" "aws:cloudformation:logical-id", "Value" "theDude"}],
      "State" {"Name" "running"}}
     {"InstanceId" "EC2789",
      "Tags"
      [{"Key" "StackType", "Value" "Dev"}
       {"Key" "junkTag", "Value" "should not be included"}
       {"Key" "aws:cloudformation:logical-id", "Value" "theDude"}],
      "State" {"Name" "running"}}]}]}
```

Buried in this response, we can see the `State` key, which gives us the status of that particular EC2 instance. This is all we need, as far as EC2 goes. That leaves us with the RDS to handle.

Relational Database Service

One might think that getting the statuses of RDS instances would be just as easy as it was with EC2. Let's see if that is the case.

The describeDBInstances endpoint

The `describeDBInstances` endpoint is equivalent to the EC2 endpoint that we just looked at in purpose. Its input supports filters, so we can pass multiple RDS instance IDs.

When given specific database instance IDs, the service will respond with the following code:

```
{"DBInstances"
  [{"DBInstanceIdentifier" "RDS123", "DBInstanceStatus" "available"}
  {"DBInstanceIdentifier" "RDS456", "DBInstanceStatus" "available"}]}
```

We get a vector with information about RDS instances.

Designing the solution

We now have all of the information that we need to start designing our application. We need to coordinate four different API calls per CloudFormation stack, as follows:

- `describeStacks`: To list all available stacks
- `describeStackResources`: To retrieve the details of all resources contained in a stack
- `describeInstances`: To retrieve the details of all EC2 instances in a stack
- `describeDBInstances`: To retrieve the details of all DB2 instances in a stack

Next, I would like you to step back for a moment and think about how you would design code like this. Go ahead; I'll wait.

Now that you're back, let's take a look at one possible approach.

If you recall the screenshot of what the dashboard will look like, you will realize that, for the purposes of our application, the differences between EC2 and RDS resources can be completely ignored as long as each one has the attributes ID, type, and status.

This means that whatever our solution may be, it has to somehow provide a uniform way of abstracting the different resource types.

Additionally, apart from `describeStacks` and `describeStackResources`, which need to be called sequentially, `describeInstances` and `describeDBInstances` can be executed concurrently, after which we will need a way to merge the results.

Since an image is worth a thousand words, the following figure shows what we would like the workflow to look like:

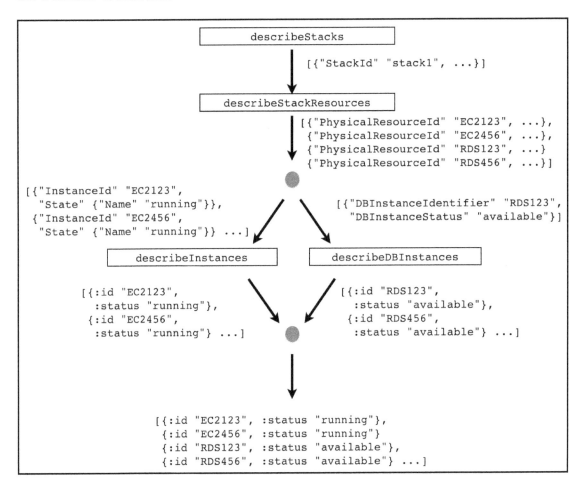

The preceding figure highlights a number of key aspects of our solution:

1. We start by retrieving stacks, by calling `describeStacks`
2. Next, for each stack, we call `describeStackResources`, in order to retrieve a list of resources for each one
3. Then, we split the list by type, ending with a list of EC2 resources, and one with RDS resources
4. We proceed by concurrently calling `describeInstances` and `describeDBInstances`, yielding two lists of results, one per resource type

5. As the response formats are different, we transform each resource into a uniform representation

6. Lastly, we merge all of the results into a single list, ready for rendering

This is quite a bit to take in, but, as you will soon realize, our solution isn't too far from this high-level description.

We can quite easily think of this problem as a flow of date. We have information about several different types of instances flowing through API calls. Each call transforms data as needed until we arrive at the information we're after. The final result is in the format we would like to work within the front-end application.

As it turns out, a great way to model this problem is to use one of the Reactive abstractions that you learned about earlier in this book: Observables.

Running the AWS stub server

Before we jump into writing our dashboard, we should make sure that our AWS stub server is properly set up. The stub server is a Clojure web application that simulates how the real AWS API behaves, and it is the backend that our dashboard will talk to.

Let's start by going into our Terminal, cloning the book repository by using Git, and then starting the stub server, as follows:

```
$ git clone
https://github.com/PacktPublishing/Hands-On-Reactive-Programming-with-Cloju
re-Second-Edition
$ cd Hands-On-Reactive-Programming-with-Clojure-Second-
Edition/Chapter09/aws-api-stub
$ lein ring server-headless 3001
2018-11-23 17:33:37.766:INFO:oejs.Server:jetty-7.6.8.v20121106 2018-11-23
17:33:37.812:INFO:oejs.AbstractConnector:Started
SelectChannelConnector@0.0.0.0:3001 Started server on port 3001
```

This will start the server on port 3001. To validate that it is working as expected, point your browser to `http://localhost:3001/cloudFormation/describeStacks`. You should see the following JSON response:

```
{
    "Stacks": [
        {
            "Parameters": [
                {
                    "ParameterKey": "DevDB",
```

```
                    "ParameterValue": null
                }
            ],
            "StackStatus": "CREATE_IN_PROGRESS",
            "StackId": "arn:aws:cloudformation:ap-
  southeast-2:337944750480:stack/DevStack-62031/1",
            "StackName": "DevStack-62031"
        }
    ]
}
```

Setting up the dashboard project

As we mentioned previously, we will be developing the dashboard by using ClojureScript, with the UI rendered with Om. Additionally, as we have chosen Observables as our main reactive abstraction, we will need RxJS, one of the many implementations of Microsoft's Reactive Extensions. We will be pulling these dependencies into our project shortly.

Let's create a new ClojureScript project called `aws-dash`, using the `figwheel` Leiningen template:

```
$ lein new figwheel aws-dash
```

This gives us a starting point, but we should make sure that all of our versions match. Open up the `project.clj` file found in the root directory of the new project, and ensure that the dependencies section looks as follows:

```
  . . .
  :dependencies [[org.clojure/clojure "1.9.0"]
                 [org.clojure/clojurescript "1.10.238"]
                 [org.clojure/core.async "0.4.474"]
                 [org.omcljs/om "1.0.0-beta4"]
                 [cljs-http "0.1.45"]
                 [com.cognitect/transit-cljs "0.8.256"]]
  . . .
```

This is the first time that we have seen the last two dependencies. `cljs-http` is a simple HTTP library that we will use to make AJAX requests to our AWS stub server. `transit-cljs` allows us to, among other things, parse JSON responses into ClojureScript data structures.

Transit is a format and a set of libraries through which applications developed in different technologies can speak to each other. In this case, we are using the ClojureScript library to parse JSON, but if you're interested in learning more, I recommend reading the official blog post announcement by Rich Hickey[2].

Next, we need RxJS, which, being a JavaScript dependency, isn't available via Leiningen. That's OK. We will simply download it from the Rx website. Go to `https://unpkg.com/rxjs@6.3.3/bundles/rxjs.umd.min.js` and save the file in `aws-dash/resources/public/js/rx.js`.

Moving on, we need to make our application aware of our new dependency on RxJS. Open the `aws-dash/resources/public/index.html` file and add a `script` tag to pull in RxJS, as follows:

```
<html>
  <head>
   <script src="js/rx.js" type="text/javascript"></script>
  </head>
  <body>
    <div id="app"></div>
    <script src="js/compiled/aws_dash.js"></script>
  </body>
</html>
```

With all of the dependencies in place, let's start the auto-compilation for our ClojureScript source files, as follows:

```
$ lein figwheel
```

Creating AWS Observables

We're now ready to start to implement our solution. If you recall Chapter 2, *A Look at Reactive Extensions*, `RxJava/RxJS/RxClojure` ships with several useful Observables. However, when the built-in Observables aren't enough, it gives us the tools to build our own.

Since it is highly unlikely that RxJS already provides Observables for Amazon's AWS API, we will start by implementing our own primitive Observables.

To keep things neat, we will do this in a new file, under `aws-dash/src/cljs/aws_dash/observables.cljs`:

```
(ns aws-dash.observables
  (:require-macros [cljs.core.async.macros :refer [go]])
  (:require [cljs-http.client :as http]
            [cljs.core.async :refer [<!]]
            [cognitect.transit :as t]))


(def r (t/reader :json))

(def  aws-endpoint "http://localhost:3001")
(defn aws-uri [path]
  (str aws-endpoint path))
```

The namespace declaration requires the dependencies that we will need in this file. Note that there is no explicit dependency on RxJS. Since it is a JavaScript dependency that we manually pulled in, it is globally available for us to use via JavaScript interoperability.

The next line sets up a `transit` reader for JSON, which we will use when parsing the stub server responses.

Then, we define the endpoint that we will be talking to, as well as a helper function to build the correct URIs. Make sure that the `aws-endpoint` variable matches the host and port of the stub server started in the previous section.

All of the Observables that we are about to create will follow a common structure: they will make a request to the stub server, extract some information from the response, optionally transform it, and then emit each item in the transformed sequence into the new Observable sequence.

To avoid repetition, this pattern is captured in the following function:

```
(defn observable-seq [uri transform]
  (.create js/rxjs.Observable
           (fn [observer]
             (go (let [response       (<! (http/get uri {:with-credentials?
false}))
                       data           (t/read r (:body response))
                       transformed    (transform data)]
                   (doseq [x transformed]
                     (.next observer x))
                   (.complete observer)))
             (fn [] (.log js/console "Disposed")))))
```

Let's break this function down, as follows:

1. `observable-seq` receives two arguments—the backend URI to which we will issue a `GET` request, and a `transform` function, which is given the raw parsed JSON response and returns a sequence of transformed items.
2. Then, it calls the `create` function of the RxJS object, `rxjs.Observable`. Note that we make use of JavaScript interoperability here—we access the `create` function by prepending it with a dot, much like in Java interoperability. Since `rxjs.Observable` is a global object, we access it by prepending the global JavaScript namespace that ClojureScript makes available to our program, `js/rxjs.Observable`.
3. The Observable's `create` function receives two arguments. One is a function that gets called with an Observer, to which we can push items to be published in the Observable sequence. The second function is a function that is called whenever this Observable is disposed of. This is the function where we can perform any cleanup that's needed. In our case, this function simply logs the fact that it is called to the console.

The first function is the one that interests us, though:

```
(fn [observer]
  (go (let [response    (<! (http/get uri
                                      {:with-credentials?
                                       false}))
            data        (t/read r (:body response))
            transformed (transform data)]
        (doseq [x transformed]
          (.next observer x))
        (.complete observer)))))
```

As soon as it gets called, it performs a request to the provided URI, using the `get` function of `cljs-http`, which returns a `core.async` channel. That's why the whole logic is inside of a `go` block.

Next, we use the transit JSON reader that we configured previously to parse the body of the response, feeding the result into the `transform` function. Remember that this function, as per our design, returns a sequence of things. Therefore, all that is left to do is push each item into the Observer in turn.

Once we're done, we will indicate that this Observable sequence won't emit any new items by invoking the `.complete` function of the `observer` object.

Now, we can proceed with creating our Observables by using this helper function, starting with the one responsible for retrieving CloudFormation stacks:

```
(defn describe-stacks []
  (observable-seq (aws-uri "/cloudFormation/describeStacks")
                  (fn [data]
                    (map (fn [stack] {:stack-id   (stack "StackId")
                                      :stack-name (stack "StackName")})
                         (data "Stacks")))))
```

This creates observable, which will emit one item per stack, in the following format:

```
({:stack-id "arn:aws:cloudformation:ap-
southeast-2:337944750480:stack/DevStack-62031/1", :stack-name
"DevStack-62031"})
```

Now that we have all Amazon stacks that we use, we need observable to describe resources of each stack, as follows:

```
(defn describe-stack-resources [stack-name]
  (observable-seq (aws-uri "/cloudFormation/describeStackResources")
                  (fn [data]
                    (map (fn [resource]
                           {:resource-id (resource "PhysicalResourceId")
                            :resource-type (resource "ResourceType")} )
                         (data "StackResources")))))
```

It has a similar purpose, and emits resource items in the following format:

```
({:resource-id "EC2123", :resource-type "AWS::EC2::Instance"}
 {:resource-id "EC2456", :resource-type "AWS::EC2::Instance"}
 {:resource-id "EC2789", :resource-type "AWS::EC2::Instance"}
 {:resource-id "RDS123", :resource-type "AWS::RDS::DBInstance"}
 {:resource-id "RDS456", :resource-type "AWS::RDS::DBInstance"})
```

Since we're following our strategy almost to the letter, we need two more observables (one for each instance type):

```
(defn describe-instances [instance-ids]
  (observable-seq (aws-uri "/ec2/describeInstances")
                  (fn [data]
                    (let [instances (mapcat (fn [reservation]
                                              (reservation "Instances"))
                                            (data "Reservations"))]
                      (map (fn [instance]
                             {:instance-id (instance "InstanceId")
                              :type        "EC2"
                              :status      (get-in instance ["State"
```

```
"Name"])})
                                    instances)))))

(defn describe-db-instances [instance-ids]
  (observable-seq (aws-uri "/rds/describeDBInstances")
                  (fn [data]
                    (map (fn [instance]
                           {:instance-id (instance "DBInstanceIdentifier")
                            :type        "RDS"
                            :status      (instance "DBInstanceStatus")})
                         (data "DBInstances")))))
```

Each of these will emit resource items in the following formats, for EC2 and RDS, respectively:

```
({:instance-id "EC2123", :type "EC2", :status "running"} ...)
({:instance-id "RDS123", :type "RDS", :status "available"} ...)
```

Combining the AWS Observables

It seems that we have all of the major pieces in place now. All that is left to do is combine the more primitive, basic Observables that we just created into more complex and useful ones. We need to combine and aggregate all the data produced by Observables in order to render our dashboard.

We will use a number of Rx functions to operate on simple Observables and create complex ones:

```
(def rx-filter js/rxjs.operators.filter)
(def rx-flat-map js/rxjs.operators.flatMap)
(def rx-map js/rxjs.operators.map)
(def rx-merge js/rxjs.merge)
(def rx-reduce js/rxjs.operators.reduce)
```

We will start by creating a function that combines both the `describe-stacks` and `describe-stack-resources` Observables, as follows:

```
(defn stack-resources []
  (-> (describe-stacks)
      (.pipe (rx-map #(:stack-name %)))
      (.pipe (rx-flat-map describe-stack-resources))))
```

Starting with the previous example, you will begin to see how defining our API calls in terms of Observable sequences pays off: it's pretty simple to combine these two Observables in a declarative manner.

Remember the role of `rxjs.operators.flatMap`: as `describe-stack-resources` itself returns an Observable, we use `flatMap` to flatten both Observables, as we did before, in various abstractions.

The `stack-resources` Observable will emit the resource items for all stacks. According to our plan, we would like to fork the processing here, in order to concurrently retrieve EC2 and RDS instance data.

By following this train of thought, we will arrive at two more functions that combine and transform the previous Observables:

```
(defn ec2-instance-status [resources]
  (-> resources
      (.pipe (rx-filter #(= (:resource-type %) "AWS::EC2::Instance")) )
      (.pipe (rx-map #(:resource-id %)))
      (.pipe (rx-reduce conj []))
      (.pipe (rx-flat-map describe-instances)))))

(defn rds-instance-status [resources]
  (-> resources
      (.pipe (rx-filter #(= (:resource-type %) "AWS::RDS::DBInstance")))
      (.pipe (rx-map #(:resource-id %)))
      (.pipe (rx-flatmap describe-db-instances)))))
```

Both of the functions receive an argument, `resources`, which is the result of calling the `stack-resources` Observable. This way, we only need to call it once.

Once again, it is fairly simple to combine the Observables in a way that makes sense, following our high-level idea that was described previously.

Starting with `resources`, we filter out the types that we're not interested in, retrieve the IDs, and request detailed information by flatmapping the `describe-instances` and `describe-db-instances` Observables.

Our simple Reactive API for Amazon AWS is now complete, leaving us with the UI to create.

Putting it all together

Now, let's turn to building our user interface. It's a simple one, so let's just jump into it. Open up `aws-dash/src/aws_dash/core.cljs` and add the following:

```
(ns aws-dash.core
  (:require [aws-dash.observables :as obs]
```

```
        [aws-dash.parser :as parser]
        [om.next :as om :refer-macros [defui]]
        [om.dom :as dom]))

(enable-console-print!)

(def app-state (atom {:instances []}))

(defui Column
       static om/IQuery
       (query [this]
              [:instance-id :type :status])
       Object
       (render [this]
         (let [{:keys [instance-id type status]} (om/props this)]
                (dom/tr #js {:key instance-id}
                        (dom/td nil instance-id)
                        (dom/td nil type)
                        (dom/td nil status)))))

(def column (om/factory Column {:keyfn :instance-id}))

(defn column-view [columns]
  (map column columns))

(defui RootView
       static om/IQuery
       (query [this]
              '[:instances])
       Object
       (render [this]
               (let [{:keys [:instances]} (om/props this)]
                 (dom/div nil
                          (dom/h1 nil "Stack Resource Statuses")
                          (dom/table #js {:style #js {:border "1px solid
black"}}
                                     (dom/tbody nil
                                       (dom/tr nil
                                           (dom/th nil "Id")
                                           (dom/th nil "Type")
                                           (dom/th nil "Status"))
                                       (column-view instances)))))))

(def reconciler
  (om/reconciler
    {:state     app-state
     :parser    parser/parser}))
```

```
(defn start []
  (om/add-root!
    reconciler
    RootView
    (.getElementById js/document "app")))

(start)

(defn on-js-reload []
  (start))
```

Our application state contains a single key, :instances, which starts as an empty vector. As you can see from each Om component, the instances will be rendered as rows in an HTML table.

We are missing our parser file. Let's create parser.cljs, and include the following code:

```
(ns aws-dash.parser
  (:require [om.next :as om])
  (:refer-clojure :exclude [read]))

(defmulti read om/dispatch)

(defmethod read :instances
  [{:keys [state query]} k _]
  (let [st @state]
    {:value (:instances st)}))

(defmulti mutate om/dispatch)

(defmethod mutate 'add/instances
  [{:keys [state]} _ {:keys [data]}]
  {:action
   (fn []
     (swap! state update-in
            [:instances]
            (fn [existing-instances]
              (concat existing-instances data))))
   :value {:keys [:instances]}})

(def parser (om/parser {:read read :mutate mutate}))
```

The read function looks up the data under the :instances key. The mutate function, 'add/instances, concatenates the passed data to existing instances.

After saving the file, make sure that the web server is running by starting it from the REPL:

```
lein figwheel
```

You should now be able to point your browser to `http://localhost:3449/index.html`; but, as you may have guessed, you will see nothing but an empty table.

That is because we haven't yet used our Reactive AWS API.

Let's fix it and bring it all together at the bottom of `core.cljs`, as follows:

```
(def resources (obs/stack-resources))

(.subscribe (-> (obs/rx-merge (obs/rds-instance-status resources)
                              (obs/ec2-instance-status resources))
              (.pipe (obs/rx-reduce conj [])))
            (fn [data]
              (let [pass {:data (filter (fn [m]
                                          (map? m))
                                        data)}]
                (om/transact! reconciler `[(add/instances ~pass)]))))
```

Yes, this is all we need! We create a `stack-resources` Observable and pass it as an argument to both `rds-instance-status` and `ec2-instance-status`, which will concurrently retrieve the status information about all instances.

Next, we create a new Observable by merging the previous two, followed by a call to `rx-reduce`, which will accumulate all of the information into a vector, convenient for rendering.

Finally, we simply subscribe to this Observable, and, when it emits its results, we update our application state, leaving Om to do the rendering for us.

Go back to your browser at `http://localhost:3449/index.html`, and you should see all of the instance statuses, as shown at the beginning of this chapter.

Exercises

With the preceding approach, the only way to see new information about the AWS resources is to refresh the whole page. Modify our implementation in such a way that it queries the stub services every so often (say, every 500 milliseconds).

 The `interval` function from RxJS can be helpful in solving this exercise. Think about how you might use it with our existing stream by reviewing how `flatMap` works.

Summary

In this chapter, we looked at a real use case for reactive applications—building a dashboard for AWS CloudFormation stacks.

You learned that considering the information needed as resources/items flowing through a graph can help you to understand how to create Observables. In addition, you saw that creating primitive Observables that do only one thing can provide a nice, declarative way to combine them into more complex Observables, providing a degree of reuse not usually found in common techniques.

Finally, we packaged it together with a simple Om-based interface to demonstrate how using different abstractions in the same application does not add to the complexity, as long as the abstractions are chosen for the problem at hand carefully.

We have written a few Clojure applications so far. In the next chapter, we will take a look at the concept of testing and learn about Clojure testing frameworks.

Further reading

Here is a list of information you can refer to:

1. Amazon, JS SDK: `https://aws.amazon.com/sdk-for-node-js/`
2. Clojure, Transit: `http://blog.cognitect.com/blog/2014/7/22/transit`

10
Reactive Microservices

So far, you've seen examples of using Reactive Programming in Clojure. We've created simple applications with Om, and we've used Amazon's API in the backend server. It's now time to investigate what we can do to create more elaborate applications.

A well-designed application can make our business successful, while a poorly designed one will certainly create many problems, from unhappy customers to the loss of prospective clients. When designing an application's architecture, we have two broad choices—we can either create one monolithic application, or we can use a microservices architecture.

In this chapter, we'll cover the following:

- Comparing and contrasting monolithic and microservices architectures
- The best practices for designing microservices
- Event-driven communication between microservices using messages and CQRS
- Common pitfalls when creating microservices
- What Clojure offers in terms of microservices

An introduction to microservices

Gone are the times when developers mainly designed simple applications that could be run in a single environment. Nowadays, we have a plethora of environments and hardware configurations. Our applications process lots of data and serve many customers, often with different needs. This has resulted in a need to create big applications. Software architects have explored ways to create such applications. They have used what we call multitier architecture[1], where there's a clear separation between data management, application processing, and presentation.

Applications that are created using one technology stack and are packaged together as one are called **monolithic**. We can contrast them with microservices architectures[2], where we structure our application as a collection of loosely coupled services. Each service is responsible for one task and can be developed independently of other services.

Advantages of microservices

There are many benefits to using microservices. Since we decompose our application into smaller parts, it improves the modularity of the whole system. As a result, each service is easier to develop, test, understand, and modify, because we change only one service and not unrelated functionalities that just happen to be bound together in a monolithic design.

Each service can be developed by a separate team, speeding up the application development life cycle. Working on smaller parts also helps the application to emerge, using continuous refactoring when needed.

Each service can be configured and deployed independently of one another. In monolithic applications, developers work on some features that are later tested by a **Quality Assurance (QA)** team. Once the bugs are fixed and the release is signed off on by the QA team, DevOps publish a new version to production. This process can take weeks, or even months, with some applications. With microservices, this process is much shorter, allowing for continuous delivery[4] of new versions and easier deployment.

Having one service allows us to address one business objective or technical capability at a time. This helps to deliver a required piece of the working application much quicker than releasing all of the features at once. Because the architecture is composed of smaller parts, each one is easier to replace, as opposed to redesigning and refactoring a part of a monolithic application.

Scalability

For some applications, there often comes a time when they need to grow in order to support more users. Monolithic applications can only scale vertically. This often means running the application on a scaled-up version of a system, with more RAM or hard drive space.

Microservices allow us to scale horizontally. Once we identify the service that needs scaling, we can design similar services to cooperate with existing ones. Microservices also allow partitioning data into smaller databases, especially when the data is used for different purposes. One service might use a relational database for user data and another service might use a NoSQL database, such as ElasticSearch[5], for text searching or geolocation.

Disadvantages of microservices

Using a microservices architecture results in building a distributed system. This can create some challenges, as follows:

- Connectivity
- Debugging
- Complexity
- Latency problems
- Security

The services need to communicate with each other. This can be done by using APIs or exchanging messages with brokers, such as Kafka[6]. With each service, the testing and debugging of the whole system increases. If each service runs in a separate runtime environment, automation testing becomes challenging.

Each service also increases the system resource and memory consumption. The costs of maintenance and monitoring of the whole system are much higher than in a monolithic system. A more complex system requires more expertise to develop and maintain. There is a high initial investment in the development, deployment, and management. Many people, not just developers, need to understand each service in order to understand the whole system.

Choosing the different technology stacks for the different services can lead to non-uniform application design and architecture. This requires a lot of documentation and the constant updating of schemata and tests.

If the application doesn't need to scale, using microservices may not provide any meaningful benefits. Even worse, when the microservices aren't implemented correctly, they can make poorly written applications even more dysfunctional.

When to use microservices

Microservices are a double-edged sword. When designing a system, it's important to weigh the pros and cons against a monolithic architecture.

Microservices are well suited for software-as-a-service applications[7], where each feature is focused on a single problem. This allows for rapid changes and for scaling to adjust to business demands.

On the other hand, a monolithic architecture is well suited for transactional-oriented applications. Such applications have clearly defined features and change less often. They provide robust access to databases with ACID properties[8].

Regardless of the initial decision, a well thought out design allows us to create a solid system. Unless a microservices design outweighs a monolithic one, it's recommended to start with a monolithic architecture that allows for faster development and deployment. When an application's complexity increases and a need to scale comes along, a well-designed system can be converted into a microservices architecture.

Microservices best practices

When building microservices, we can use a number of best practices to build a robust system. It is important to think about not only one service, but how the service connects to a larger system. We'll go over some best practices in the next sections.

Domain Driven Design

Domain Driven Design[9] is a software design technique that's used to understand and solve complex problems. It advocates for decomposing the problem into smaller and more understandable pieces. Services should be modeled around business domains. Problems are seen as various domains and subdomains.

Each business domain should have a clearly defined role and a boundary separating it from other domains. Hence, each model gets bound by a single application context, called a **bounded context**[10]. The following diagram shows two contexts in an ordering app, and how we can divide each context into smaller parts:

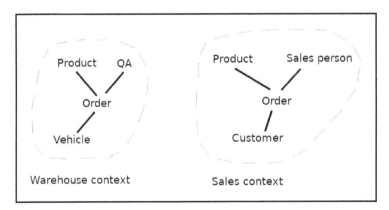

If we develop an application where customers can place orders for various products, instead of thinking about it as a monolithic application, we can divide it into various business domains, such as a warehouse or sales. Each domain has a clearly defined context that is separate from others. The sales context is responsible for handling customer orders and transactions and for placing orders for different products to the warehouse. The warehouse context is responsible for obtaining products using different vehicles (such as a forklift), checking the quality of the product before sending it further for the processing of customer orders, and so on.

Separate data storage

Each microservice should become the owner of its data, as the data should be made private for each microservice. Any data access should only happen through the APIs for each particular service. If this isn't the case and some services access data directly, it will introduce unnecessary coupling between services.

Team building and structure

Teams in the organization should be divided based on the microservices, where one team works on each microservice. When each team consists of development, QA, DevOps, and a manager, they can focus on creating smaller services that are developed and released faster than in monolithic applications.

Deployment

Microservices should be easy to deploy independently. Releasing one service shouldn't result in the need to release changes in other services. Teams should strive to have an automatic build and release deployment process. Tools such as CircleCI[11] can help to manage the deployment process by automating it. Microservices are often wrapped in containers, such as Docker[12], that allow for deployment to many environments.

Failure isolation

Microservices allow for failure isolation, as each service runs independently of the others; when there is a problem in the application, the DevOps team can track which service is responsible for it.

Cross-cutting concerns

When many services use the same functionality, it's advisable to move them to a separate service. Authentication and authorization are often realized in this manner. Other services won't need to re-implement the same functionality all over again but can rely on shared tools and APIs.

This brings us to the end of our overview of the best practices. In the next section, we will look at the ways in which services can communicate with each other.

Communication between services

Now we know that the main goal of creating microservices is to provide a single business context that is independent of other contexts. Although these services can be deployed in isolation, they need to communicate with each other. In this section, we will look at event-driven communication and the concept of CQRS.

Event-driven communication

The key concept in event-driven communication is an event. We can define an event as the outcome of the action taken by a microservice. When an event happens, some other part of the microservice architecture should react. The question is, what part should react? Stay tuned for the answer.

The following diagram will help us to understand event-driven communication:

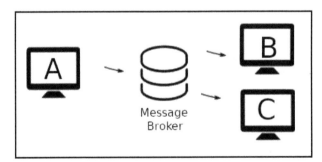

Service A emits an event and sends a message. This message is received by the **Message Broker**. The broker then passes the message to **Service B** and **Service C**. The broker acts as a bridge between the sender and the receivers. The answer for our question is the broker. It reacts to events from the sender and passes messages to the receivers.

The communication that occurs when using a message broker is asynchronous. An event can be published by a sender service and later consumed by receiving services.

Because senders and receivers are decoupled, more than one receiver can obtain messages that are sent by the sender. The sender is not blocked when waiting for receivers to get messages. Once the message reaches the broker, it keeps the message. Receivers can consume this message when they are ready. Receivers do not need to be running when the message is created. Similarly, in the case of a failure, a receiver can start consuming messages where it left off.

The byproduct of using event-driven communication is that the state of the whole application can be rebuilt by processing the events in the sequence that they have been published. We can simulate the current state or some other state at a particular time in the past.

This ability to rebuild the application state helps us in the following situations:

- Running the system on a daily basis
- Recovering from failures
- Auditing the system at specified times
- Debugging the system

In the next section, we will learn about CQRS—another microservices communication pattern.

The CQRS communication pattern

The **Command Query Responsibility Segregation (CQRS)** pattern advises splitting an application into **query** and **command** parts.

A service should be either responsible for a query or command, but not both. The query side is responsible for returning the data that's been queried. The command side is responsible for performing some actions. Often, an action change the state of the application, such as creating, deleting, or updating stored resources.

The CQRS pattern fits well with a microservices-based architecture that splits various business functionalities into smaller services. It is easy to imagine one service providing various metrics about products while another service is used to update the products catalog.

We have to bear in mind that, with microservices, it can be challenging to keep all of the services consistent. For example, a change in a service that's responsible for creating a product, such as it being able to add a new feature, can result in changes in the query service. The query service now needs to return products with the newly added feature. If we keep the schema or resources consistent between services, the CQRS pattern can greatly help us design communication between services.

The need to keep microservices consistent between each other is an example of a pitfall that's encountered when designing microservices-based architectures. In the next section, we will explore other common pitfalls.

Common pitfalls

When designing a microservices-based architecture, many things can go wrong. We'll now explore some of the pitfalls that can happen to unaware or unprepared teams.

Attitudes towards microservices

When it comes to application design using microservices, we can divide people into three broad categories, as follows:

- Enthusiast
- Hater
- Indifferent

The first two types have very strong opinions about microservices and monolithic application design. Both camps can be dogmatic and can enter into heated debates. Some have solid arguments to support their decisions, but for various reasons, don't want to acknowledge the other camp.

It's natural to have some disagreement if it leads to constructive decisions. A healthy team structure allows for room to discuss ideas, but in the end, the decision should be made by a designated person in charge. Democratic team management, where all (or most) of the developers can influence decisions can result in debates that take lots of time and effort, often causing emotional friction.

The third camp of engineers can be a problem for teams implementing microservices. Such developers are often not well-equipped technically to build services. They can implement them incorrectly, such as by introducing unnecessary coupling with other services, over-engineering some services, or making communication with services more challenging.

Testing, deployment, and monitoring are different than in monolithic application design. They require more time and effort investment on the part of each team. In a traditional approach, the developers hand applications to QA for testing, and later, to the admin or DevOps team, to deploy and monitor it. With microservices, each task is shared in a team. Each team needs an initial training investment for learning the best design practices.

Service boundaries

With a design that encourages granularity, it's easy to make the mistake of assigning each service to a person. This can result in a developer taking ownership of service, feeling personally responsible for it, and often identifying with it. Some developers might take criticism of the service as a personal attack. Introducing changes might also be seen not as a technical decision, but a personal one.

Separation of services also leads to detachment. Developers lose sight of the system and focus on their own services. They stop trying to understand the other services and the system as a whole and choose to focus on their own service.

Service granularity

It's tempting to get too granular with a microservices design. Each service is a separate build and deploy unit. This introduces a burden to the DevOps team. Also, when the traffic is still low, services incur extra latency, due to communication.

It's advisable to start with a few services and introduce more when one part of a service needs to be scaled.

Service separation

When designing services, it is common to encounter problems in a number of areas. Let's take a look at some of those problems.

Build dependencies

When designing microservices, we often have two conflicting goals. First is a desire to share common code between services often arises. Second is that each service should be built independently of others. The two goals need to be balanced, as they come with trade-offs. Teams can either replicate functionality in services, lessening the need for the shared code at the expense of increasing build time and maintenance, or they can try to design shared libraries, at the expense of introducing conflicts between services that need to use the shared code in slightly different manners. A resolution of such conflicts is required.

Services contracts

As services need to communicate with each other, it is important to establish an API's contracts. Data shared between services needs to conform to a common schema and be useful for the services concerned. If one service is designed to send arrays and the other expects `String`, this can cause issues and result in unnecessary changes to services.

Services communication

The ways that the services communicate need to be explicitly defined. The documentation for each service should clearly state the following:

- The list of expected responses
- How it handles errors
- Request options

There are various options for sharing data between services, such as AMQP[13] or CQRS[14]. It's unlikely that one way of sharing data will be best suited among many services. Often, using a combination of various models is necessary.

DevOps

A good DevOps team and strong skills are needed, due to the increased complexity of having a microservices architecture.

With many services, the cost of manual deployment increases. **Continuous Integration (CI)** tools, such as CircleCI, allow us to automate the build and deployment process.

Each service needs to be monitored and maintained. Failing to do so may result in countless hours spent investigating which service is failing.

RESTful microservices in action

Having investigated the pros and cons of microservices, we can start to work on implementing a microservices architecture in Clojure.

Application overview

In Chapter 7, *The UI as a Function,* we created a simple Trello-like application to manage an agile board. We stored the data in a Clojure atom. In a more realistic example, we would store the data in a database. Let's suppose that we need to create a native app for such a board. On top of having a web application, we need a phone app. Storing the data directly in an app is not an option, as we need to synchronize the phone and web apps. The board's data that's used by both applications are a good candidate for a separate microservice.

The following diagram shows what our system looks like:

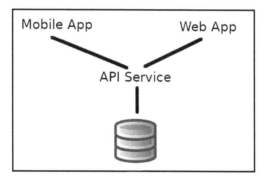

Services messaging

Both of our frontend services need to manipulate the cards' data. They need to do **CRUD** (short for **Create, Read, Update, and Delete**) operations[15]. Each service will initiate operations to manipulate cards. We'll use a REST architectural style[16] to implement messaging between services. REST is based on the HTTP protocol, and it provides methods such as GET, PUT, POST, and DELETE, to manipulate resources such as cards. Services that conform to a REST style are called **RESTful**.

A Clojure RESTful service

We'll use the following command to create a new Clojure project, using a Leiningen template:

```
lein new app restful
```

Setting up the project structure

Next, we'll add the necessary dependencies to `project.clj`, as follows:

```
:dependencies [[org.clojure/clojure "1.9.0"]
               [org.postgresql/postgresql "42.2.4"]
               [prismatic/schema "1.1.9"]
               [metosin/compojure-api "2.0.0-alpha26"]
               [ring/ring-jetty-adapter "1.6.3"]
               [toucan "1.1.9"]]
```

We'll use the **Prismatic** schema to provide object validation in our RESTful API and `compojure-api`. `compojure-api`, which provides a number of helper functions that make creating web APIs easier than if we were to write them by ourselves. In the following sections, we'll see methods such as `POST` or `DELETE` in action.

In this example, I'm using the Postgres database. If you have another database set up already, you can use it. We use the `toucan` library to provide an interface for the database operations that build on top of `clojure.java.jdbc`. To keep things simple, we'll create a database and table using `psql`:

```
$ createdb restful
$ psql -d restful

restful=# CREATE TABLE "cards" (
            id SERIAL PRIMARY KEY,
            name VARCHAR(50) UNIQUE NOT NULL,
            description VARCHAR(255) UNIQUE NOT NULL
          );
```

Database operations with Toucan

In order to use Toucan, we need to provide it with the following:

- Database connection data
- A root namespace for defined data models

In `core.clj`, add the following code:

```
(ns restful.core
  (:require [toucan.db :as db]
            [toucan.models :as models])
  (:gen-class))

(def db-spec
  {:dbtype "postgres"
   :dbname "restful"})

(defn -main [& args]
  (db/set-default-db-connection! db-spec)
  (models/set-root-namespace! 'resultful.models))
```

Create a folder, `models`, with a new file, `card.clj`, inside of it:

```
(ns restful.models.card
  (:require [toucan.models :refer [defmodel]]))

(defmodel Card :cards)
```

The `:cards` keyword refers to the `cards` table that we created earlier, in `psql`.

Coercion with the schema

Very often, we want to validate our data against some schema. `compojure-api` allows us to provide custom schema with constraints for our data.

For our `cards` entities, we can add the following constraints:

- The name should not be blank and should not have more than 50 characters
- The description should have at least five characters but not more than 100

Create a `util.clj` file, where we'll include convenience functions:

```
(ns restful.util
  (:require [clojure.string :as str]))

(def non-blank? (complement str/blank?))

(defn max-length? [length text]
  (<= (count text) length))

(defn non-blank-with-max-length? [length text]
  (and (non-blank? text) (max-length? length text)))
```

```
(defn min-length? [length text]
  (>= (count text) length))

(defn length-in-range? [min-length max-length text]
  (and (min-length? min-length text) (max-length? max-length text)))
```

We'll use these functions to define the schema for `CardReqest`, in `cards.clj`:

```
(ns restful.cards
  (:require [compojure.api.sweet :refer [GET POST PUT DELETE]]
            [restful.models.card :refer [Card]]
            [restful.util :as str]
            [ring.util.http-response :refer [ok not-found created]]
            [schema.core :as s]
            [toucan.db :as db]))

(defn valid-name? [name]
  (str/non-blank-with-max-length? 50 name))

(defn valid-description? [description]
  (str/length-in-range? 5 100 description))

(s/defschema CardRequestSchema
  {:name (s/constrained s/Str valid-name?)
   :description (s/constrained s/Str valid-description?)})
```

We've defined the schema for `CardRequest`, which should contain a valid `:name` and `:description`.

The Card API

Inside of the `cards.clj` file, we'll add a handler for requests creating a new card:

```
(defn id->created [id]
  (created (str "/cards/" id) {:id id}))

(defn create-card-handler [create-card-req]
  (->> create-card-req
       (db/insert! Card)
       :id
       id->created))
```

create-card-handler inserts data into the database using Toucan's insert! function then takes id of a newly created card and returns a created HTTP response.

Compojure HTTP API

Compojure (https://github.com/weavejester/compojure) is a routing library for web applications. It provides a number of methods to handle HTTP requests. There are functions, such as POST, GET, and PUT, that correspond to HTTP methods.

The final step in writing our microservice is to wire the handler with the compojure-api route:

```
(def card-routes
  [(POST "/cards" []
     :body [create-card-req CardRequestSchema]
     (create-card-handler create-card-req))])
```

The first argument is the URI of the route ("/cards"). It matches the URI of a request. The second argument provides a way to retrieve information from the request map if we need it. Next, we instruct Compojure to validate the passed data in body, against CardRequestSchema. The last argument is a handler, which we saw earlier.

In core.clj, we'll use the ring-jetty adapter to expose the card routes:

```
(ns restful.core
  (:require ; ...
    [ring.adapter.jetty :refer [run-jetty]]
    [compojure.api.sweet :refer [api routes]]
    [restful.cards :refer [card-routes]]))
; ...

(def app (apply routes card-routes))

(defn -main
  [& args]
  ; ...
  (run-jetty app {:port 3000}))
```

The GET Card API

We've added an API for creating a card. We'll now add the code for getting card data in `cards.clj`:

```
(defn card->response [card]
  (if card
    (ok card)
    (not-found)))

(defn get-card-handler [card-id]
  (card->response (Card card-id)))

(def card-routes
  [ ; ...
  (GET "/cards/:id" []
  :path-params [id :- s/Int]
  (get-card-handler id))])
```

The preceding implementation is made from a few parts, as follows:

- A route to get `Card` with an `id` parameter
- The Prismatic schema's `Int` predicate, to check that `id` is an integer type
- Passing `id` to the handler
- Returning an `ok` response if we have a card in the database, otherwise, `not-found`

The GET Cards API

Similarly, we'll create functions and routes to get cards, as follows:

```
(defn get-cards-handler []
  (ok (db/select Card)))

(def card-routes
  [ ; ...
  (GET "/cards" []
  (get-cards-handler))])
```

In this implementation, we did the following:

- Defined a route for getting cards
- Called a handler when this route was requested
- Accessed the cards' data inside of the handler

The UPDATE Card API

The next step is to implement the part of the code responsible for updating existing cards, as follows:

```
(defn update-card-handler [id update-card-req]
  (db/update! Card id update-card-req)
  (ok))

(def card-routes
  [ ; ...
  (PUT "/cards/:id" []
  :path-params [id :- s/Int]
  :body [update-card-req CardRequestSchema]
  (update-card-handler id update-card-req))])
```

The DELETE Card API

The final HTTP method to implement is the delete route, as follows:

```
(defn delete-card-handler [card-id]
  (db/delete! Card :id card-id)
  (ok))

(def card-routes
  [ ; ...
  (DELETE "/cards/:id" []
  :path-params [id :- s/Int]
  (delete-card-handler id))])
```

The Swagger UI

The Compojure API offers Swagger[17] integration, in order to view and organize the APIs. In order to enable Swagger in Compojure, we need to wrap api with the Swagger configuration in core.clj:

```
(def swagger-conf
  {:ui "/swagger"
   :spec "/swagger.json"
   :options {:ui {:validatorUrl nil}
             :data {:info {:version "1.0.0", :title "Restful Microservice
CRUD API"}}}})

(def app (api {:swagger swagger-conf} (apply routes card-routes)))
```

We can now run the application (`lein run`) and explore our new API
at `http://localhost:3000/swagger`:

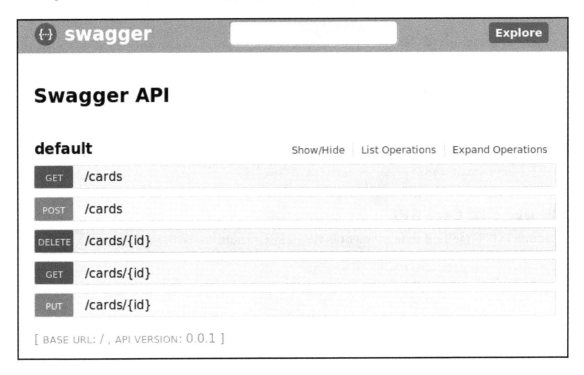

The Swagger UI allows us to test our CRUD operations in the browser. It provides example
requests and gives detailed responses for requests.

If we try to create a card violating the schema that has been defined, Swagger will pass
information about the exception and the schema violation. When a request is successful,
we'll be informed, as well.

Summary

In this chapter, we explored microservices. First, you saw what distinguishes a microservice
from a monolithic application. You learned about the pros and cons of using microservices.
Next we explored the topic of even-driven communication. We saw how microservices can
communicate with each other using messages and CQRS. We also covered the best
practices for designing microservices and some common pitfalls.

You also learned how to implement microservices APIs in Clojure, using the Compojure API. We used the Clojure library, Toucan, to interface with the database, in order to expose data. We used Prismatic's schema to validate data for the API and the Swagger UI to explore the API services.

In the next chapter, we'll look at some ways to test Clojure applications.

Further reading

Here is a list of information you can refer to:

1. Multitier architecture, Wikipedia: `https://en.wikipedia.org/wiki/Multitier_architecture`
2. Microservices architecture, Wikipedia: `https://en.wikipedia.org/wiki/Microservices`
3. *Microservices: The Good, the Bad and the Hype*: `https://thenewstack.io/beauty-beast-justgivings-microservices-transformation/`
4. Continuous delivery: `https://en.wikipedia.org/wiki/Continuous_delivery`
5. ElasticSearch: `https://www.elastic.co/products/elasticsearch`
6. Apache Kafka: `https://kafka.apache.org/`
7. SaaS, Wikipedia: `https://en.wikipedia.org/wiki/Software_as_a_service`
8. ACID, Wikipedia: `https://en.wikipedia.org/wiki/ACID_(computer_science)`
9. Domain Driven Design, Thoughtworks: `https://www.thoughtworks.com/insights/blog/domain-driven-design-services-architecture`
10. Bounded Context, Martin Fowler: `https://martinfowler.com/bliki/BoundedContext.html`
11. CircleCI: `https://circleci.com/`
12. Docker: `https://www.docker.com/`
13. AMQP: `https://www.amqp.org/`
14. CQRS, Martin Fowler: `https://www.martinfowler.com/bliki/CQRS.html`
15. CRUD, Wikipedia: `https://en.wikipedia.org/wiki/Create,_read,_update_and_delete`
16. REST, Wikipedia: `https://en.wikipedia.org/wiki/Representational_state_transfer`
17. Swagger UI: `https://swagger.io/`

11
Testing Reactive Apps

We have now written a few applications, but we have not written any tests for them. While some people argue that testing puts an unnecessary burden on teams[1], there are some benefits to software testing[2], such as ensuring the quality of the product and shortening the product delivery time by catching bugs early in the development process. Clojure provides a number of unit testing frameworks that can help us to organize, write, and test code.

This chapter will cover the following topics:

- Why testing is important
- Different approaches to testing
- An introduction to Clojure unit testing frameworks

The Clojure unit testing frameworks that we will investigate are as follows:

- clojure.test
- expectations
- Midje
- Speclj

Why testing is important

At the beginning of this chapter, I pointed out that software testing is important. Why? In order to answer that, you will need to understand what software testing is. It can be defined as a process that ensures that a particular piece of software is bug-free. Testing is a step-by-step process that ensures that the software passes expected standards of performance, set by customers or the industry. These steps can also help to identify errors, gaps, or missing requirements.

The benefits of software testing are as follows:

- Providing a high-quality product with low maintenance costs
- Ensuring the accuracy and consistency of the product
- Discovering defects and errors that are not recognized during the developmental phase
- Checking whether the application produces the expected output
- Providing us with knowledge of customers' satisfaction with the product

Testing approaches

There are a number of software testing methodologies, depending on the angle from which we look at the software[3]. The most common distinction is between functional testing and non-functional testing. We will now discuss what makes tests functional or non-functional, and when it is appropriate to use one type or the other.

Functional testing

Functional tests try to capture the functional requirements (such as security, usability, and performance) of the software being tested[4]. The requirements are taken from the specifications of the software component.

Typically, functional testing involves the following steps:

1. Identifying what functions and features a software component has, based on the requirement specification document
2. Creating input data based on the requirements
3. Determining the expected output
4. Executing the tests
5. Comparing the expected results with the actual output

Functional testing is beneficial when the following conditions are true:

- The requirements are clearly specified in the documentation
- It is possible to define the input and the expected output of tests
- The usability of the system is important
- There are clearly defined and known error conditions

Functional testing types include the following:

- Unit testing
- Integration testing
- System testing
- Sanity testing
- Smoke testing
- Interface testing
- Regression testing
- Beta/acceptance testing

While functional testing has advantages, there are some testing areas that are not covered by functional tests. In such cases, so-called non-functional tests are performed.

Non-functional testing

Non-functional tests check things that are not directly related to the functional requirements. To put it another way, non-functional tests are concerned with the way that software operates as a whole, rather than with the specific behaviors of the software or its components.

Non-functional testing types include the following:

- Performance testing
- Load testing
- Stress testing
- Volume testing
- Security testing
- Compatibility testing
- Installation testing
- Recovery testing
- Reliability testing
- Usability testing
- Compliance testing
- Localization testing

As you can see in the preceding list, with non-functional tests, we are concerned with areas such as security, how a system behaves under various load conditions, whether it is user-friendly, and whether it provides localization to run in different countries.

While we have discussed functional and non-functional testing separately, they should not be seen as opposing testing methodologies, but rather complementary approaches. They are often performed together, to provide the assurance that the software has a high standard and can operate under various conditions.

Testing and catching bugs in software is not free. It requires time and resources from developers and testers. Having said that, fixing bugs late in development is more expensive than catching them early in the development phase. Unit testing allows us to catch many bugs early on, while not requiring too many resources from developers[5]. In the next section, we will examine what unit testing is, and the most popular unit testing frameworks in Clojure.

Clojure unit testing frameworks

Unit testing[6] is the testing of an individual software component or module. Clojure provides a number of testing frameworks for unit testing.

Let's create a Clojure project where we can write our tests, using the following command: `lein new testing-example`.

The clojure.test framework

The **clojure.test** framework (`http://clojure.github.io/clojure/clojure.test-api.html`) is the default Clojure unit testing framework that comes with the Clojure standard library. By default, Leiningen creates a testing directory with each new project:

```
$ tree test

├── test
│   └── testing_example
│       └── core_test.clj
```

This directory has one test file, called `core_test.clj`:

```
(ns testing-example.core-test
  (:require [clojure.test :refer :all]
            [testing-example.core :refer :all]))
```

```
(deftest a-test
  (testing "FIXME, I fail."
    (is (= 0 1))))
```

This file imports the Clojure testing namespace, as well as the core file from the `src` directory. The file contains one test method. Let's run the test using Leiningen, as follows:

$ lein test

```
lein test testing-example.core-test

lein test :only testing-example.core-test/a-test

FAIL in (a-test) (core_test.clj:7)
FIXME, I fail.
expected: 0
  actual: 1
    diff: - 0
          + 1

Ran 1 tests containing 1 assertions.
1 failures, 0 errors.
Tests failed.
```

The test fails, as we have not yet implemented it. Let's change the `a-test` function, as follows:

```
(deftest a-test
  (testing "Testing equality of a number."
    (is (= 1 1))))
```

The test will now pass, as shown in the following code snippet:

$ lein test

```
lein test testing-example.core-test

Ran 1 tests containing 1 assertions.
0 failures, 0 errors.
```

In Chapter 10, *Reactive Microservices*, we wrote the schema code for the description of `card` and the name, using some helper functions. These functions are ideal candidates for unit testing. Put the following code into `core.clj`:

```
(ns testing-example.core
  (:require [clojure.string :as str]))

(def non-blank? (complement str/blank?))
```

The is macro

The `clojure.test` object provides the `is` macro for testing. It takes a predicate test and an optional assertion message. Add the following code to `core_test.clj`:

```
(deftest non-blank-test
  (testing "Testing non-blank? function"
  (is (true? (non-blank? "")))
  "Tested string is blank.")))
```

If we run the test now, we will get the following result:

```
$ lein test

lein test testing-example.core-test

lein test :only testing-example.core-test/non-blank-test

FAIL in (non-blank-test) (core_test.clj:11)
Testing non-blank function
Tested string is blank.
expected: (true? (non-blank? ""))
  actual: (not (true? false))

Ran 2 tests containing 2 assertions.
1 failures, 0 errors.
Tests failed.
```

As you can see, the test failed, and the `Tested string is blank` message was printed out. We will fix it now, as follows:

```
(deftest non-blank-test
   (testing "Testing non-blank? function"
     (is (true? (non-blank? "Some text"))
         "Tested string is blank.")))
```

When the test is run again, it will pass, as shown in the following code snippet:

```
$ lein test

lein test testing-example.core-test

Ran 2 tests containing 2 assertions.
0 failures, 0 errors
```

The are macro

The `are` macro is a convenience macro, when we plan to write multiple tests using the `is` macro.

Consider the following code snippet:

```
(deftest non-blank-test-with-is
  (testing "Testing non-blank? function"
    (is (true? (non-blank? "Some text")))
    (is (false? (non-blank? "")))
    (is (false? (non-blank? nil)))))
```

Instead of using the preceding code, we can write the test as follows:

```
(deftest non-blank-test-with-are
  (testing "Testing non-blank? function"
    (are [predicate text] (predicate (non-blank? text))
        true? "Some text"
        false? ""
        false? nil)))
```

The `are` macro checks multiple assertions against the template assertion provided by us.

Running the test provides us with the following result:

```
$ lein test

lein test testing-example.core-test

Ran 4 tests containing 8 assertions.
0 failures, 0 errors
```

The expectations framework

An alternative to clojure.test is the expectations framework (you can read more about it at `https://clojure-expectations.github.io/`).

In order to use it, we need to add it to `project.clj`. The file should look as follows:

```
(defproject testing-example "0.1.0-SNAPSHOT"
  :license {:name "Eclipse Public License"
            :url "http://www.eclipse.org/legal/epl-v10.html"}
  :dependencies [[org.clojure/clojure "1.9.0"]
                 [expectations "2.2.0-rc3"]]
  :plugins [[lein-expectations "0.0.8"]])
```

`lein-expectations` is a Leiningen plugin to run expectations tests.

Create a `testing_example/expectations_tests.clj` file in the `test` directory, as follows:

```
(ns testing-example.expectations-tests
  (:require [expectations :refer :all]
            [testing-example.core :refer :all]))

(expect true (non-blank? "Some text"))
```

The tests are run by using the Leiningen plugin that we included earlier:

```
$ lein expectations

Ran 1 tests containing 1 assertions in 1 msecs
0 failures, 0 errors
```

The `expectations` object is built with the idea that unit tests should contain one assertion per test. A result of this design choice is that expectations have very minimal syntax, and reduces the amount of code needed to perform the tests.

The `expectations` object allows us to test things like the following:

- Errors are thrown by the code
- The function's return value
- A substring using a regular expression

The following code uses the `expect` function to test the three scenarios that we just mentioned:

```
(expect ClassCastException (non-blank? 1234))

(expect Boolean (non-blank? ""))

(expect #"Dev" "DevOps")
```

With expectations, we can also test Clojure collections, as follows:

```
(expect 2 (in [1 2 3 4 5 6]))

(expect {:surname "Doe"} (in {:name "John" :surname "Doe"}))

(expect 3 (in #{1 2 3 4}))
```

Running all of the tests provides us with the following output:

```
lein expectations

Ran 7 tests containing 7 assertions in 5 msecs
0 failures, 0 errors.
```

The Midje framework

The **Midje** testing framework (https://github.com/marick/Midje) builds on top of the clojure.test bottom-up testing, adding support for top-down testing.

In order to use Midje, add it as a dependency ([midje "1.9.4"] to project.clj).

Next, create a new file, testing_example/midje_tests.clj, in the test directory:

```
(ns testing-example.midje-tests
  (:require [midje.sweet :refer :all]
            [testing-example.core :refer :all]))

(fact (non-blank? "Some text") => true)
```

The Midje framework provides a number of macros; the ones that we will learn are as follows:

- fact
- facts
- throws
- contains
- just

The fact macro

Midje uses a fact macro, which states certain facts about a future version of our program. The macro takes a single argument on both sides of the => symbol. The fact macro states that the left side is to be expected on the right side of the symbol.

Midje supports auto-testing in repl, as follows:

```
$ lein repl
user=> (use 'midje.repl)
user=> (autotest)
```

```
================================================================
Loading (testing-example.core testing-example.midje-tests testing-
example.core-test)
>>> Midje summary:
All checks (1) succeeded.

>>> Output from clojure.test tests:

Ran 4 tests containing 8 assertions.
0 failures, 0 errors.
```

The auto-runner gives us the information that one `midje` test passed, as well as all of the previously written `clojure.test` tests.

The facts macro

It is often that we create a number of tests using `fact` macro. `facts` macro allows us to group related tests together. The first argument is a description of a group of tests, as follows:

```
(facts "nil or blank strings are invalid values"
      (fact (non-blank? nil) => false)
      (fact (non-blank? "") => false))

(facts "alpha-numeric are possible values"
      (fact (non-blank? "Some text") => true)
      (fact (non-blank? "1234") => true))
```

The auto-test running in `repl` gives us the following information:

```
================================================================
Loading (testing-example.midje-tests)
nil
All checks (5) succeeded.
```

Top-down testing

In bottom-up testing, you write a function and the tests for it, then write other functions that use your first function. In the previous chapter, you saw the `non-blank-with-max-length?` function:

```
(defn non-blank-with-max-length? [length text]
      (and (non-blank? text) (max-length? length text)))
```

The `non-blank-with-max-length?` function uses `non-blank?` internally, which we just tested. We can now write an implementation and tests for `non-blank-with-max-length?`. This is an example of bottom-up testing.

Top-down testing uses the opposite approach, where we write top-level code, and if it uses other functions, we provide stubs for them:

```
(unfinished max-length?)

(def text-title "Some title")
(def text-max-length 20)

(defn non-blank-with-max-length? [length text])

(fact "Title should be non blank and 20 characters maximum"
 (non-blank-with-max-length? text-max-length text-title) => true
 (provided
   (max-length? text-title text-max-length) => true))
```

We state that `max-length?` is an `unfinished` function that we will implement in the future. We use the `provided` function to stub `max-length?` with the `true` value that we expect from it.

Midje's `autorun` provides us with the following output:

```
==================================================================
Loading (testing-example.core testing-example.midje-tests testing-
example.core-test)

FAIL at (midje_tests.clj:25)
These calls were not made the right number of times:
    (max-length? text text-max-length) [expected at least once, actually
never called]

FAIL "Title should be non blank and 20 characters maximum" at
(midje_tests.clj:23)
Expected:
true
Actual:
nil
>>> Midje summary:
FAILURE: 2 checks failed.   (But 5 succeeded.)
```

The output from the auto-runner tells us that our test failed, as max-length? was expected to be called but never was. If we provide a definition for non-blank-with-max-length?, the tests will pass again, as follows:

```
(defn non-blank-with-max-length? [length text]
  (and (non-blank? text) (max-length? text length)))
```

After adding the preceding function, the tests will pass, as follows:

```
=====================================================================
Loading (testing-example.midje-tests)
nil
All checks (6) succeeded.
```

The next step is to write tests for the max-length? function:

```
(defn max-length? [length text])

(fact "Text max length should not exceed provided number"
  (max-length? text-max-length text-title) => true)
```

When the tests are run, we will get the following output:

```
=====================================================================
Loading (testing-example.midje-tests)

FAIL "Text max length should not exceed provided number" at
(midje_tests.clj:33)
Expected:
true
Actual:
nil
nil
FAILURE: 1 check failed.   (But 6 succeeded.)
```

The tests failed, as was expected because we have not yet implemented max-length?:

```
(defn max-length? [length text]
  (<= (count text) length))
```

Now, the tests will pass:

```
=====================================================================
Loading (testing-example.midje-tests)
nil
All checks (7) succeeded
```

So far, we have one test for `max-length?`. We will now add a test, checking the situation when text is longer than the allowed value:

```
(fact "Passing text longer than max value"
  (max-length? (- (count text-title) 1) text-title) => false)
```

The auto-runner tells us that our new test has passed:

```
==================================================================
Loading (testing-example.midje-tests)
nil
All checks (8) succeeded
```

Midje allows us to check various conditions and behaviors in our program. We will look at how we can check for exceptions or collections in the following subsections.

Checking for exceptions

With Midje, we can check whether a certain exception is being thrown in our code:

```
(fact "Passing a number throws an exception"
  (non-blank? 1234) => (throws ClassCastException))
```

The auto-runner tells us that our test checking `ClassCastException` was implemented correctly:

```
==================================================================
Loading (testing-example.midje-tests)
nil
All checks (9) succeeded
```

Checking collections

Midje provides us with a number of macros that allows us to check our collections.

The macros that you will learn about are as follows:

- `contains`
- `just`

The contains macro

The `contains` macro allows us to check the elements in a collection:

```
(fact "Check if a collection contains some elements"
  [:bread :butter :lemon] => (contains [:bread :butter :lemon]))

(fact "The order of elements matters"
  [:bread :butter :lemon] => (contains [:lemon :bread :butter]))
```

The test's auto-runner produces the following output:

```
================================================================
Loading (testing-example.midje-tests)

FAIL "The order of elements matters" at (midje_tests.clj:48)
Actual result did not agree with the checking function.
Actual result:
[:bread :butter :lemon]
Checking function: (contains [:lemon :bread :butter])
    The checker said this about the reason:
        Best match found: [:lemon]
nil
FAILURE: 1 check failed.   (But 10 succeeded.)
```

By default, the `contains` function will check the order of items and will fail if the order specified in the expected collection differs from the order of items in the tested collection. In the preceding test, the order that we provided (and expect) is as follows:

```
[:bread :butter :lemon]
```

If we are not interested in the order, but only in the membership in a collection, we can use the `:in-any-order` modifier, as follows:

```
(fact "The order of elements matters in not taken into account"
      [:bread :butter :lemon] => (contains [:lemon :bread :butter] :in-any-
order))
```

This will produce the following output:

```
================================================================
Loading (testing-example.midje-tests)
nil
All checks (11) succeeded.
```

Suppose that there are more elements in the collection, as follows:

```
(fact "Collection has more elements"
      [:bread :butter :cake :lemon] => (contains [:bread :butter :lemon]))
```

The preceding tests will fail, as shown in the following code snippet:

```
====================================================================
Loading (testing-example.midje-tests)

FAIL "Collection has more elements" at (midje_tests.clj:53)
Actual result did not agree with the checking function.
Actual result:
[:bread :butter :cake :lemon]
Checking function: (contains [:bread :butter :lemon])
    The checker said this about the reason:
        Best match found: [:bread :butter]
nil
FAILURE: 1 check failed.  (But 11 succeeded.)
```

We can use the :gaps-ok modifier to fix the failing test:

```
(fact "Collection has more elements"
      [:bread :butter :cake :lemon] => (contains [:bread :butter :lemon]
:gaps-ok))
```

This allows the test to pass, as follows:

```
====================================================================
Loading (testing-example.midje-tests)
nil
All checks (12) succeeded
```

We can also combine both modifiers together, as follows:

```
(fact "Collection has more elements and not in order"
      [:lemon :bread :butter :cake] => (contains [:bread :butter :lemon]
:gaps-ok :in-any-order))
```

With both modifiers in use, our last test passes, as follows:

```
====================================================================
Loading (testing-example.midje-tests)
nil
All checks (13) succeeded
```

The just macro

The `just` macro is a variation of `contains`, which will fail if the tested expression on the left-hand side of the `=>` symbol has any extra values:

```
(fact "Collection has too many elements"
  [:bread :butter :cake] => (just [:bread :butter]))
```

Adding this code will produce the following output:

```
================================================================
Loading (testing-example.midje-tests)

FAIL "Collection has too many elements" at (midje_tests.clj:63)
Actual result did not agree with the checking function.
Actual result:
[:bread :butter :cake]
Checking function: (just [:bread :butter])
    The checker said this about the reason:
        Expected two elements. There were three.
nil
FAILURE: 1 check failed.  (But 13 succeeded.)
```

Suppose that we change the test to the following:

```
(fact "Collection has exact number of elements"
  [:bread :butter] => (just [:bread :butter]))
```

The preceding test will pass, as shown in the following code snippet:

```
================================================================
Loading (testing-example.midje-tests)
nil
All checks (14) succeeded
```

The Speclj framework

The **Speclj** framework (`https://github.com/slagyr/speclj`) is a TDD/BDD[7] testing framework based on RSpec[8]. **Behavior Driven Development (BDD)** is a type of **Test Driven Development (TDD)** that allows business and development teams to collaborate on software building. In BDD, the tests are described using English-like sentences that express the behavior of a program and the expected outcomes. In TDD, the tests are written first, before the actual code is implemented.

In order to use Speclj, we need to add it to `project.clj`:

```
(defproject testing-example "0.1.0-SNAPSHOT"
  :license {:name "Eclipse Public License"
            :url "http://www.eclipse.org/legal/epl-v10.html"}
  :dependencies [[org.clojure/clojure "1.9.0"]
                 [expectations "2.2.0-rc3"]
                 [midje "1.9.4"]
                 [speclj "3.3.2"]]
  :plugins [[lein-expectations "0.0.8"]
            [speclj "3.3.2"]])
```

Next, we will create a file, `testing_example/speclj_tests.clj`, in the `test` directory:

```
(ns testing-example.speclj-tests
  (:require [speclj.core :refer :all]
            [testing-example.core :refer :all]))
```

The Speclj framework provides a number of macros, such as `context`, `describe`, `it`, `should`, and `should=`, which help to create tests. Macros are composable, allowing developers to create tests that are read like English sentences.

The `describe` container is the outermost container for specs. It takes a string name and any number of spec components. `context` is used to nest the testing contexts inside of the outer `describe`:

```
(describe "Testing non-blank? function"
          (context "Passing invalid values"
                   (it "is passed an empty string"
                       (should-not (non-blank? "")))
                   (it "is passed a nil"
                       (should-not (non-blank? nil))))
          (context "Passing valid values"
                   (it "accepts letters"
                       (should (non-blank? "Some text")))
                   (it "accepts number strings"
                       (comment (should (non-blank? 1234)))
                       (should (non-blank? 1234)))))
```

When we run the tests, some of them will fail:

```
$ lein spec
...F

Failures:

  1) Testing non-blank? function Passing valid values accepts numbers
```

```
        java.lang.Long cannot be cast to java.lang.CharSequence
        java.lang.ClassCastException: java.lang.Long cannot be cast to
java.lang.CharSequence
            ... 3 stack levels elided ...
            at
testing_example.speclj_tests$eval10197$fn__10198$fn__10219$fn__10227.invoke
(/testing-example/test/testing_example/speclj_tests.clj:16)
            ;;;
            ... 15 stack levels elided ...

    Finished in 0,00071 seconds
    4 examples, 1 failures
```

The stack trace tells us that our tests fail on line 16, where we used a number. Let's change the code, as follows:

```
(it "accepts number strings"
    (should (non-blank? "1234")))
```

Now, the tests will pass, as shown in the following code snippet:

```
$ lein spec
....

Finished in 0,00044 seconds
4 examples, 0 failure
```

When we look at the tests, we can see that by using different macros, we can create tests that are read like English sentences.

The speclj.core namespace provides a number of should-like macros. The macros that we will cover are as follows:

- should-contain
- should=
- should==
- should-throw
- should-be-a

These macros can help to create many tests. We will see them in action in the following sections.

The should-contain macro

The `should-contain` macro is a multipurpose assertion macro. It works with strings or collections. In collections, the macro will search for a given value. In strings, the macro will search for a substring:

```
(describe "Testing containment"
        (context "Using a string"
                (it "looks for a substring"
                        (should-contain "Text" "Some Text"))
                (it "looks for regular expression"
                        (should-contain #"Some.*" "Some text")))
        (context "Using collections"
                (it "looks for a key in a map"
                        (should-contain :bird {:color :red :bird :parrot}))
                (it "looks for a value in a collection"
                        (should-contain :orange [:blue :green :orange
:pink])))))
```

Running the examples will provide us with the following output:

```
$ lein spec
. . . . . . . .

Finished in 0,00170 seconds
8 examples, 0 failures
```

The should= and should== macros

The `should=` and `should==` macros take two test forms as arguments. Both macros allow us to test forms for equality. The difference between them is that `should==` does not take the order of items in a collection into account, while in `should=`, the order of items is important:

```
(describe "Testing equivalency"
        (context "same order of items in collections"
                (it "compares collections"
                        (should= [:bread :cake :juice] [:bread :cake
:juice])))
        (context "different order of items in collections"
                (it "compares collections"
                        (should==  [:bread :cake :juice] [:juice :cake
:bread])))))
```

When the new tests are run, they will pass, as shown in the following code snippet:

```
lein spec
. . . . . . . . . . . .

Finished in 0,00368 seconds
10 examples, 0 failures
```

The should-throw macro

The `should-throw` macro tests whether a provided test throws an exception:

```
(describe "Testing exceptions"
        (it "throws ClassCastException"
            (should-throw ClassCastException (non-blank? 1234))))
```

Running the tests catches the `ClassCastException` thrown, as follows:

```
lein spec
. . . . . . . . . .

Finished in 0,00482 seconds
11 examples, 0 failures
```

The should-be-a macro

The `should-be-a` macro allows us to test types such as Booleans or Integers. This macro takes two arguments. First is the type we expect and the other argument is the tested function:

```
(describe "Testing return type"
        (it "return boolean"
            (should-be-a Boolean (non-blank? "text"))))
```

When the tests are run, they will pass, as shown in the following code snippet:

```
lein spec
. . . . . . . . . . .

Finished in 0,00335 seconds
12 examples, 0 failures
```

Summary

In this chapter, we explored testing in Clojure. First, we discussed the benefits of testing, and then we covered some different testing methodologies, such as load testing and integration testing.

Finally, we explored four Clojure unit testing frameworks. While each framework allows us to test our code, each does so in a different way. Each framework was designed with a particular use case in mind. While showing the testing frameworks in action, we explained why each one was created, and what situations to use it in.

Often, the decision of whether to use one framework or another is a matter of preferred testing style. We advise developers to try each framework out and decide which one suits them best.

In the next chapter, we will look at concurrency in Clojure.

Further reading

Here is a list of information you can refer to:

1. Why testing is important, Atlassian: `https://www.atlassian.com/blog/software-teams/why-software-testing-is-important`

2. *Why is software testing necessary?*, TryQA: `http://tryqa.com/why-is-testing-necessary/`

3. *Types of Software Testing: Different Testing Types with Details*, Software Testing Help: `https://www.softwaretestinghelp.com/types-of-software-testing/`

4. Software testing, functional testing: `http://softwaretestingfundamentals.com/functional-testing/`

5. *Test early and Often*, Microsoft: `https://docs.microsoft.com/en-us/previous-versions/visualstudio/visual-studio-2012/ee330950(v=vs.110)`

6. Unit Testing, Martin Fowler: `https://www.martinfowler.com/bliki/UnitTest.html`

7. BDD, Wikipedia: `https://en.wikipedia.org/wiki/Behavior-driven_development`

8. RSpec: `http://rspec.info/`

12
Concurrency Utilities in Clojure

Writing multithreaded programs is not an easy task. Such programs are often difficult to reason about and debug. Sometimes, they provide different output due to changes in the execution order. Yet many programmers write multithreaded software, because today's demands require utilizing available CPU cores.

In Java, developers can use threads and locks. Such tools are not easy to use. We can see this by examining how thick the books on concurrency in Java[1] are. While Clojure does not provide a silver bullet to solve all concurrency issues, it does provide well-thought-out tools to manage multithreading.

In this chapter, we will do the following:

- Explain why concurrency is important in Clojure
- Examine the often overlooked difference between concurrency and parallelism
- Discuss problems with mutable states
- Explore Clojure's approach to states
- Investigate Clojure's concurrency constructs—refs, agents, atoms, and vars
- Look at how to use promises and futures

Introduction to concurrency

Rich Hickey spent around two and a half years working on Clojure before releasing it to a wider audience[2]. One of his design goals was to create a programming language with first-class support for concurrency[3]. As a result, Clojure has well-thought-out concurrency tools.

Concurrency or parallelism

While some people use the terms concurrency and parallelism interchangeably, we need to make it clear that they are related, but are not the same[4].

Concurrency is about the coordination and composition of independent processes, while **parallelism** is the simultaneous execution of processes.

The following diagram illustrates how concurrency and parallelism handle processes during a program's execution time:

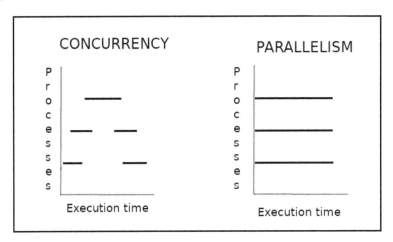

State, identity, and value

Many programs operate on states. For example, the following Java class introduces a `Car` object:

```
class Car {
    public String type;
    public String color;
    public int age;
}

public Car (String type, String color, int age) {
    this.type = type;
    this.color = color;
    this.age = age;
}

Car sedan = new Car("Sedan", "red", 5);
```

Programs written in many languages, such as Java, C#, Ruby, or Python, are full of similar classes. We are so used to this approach that we rarely consider how problematic it can be.

We created an instance of `Car`, represented by a particular type, `sedan`. We might have bought this car when it was already five years old. The car can exist in many states—as a brand new car with an age of `1`, or as an antique car with an age of over `25`. At each point in time, the car has precisely one valid state. Its state might change from time to time, but that does not invalidate the previous states.

If we want to change our car in a Java program, we alter the existing state, as follows:

```
sedan.age++;
```

What's more troubling is that with the way we designed `Car`, it is possible to do the following:

```
sedan.type = "minivan";
```

Now, `sedan` is not a sedan anymore; it represents a different type. As you can see, it is easy to mix the state, identity, and values.

Values are things that never change. The `minivan` string and the number `16` are constants. They always mean the same thing. We can define the **state** as a current set of values associated with data in a program. The **identity**, on the other hand, is a stable, logical entity associated with a series of different values over time.

Next, we will explore what happens when the state and identity are conflated, and what solutions most object-oriented languages, like Java, provide.

Common problems with states

Most of the problems in multithreaded programs happen because the changes to shared data are not properly protected.

The problems can be divided into three categories, as follows:

- Lost updates
- Unrepeatable reads
- Phantom reads

Lost updates

Lost updates happen when two or more threads update the same data, one after another. Suppose that we update the color of a car, as follows:

```
sedan.color = "orange";
```

Then, suppose that another thread updates the color during the first update, as follows:

```
sedan.color = "pink";
```

We will lose the information that the `sedan` color was `"orange"` at one point in time. The update that was done by one thread will be lost.

Unrepeatable reads

An unrepeatable read happens when an instance is read by one thread while being changed by another thread. The reading thread can access that instance in an incomplete state, as follows:

```
sedan.age++;
sedan.color = "green";
```

We end up with a situation where the age is incremented, while the color is not updated. Reading the content again might not give us this particular inconsistent state, making debugging such code very difficult.

Phantom reads

A **phantom read** happens when a thread reads a state that is altered, either by adding more data or by deleting it. As a result, the thread has accessed a state with data that no longer exists.

Programmers are aware of such situations in multithreaded programs and have designed a number of solutions, which we will explore in the next section.

The traditional solution to the problem with states

The traditional solution to the problems involved in sharing data among many threads is to add some level of access control to shared data. This is done using **locks**. With locks, the programmers control the execution of parts of the code, ensuring that only one thread can access a protected part of the code at one time. When a thread tries to execute the protected part of the code, it first needs to obtain the lock. When another thread holds the lock, the new thread is blocked until the lock is available again. The blocked thread resumes execution only after it has obtained the lock.

While this approach is easy to understand and explain, its actual implementation is often challenging. With more than one piece of data needing coordination, the programs grow in complexity. Using locks leads to contention, as all other threads need to wait till the one holding a lock finishes. Fixing bugs in such programs is difficult, as by design threads are not coordinated, and anyone can request a lock on data.

A few issues can arise when threads try to access locks, as follows:

- Deadlock
- Starvation
- Livelock
- Race conditions

Deadlock

Deadlock arises when two or more threads wait for another to release the lock that they need. Imagine a situation where thread A has a lock on data (a1), and thread B has a lock (b1). Thread A wants to finish executing its part of the code and needs resources protected by lock b1. At the same time, thread B cannot release lock b1, as it has not finished the execution of its part of the code because it needs access to resources protected by lock a1. With this circular dependency, both threads are unable to proceed.

Starvation

Starvation occurs when a thread is not allocated enough resources for an assigned task. In this case, the thread starves and never completes.

Livelock

Livelock happens when two or more threads continue to execute and change their states, while not making progress towards finishing. The most vivid example is a situation wherein two people meet in a hall and block each other's way. As one moves to the left, the other moves too. As a response, the first person moves to the right, and the second person moves to the right as well. In this situation, both make movements, either to the left or right, but this does not result in them finishing their tasks and passing each other.

Race conditions

A **race condition** is a situation in which the timing of the execution of threads causes an unexpected result. The order in which the threads finish their execution should not influence the overall result. In race conditions, the final result (or state) varies, depending on which thread finishes first. Bugs arising from race conditions are difficult to debug and reproduce, as they happen relatively rarely, and the timing of threads is important. During some program executions, we get expected results, while at other times, when a race condition is taking place, we get unexpected results.

Other problems with locks

The other problems with locks are as follows:

- Developing programs with locks consume more resources, such as time and money
- Maintaining such software is more expensive
- Debugging the software takes more time
- Code with locks is less multithreaded than lock-free code

Having explored some problems (and potential solutions) involved in writing multithreaded code, we will now investigate how Clojure approaches this topic.

The Clojure approach to concurrency

Clojure provides four constructs that can help developers to write concurrent programs, as follows:

- Refs
- Agent

- Atoms
- Vars

Each construct serves a different purpose. In order to understand when to use each one, we will need some ways to classify them. We will provide these in the next sections.

Classifying constructs

If we want to classify Clojure concurrency constructs we can use two continua—coordination and synchronization. When used together, they will help us decide which Clojure concurrency construct to use.

Synchronization

Operations on data are classified as **synchronous** when one thread waits until it has exclusive access to the required data. On the other hand, **asynchronous** operations can be performed without blocking access to data by one thread.

Coordination

In a **coordinated** operation, multiple threads cooperate in order to yield the correct results. In an **uncoordinated** operation, multiple threads execute in separated contexts, and they cannot impact each other in a negative way.

Both concepts (coordination and synchronization) allow us to categorize three of Clojure's concurrency constructs. **Vars** are not included in the following table, as they are primarily used in thread-local changes, and not in multithreaded contexts:

	Coordinated	Uncoordinated
Synchronous	Refs	Atoms
Asynchronous		Agents

We can describe all of the Clojure concurrency constructs by showing their usefulness, as follows:

Type	Useful for
Refs	Synchronous, coordinated changes in a shared context
Agents	Asynchronous, uncoordinated changes in a shared context
Atoms	Synchronous, uncoordinated changes in a shared context
Vars	Isolated changes

This classification can help us to choose the most appropriate construct for our problem.

We can now explore each construct in detail. We will start with atoms.

Atoms

Atoms allow for synchronous (immediate) and independent changes to data. Also, the changes are not coordinated with other threads. Either all of them happen or none of them do.

Start `repl` to follow along, and type the following code:

```
lein repl
```

We can create `atom` in the following way:

```
(def basket-counter (atom 0))
```

We created `atom` to hold a number of items in a shopping basket. The initial value is 0.

Dereferencing atoms

In order to read the value of `atom`, we dereference it, as follows:

```
(deref basket-counter)
```

This gives us the actual value, as follows:

```
=> 0
```

We could use the @ reader macro to dereference `atom`, as follows:

```
@basket-counter
```

Again, the value will be printed for us:

```
=> 0
```

In the following sections, we will look at how we can alter atoms.

Mutating atoms

There are three functions used to update atom, as follows:

- reset!
- swap!
- compare-and-set!

reset!

The reset! function sets the provided value as the new value of atom. This way, we override an existing value:

```
(reset! basket-counter 3)
```

This will set the basket-counter value to be 3. Dereferencing atom shows that this is the case:

```
@basket-counter
```

The output is as follows:

```
=> 3
```

swap!

The swap! function is used whenever we want to update the atom's value by using an existing value as a base:

```
(swap! basket-counter + 1)
```

Here, we use Clojure's built-in + function to add 1 to the existing atom's value.

We can dereference atom as follows:

```
@basket-counter
```

This provides us with the following number:

```
=> 4
```

In the preceding example, we used the + function from Clojure's core library. We can use a custom function, as well:

```
(swap! basket-counter (fn [existing-value] (+ existing-value 3)))
```

Here, we add the number 3 to the existing value. We then dereference it, as shown in the following code snippet:

```
@basket-counter
```

This shows that the current number is 7:

```
=> 7
```

It is important to note that the functions that are used to update the value should be free of side effects, as they can be called multiple times.

compare-and-set!

The `compare-and-set!` function is a lower-level function. It is used internally, by `swap!`. The reason that this function exists is that it atomically sets the value of `atom` to the new value when the current value is equal to the old value. This function returns `true` when the operation succeeds, and `false` otherwise:

```
(compare-and-set! basket-counter 7 8)
```

In the preceding code, we set the new value to 8. We supplied 7 as the old value. `compare-and-set!` will use the supplied number, 7, against the existing value; if they are equal, it will set the new atom's value to 8.

Dereference the atoms, as follows:

```
@basket-counter
```

This provides us with the following result:

```
=> 8
```

A typical scenario for using `compare-and-set!` is when we dereference `atom`, do some work with the value, and use the function to change it to the new value. If the changes have been made to `atom` by another thread, then `compare-and-set!` will fail.

Agents

Agents are an uncoordinated, asynchronous reference type. Changes to one agent's state are independent of changes to another agent's state.

We can create `agent` in the following way:

```
(def play-time (agent 0))
```

We have created `agent` to hold the time that a player spends in a game.

Dereferencing agents

In order to read the value from `agent`, we need to dereference it, as follows:

```
(deref play-time)
```

We get the initial value that we set, as follows:

```
=> 0
```

We can also use the @ reader macro to dereference `agent`, as follows:

```
@play-time
```

This will give us the same value as the previous code:

```
=> 0
```

In the following sections, we will look at how to update `agent`.

Mutating agents

There are two functions that are used to update agents, as follows:

- `send`
- `send-off`

send

The `send` function is the first function that you will learn. Consider the following code:

```
(send play-time + 2)
```

In the preceding code, we applied the + function, with the value 2, to our `play-time` `agent`. Dereferencing `agent` shows us the updated value:

```
@play-time
```

The result is as follows:

```
=> 2
```

send-off

`send-off` is the other function that we can use to update agents:

```
(send-off play-time - 1)
```

In the preceding example, we have subtracted 1 using Clojure's function - . The - function uses current value of `play-time` to subtract 1 that we passed as an argument to `send-off`.

We can check the current value of `play-time`:

```
@play-time
```

Dereferencing `agent` gives us an updated state, as follows:

```
=> 1
```

We used the `send-off` function in the same manner that we used `send`. The difference between them is that `send-off` uses a different thread pool than the one used by `send`. The `send-off` thread pool can also grow in size.

Refs

Refs are Clojure's coordinated reference type. They allow for synchronous and coordinated changes to mutable data.

We can create `ref` as follows:

```
(def basket-items (ref []))
```

We just initialized the `ref` holding `basket-items` with an empty vector.

Dereferencing refs

If we want to obtain a ref's value, we need to dereference it, as follows:

```
(deref basket-items)
```

This gives us an empty vector, as follows:

```
=> []
```

We can also use the @ reader macro:

```
@basket-items
```

This gives us the same result, as follows:

```
=> []
```

In the following section, we will look at how to update refs.

Mutating refs

Clojure provides three functions to alter refs, as follows:

- `ref-set`
- `alter`
- `commute`

Both `ref-set` and `alter` are used in situations in which two or more threads try to mute `ref`, and one of them succeeds. This causes the others to fail. In this situation, the other transactions will start again, with the newly updated value of `ref`. This mechanism ensures that transactions work with consistent states.

The `commute` function is used in situations in which it does not matter what the most recent value is (only that it is recent).

Before we look at the functions in action, you will need to learn about Clojure's implementation of Software Transactional Memory, used to manage all of the changes that are applied to refs.

Software Transactional Memory

Software Transactional Memory (STM) is any method of coordinating multiple concurrent modifications to a shared set of storage locations. Clojure's STM is analogous to a database transaction, but for changes to Clojure's data.

Refs are meant for situations in which multiple threads need to coordinate their changes. Clojure provides a `dosync` macro for running STM transactions. You will now see this macro in action.

ref-set

The `ref-set` function allows us to update a ref's value. This function takes two arguments. First one is `ref` to be updated and the second argument is a new value for `ref` :

```
(ref-set basket-items ["vegetables"])
```

Running this code gives us an error message:

```
IllegalStateException No transaction running
clojure.lang.LockingTransaction.getEx (LockingTransaction.java:208)
```

This happens because we have not run the transaction inside of STM. Suppose that we try to alter `ref` inside of the `dosync` block, as follows:

```
(dosync
  (ref-set basket-items ["vegetables"]))
```

`ref` will be updated. Dereference it, as shown in the following code snippet:

```
(deref basket-items)
```

This will show us the updated value, as follows:

```
=> ["vegetables"]
```

alter

Another function that is used to update refs is `alter`. With it, we pass a mutating function that takes a ref's current value, applies the function to it, and stores the new value in `ref`:

```
(dosync
  (alter basket-items (fn [current-value]
                        (conj current-value "fruits"))))
```

Dereference `ref`, as follows:

```
@basket-items
```

This will give us the updated vector:

```
["vegetables" "fruits"]
```

Note that we used `dosync` again, in order to update `ref`.

commute

At the beginning of the `ref` section, we discussed how `commute` differs from `ref-set` and `alter`, as it is not checking whether a ref's value has been updated by other threads. `commute` is suited for situations in which our updating functions are commutative.

A **commutative function** is a function in which the order of arguments does not change the final value. Addition is commutative.

Consider the following statements:

```
(+ 1 2)
(+ 2 1)
```

The two preceding statements give us the same results:

```
=> 3
```

Let's create a new `ref` holding the number of players, as follows:

```
(def players-count (ref 0))
```

Dereferencing it will show the following:

```
@players-count
```

This means that we currently have 0 players:

```
=> 0
```

Suppose that we apply `commute` from one thread, as follows:

```
(dosync
  (commute players-count
            (fn [current-value] (+ current-value 1))))
```

Then, suppose that we apply `commute` from a second thread, as follows:

```
(dosync
  (commute players-count
            (fn [current-value] (+ current-value 2))))
```

Dereferencing it would show us the following:

```
@players-count
```

Currently, we have 3 players, as shown in the following output:

```
=> 3
```

In the final subsection, you will learn about vars, the fourth reference type in Clojure.

Vars

Vars is the last reference type that you will learn about. Vars are like global objects in other programming languages. They are created at the top level of a namespace. Vars provide a mechanism to refer to a mutable storage location that can be dynamically rebound (to a new storage location) on a per-thread basis.

We can create a var by using a special form of `def`, as follows:

```
(def player-max-level 100)
```

If we want to obtain its value, we call the var, as follows:

```
player-max-level
```

We then get the value shown in the following output:

```
=> 100
```

Var bindings

At the beginning of the section, we mentioned that vars can be rebound on a per-thread basis. Clojure provides a mechanism for doing that. When we create a var and give it an initial value, as we did with `player-max-level`, it is called a **root binding**. When we update the var, the other threads will see the initial value, while the thread that updated it works with a new value. We can rebind the var by using a special form of `binding`:

```
(binding [player-max-level 101]
    (println "player max level is: " player-max-level))
```

If we do this, we will get an error, as follows:

```
IllegalStateException Can't dynamically bind non-dynamic var: user/player-
max-level  clojure.lang.Var.pushThreadBindings (Var.java:320)
```

Clojure only allows us to rebind the var if it was declared `dynamic`. Let's create a new `dynamic` var, as follows:

```
(def ^:dynamic player-max-health 50)
```

Suppose that we access its value, as follows:

```
player-max-health
```

The result will then be as follows:

```
=> 50
```

Suppose that we try to rebind it:

```
(binding [player-max-health 55]
  (println "player max health is: " player-max-health))
```

We will get the information that `player-max-health` is now 55:

```
=> player max health is: 55
```

In addition to making vars `dynamic`, we can declare them as `private` or `constant`. We will explore these features in the following sections.

Private vars

Private vars allow us to hide the parts of the code that we want to keep internal. This is done during the var's definition, as follows:

```
(def ^:private items-count 14)
```

We have declared `items-count` as `private`. Suppose that we try to access it from the current namespace:

```
items-count
```

If we do this we will get its value, shown as follows:

```
=> 14
```

If we try to access it from another namespace, however, we will get an error. Note that if you try this in `repl`, you will have to substitute `other-ns` with the actual namespace from your project:

```
(ns other-ns)
(refer 'user)
items-count
```

Because we are in a different namespace, accessing the `private` var throws an error, as shown in the following code snippet:

```
<CompilerException java.lang.RuntimeException:
;= Unable to resolve symbol: items-count in this context,
compiling:(NO_SOURCE_PATH:0)>
```

The error message states that Clojure could not find `items-count` in the current context.

Constant vars

Clojure allows us to declare vars as constant, in order to protect them from changes. First, we will look at what can happen if a var is not defined as constant:

```
(def admin-name "John")
```

We have created the `admin-name` var, with the value `"John"`. We will use it to greet new players, as follows:

```
(defn greet-player [player]
  (println admin-name " welcomes " player))

(greet-player "Alice")

(greet-player "Zack")
```

So far, so good; we get the greetings that we expect:

```
=> John welcomes Alice
=> John welcomes Zack
```

Now, let's try to create a var again, as follows:

```
(def admin-name "Terry")
```

No exception is thrown if we try to do this. What about greeting the players again? Consider the following code:

```
(greet-player "Zack")
```

It tells us that the new admin is `Terry`:

```
=> Terry welcomes Zack
```

This is not what we wanted. We can protect ourselves from such situations by declaring var as constant:

```
(def ^:const support-name "Stu")

(defn support-player [player]
  (println "Hi" player "it is" support-name "from support"))

(support-player "Zack")
```

This code shows us that `Stu` is our support person:

```
=> Hi Zack it is Stu from support
```

Suppose that we try to redefine the `support-name` var and call the `support` function again, as follows:

```
(def support-name "Debbie")

(support-player "Zack")
```

We will see that `Stu` is still our support person and not `Debbie`:

```
=> Hi Zack it is Stu from support
```

You have now seen four reference types in Clojure. Now, we will explore futures and promises.

Futures and promises in Clojure

A **future** is an object that represents the result of running a function on a different thread. A **promise** is an object that represents a value that will be delivered at some point in time.

Futures

Futures are useful for long-running computations, or code that can block main threads. Let's create a function that runs for a relatively long time, as follows:

```
(defn get-user-accounts []
  (Thread/sleep 5000)
  [{:user "John"}{:user "Debbie"}])
(defn get-recent-purchases []
  (Thread/sleep 5000)
  ["vegetables" "fruits"])
```

The `get-user-accounts` and `get-recent-purchases` functions can potentially take a long time, depending on the amount of data. Here, we use `Thread/sleep` for five seconds, in order to simulate a long-running process. We can try to use these functions, as follows:

```
(defn long-process []
  (let [users (get-user-accounts)
        purchases (get-recent-purchases)]
    {:purchases purchases
     :users users}))
```

Our `long-process` function relies on data from functions that take a long time to execute. Let's see how long it can take, as follows:

```
(time (long-process))
```

On my machines, it takes 10 seconds:

```
=> "Elapsed time: 10000.668403 msecs"
=> {:purchases ["vegetables" "fruits"], :users [{:user "John"} {:user
"Debbie"}]}
```

Using futures can help us to speed up the process, as follows:

```
(defn fast-process []
  (let [users (future (get-user-accounts))
        purchases (future (get-recent-purchases))]
    {:purchases @purchases
     :users @users}))
```

We use the `future` function, which takes a body of code that will be run in a separate thread. In the preceding example, `users` and `purchases` can be run in parallel. We dereference `future` with `@`, in order to obtain a computed value.

On my four-core computer, I ran `fast-process` as follows:

```
(time (fast-process))
```

The `fast-process` took five seconds, as shown in the following output:

```
=> "Elapsed time: 5001.149672 msecs"
=> {:purchases ["vegetables" "fruits"], :users [{:user "John"} {:user
"Debbie"}]}
```

As you can see, using `future` can help us to run the code more quickly.

Promises

`promise` is an object that represents a value that will be delivered at some point in time. A `promise` object is read by using `deref` or the `@` reader macro. The values are set by using the `deliver` function, as follows:

```
(let [prom (promise)]
  (future
    ;; do some work in the future
    (deliver prom :finished))
  @prom)
```

A number of things happen in the preceding code, as follows:

1. We create `promise`.
2. Then, we use `future` to simulate doing some work.
3. We dereference `prom` by using the `@` reader macro. This will block the calling thread until a value is delivered.
4. Back in the `future`, once the work is done, we use `deliver` to let the calling thread know that the work in the `future` has completed.
5. This unblocks the calling thread, and the value becomes available to us.

Using futures and promises can help us to create concurrent programs, in which we can pass data between threads.

Summary

In this chapter, we looked at how Clojure approaches concurrency and parallelism. First, you learned about the differences between concurrency and parallelism. Then, we looked at the state, identity, and values in programming languages. This allowed us to investigate how the data and states are managed in concurrent programs in Java.

Finally, having seen how difficult concurrency is, we moved on to the Clojure approach to concurrency. We looked at how (and when) to use agents, atoms, refs, and vars. We finished the chapter by looking at futures and promises in Clojure.

Contrary to many object-oriented languages, Clojure provides clear distinctions between states and identities. Along with some tools, this allows developers to write and maintain concurrent programs in an easier way.

This brings us to the end of what was hopefully an enjoyable and informative journey through the different methods of Reactive Programming.

Far from being a complete reference, this book aims to provide you, the reader, with enough information, as well as some concrete tools and examples that you can apply today.

It is our hope that the references and exercises included in this book will prove themselves useful, should you wish to expand your knowledge and seek out more details.

Lastly, we strongly encourage you to turn the page and read the Appendix, *The Algebra of Library Design*, as we truly believe it will, if nothing else, make you consider the importance of composition in programming.

We sincerely wish that this book has been as entertaining and instructional to read as it was to write.

Thank you for reading. We look forward to seeing the great things that you build.

Further reading

Here is a list of information you can refer to:

1. *Java Concurrency in Practice*, Brian Goetz: http://jcip.net/
2. Wikipedia, Clojure: https://en.wikipedia.org/wiki/Clojure
3. Clojure, Rationale: https://clojure.org/about/rationale
4. *Concurrency is not parallelism*, Rob Pike: https://blog.golang.org/concurrency-is-not-parallelism

Appendix - The Algebra of Library Design

You might have noticed that all of the reactive abstractions that you have encountered in this book have a few things in common. For one, they work as container-like abstractions, which can be described as follows:

- Futures encapsulate a computation that eventually yields a single value
- Observables encapsulate computations that can yield multiple values over time, in the shape of a stream
- Channels encapsulate the values pushed to them, and they can have the values being popped from the channel, working as a concurrent queue through which concurrent processes can communicate

Once we have a container, we can operate on it in a number of ways, which are very similar across the different abstractions and frameworks. We can `filter` the values contained in them; transform them by using `map`; combine abstractions of the same type by using `bind`, `flatMap`, or `selectMany`; execute multiple computations in parallel; aggregate the results by using `sequence`; and much more.

As such, even though the abstractions and their underlying functionalities are fundamentally different, it still feels as if they belong to some type of higher-level abstractions.

In this appendix, we will explore what these higher-level abstractions are, the relationships between them, and how we can take advantage of them in our projects.

The semantics of map

We will get started by taking a look at one of the most used operations in these abstractions: `map`.

We've been using `map` for a long time, in order to transform sequences. Thus, instead of creating a new function name for each new abstraction, library designers simply abstract the `map` operation over its own container type.

Imagine the mess that we would end up in if we had functions such as `transform-observable`, `transform-channel`, `combine-futures`, and so on.

Thankfully, this is not the case. The semantics of `map` are well understood, to the point that even if a developer hasn't used a specific library before, he will almost always assume that `map` will apply a function to the value(s) contained within whatever abstraction the library provides.

Let's look at three examples that we have encountered in this book. We will create a new Leiningen project, in which to experiment with the contents of this appendix:

```
$ lein new library-design
```

Next, let's add a few dependencies to our `project.clj` file, as follows:

```
...
:dependencies [[org.clojure/clojure "1.9.0"]
               [com.leonardoborges/imminent "0.1.1"]
               [com.netflix.rxjava/rxjava-clojure "0.20.7"]
               [org.clojure/core.async "0.4.474"]
               [uncomplicate/fluokitten "0.3.0"]]
...
```

Don't worry about the last dependency; we'll get to that later on.

Now, start a `repl` session, so that you can follow along. Type the following code:

```
$ lein repl
```

Then, enter the following into your REPL:

```
(require '[imminent.core :as i]
         '[rx.lang.clojure.core :as rx]
         '[clojure.core.async :as async])
(def  repl-out *out*)
(defn prn-to-repl [& args]
  (binding [*out* repl-out]
    (apply prn args)))
(-> (i/const-future 31)
    (i/map #(* % 2))
    (i/on-success #(prn-to-repl (str "Value: " %))))
(as-> (rx/return 31) obs
      (rx/map #(* % 2) obs)
      (rx/subscribe obs #(prn-to-repl (str "Value: " %))))
(def c          (async/chan))
(def mapped-c (async/map< #(* % 2) c))
(async/go (async/>! c 31))
```

```
(async/go (prn-to-repl (str "Value: " (async/<! mapped-c))))
"Value: 62"
"Value: 62"
"Value: 62"
```

The three examples (using `imminent`, `RxClojure`, and `core.async`, respectively) look remarkably similar. They all follow a simple recipe:

1. Put the number `31` inside of their respective abstractions
2. Double that number by mapping a function over the abstraction
3. Print its result to the REPL

As expected, this will provide the value `62` as the output to the screen, three times.

It would seem that `map` performs the same abstract steps in all three cases—it applies the provided function, puts the resulting value in a fresh new container, and returns it. We could continue to generalize, but we would just be rediscovering an abstraction that already exists—functors.

Functors

Functors are the first abstraction that we will look at, and they are rather simple—they define a single operation, called `fmap`. In Clojure, functors can be represented by using protocols, and they are used for containers that can be mapped over. Such containers include (but are not limited to) lists, futures, observables, and channels.

The *Algebra* in the title of this appendix refers to **abstract algebra**, a branch of mathematics that studies algebraic structures. An algebraic structure is, to put it simply, a set with one or more operations defined on it.

As an example, consider **semigroups**, which is one such algebraic structure. A semigroup is defined as a set of elements together with an operation. This operation combines any two elements of this set. Therefore, the set of positive integers, along with the addition operation, form a semigroup.

Another tool that is used to study algebraic structures is called **category theory**, of which functors are a part[1].

We won't delve too deeply into the theory behind all of this, as there are plenty of books[1][2] available on the subject. It was, however, a necessary detour, to explain the title used in this appendix.

Does this mean that all of these abstractions implement a functor protocol? Unfortunately, that is not the case. As Clojure is a dynamic language and didn't have protocols built in (they were added in version 1.2 of the language), these frameworks tend to implement their own versions of the `map` function, which doesn't belong to any protocol in particular.

The only exception is `imminent`, which implements the protocols included in `fluokitten`, a Clojure library providing concepts from category theory, such as functors[2].

The following is a simplified version of the functor protocol found in `fluokitten`:

```
(defprotocol Functor
  (fmap [fv g]))
```

As we mentioned previously, functors define a single operation. `fmap` applies the function g to whatever value is inside of the container (functor), `fv`.

However, implementing this protocol does not guarantee that we have actually implemented a functor. This is because, in addition to implementing the protocol, functors are also required to obey a couple of laws, which we will examine briefly.

The `identity` law is as follows:

```
(= (fmap a-functor identity)
   (identity a-functor))
```

The preceding code is all that we need to verify this law. It simply says that mapping the `identity` function over `a-functor` is the same as simply applying the `identity` function to the functor itself.

The composition law is as follows:

```
(= (fmap a-functor (comp f g))
   (fmap (fmap a-functor g) f))
```

The composition law, in turn, says that if we compose two arbitrary functions, f and g, take the resulting function, and apply that to `a-functor`, that is the same as mapping g over the functor, and then mapping f over the resulting functor.

No amount of text will be able to replace practical examples, so we will implement our own functor, which we will call `option`. We will then revisit the laws, to ensure that we have respected them.

The option functor

As Tony Hoare once put it, null references were his one billion dollar mistake[3]. Regardless of your background, you will no doubt have encountered versions of the dreadful `NullPointerException`. This usually happens when we try to call a method on an object reference that is null.

Clojure deals with null values due to its interoperability with Java. In this section we will learn how Clojure provides improved support for dealing with null values.

The `core` library is packed with functions that do the right thing if passed a `nil` value (Clojure's version of Java's null). For instance, how many elements are there in a `nil` sequence? Consider the following code snippet:

```
(count nil) ;; 0
```

Thanks to conscientious design decisions regarding `nil`, we can, for the most part, afford not to worry about it. For all other cases, the `option` functor might be of some help.

The remaining examples in this appendix should be in a file called `option.clj`, under `library-design/src/library_design/`. You're welcome to try this in the REPL, as well.

Let's start our next example by adding the namespace declaration, as well as the data that we will be working with:

```
(ns library-design.option
  (:require [uncomplicate.fluokitten.protocols :as fkp]
            [uncomplicate.fluokitten.core :as fkc]
            [uncomplicate.fluokitten.jvm :as fkj]
            [imminent.core :as i]))

(def pirates [{:name "Jack Sparrow"     :born 1700 :died 1740 :ship "Black
Pearl"}
              {:name "Blackbeard"       :born 1680 :died 1750 :ship "Queen
Anne's Revenge"}
              {:name "Hector Barbossa" :born 1680 :died 1740 :ship nil}])

(defn pirate-by-name [name]
  (->> pirates
       (filter #(= name (:name %)))
       first))

(defn age [{:keys [born died]}]
  (- died born))
```

As a *Pirates of the Caribbean* fan, I thought it would be interesting to play with pirates in this example. Let's suppose that we would like to calculate Jack Sparrow's age. Given the data and functions that we just covered, this is a simple task:

```
(-> (pirate-by-name "Jack Sparrow")
    age) ;; 40
```

However, what if we would like to know Davy Jones' age? We don't actually have any data for this pirate, so if we run our program again, the following is what we'll get:

```
(-> (pirate-by-name "Davy Jones")
    age) ;; NullPointerException    clojure.lang.Numbers.ops
(Numbers.java:961)
```

There it is. The dreadful `NullPointerException`. This happens because, in the implementation of the `age` function, we end up trying to subtract two `nil` values, which is incorrect. As you might have guessed, we will attempt to fix this by using the `option` functor.

Traditionally, `option` is implemented as an algebraic data type—more specifically, a sum type with two variants: `Some` and `None`. These variants are used to identify whether a value is present, without using nils. You can think of both `Some` and `None` as subtypes of `option`.

In Clojure, we will represent them by using records, as follows:

```
(defrecord Some [v])

(defrecord None [])

(defn option [v]
  (if (nil? v)
    (None.)
    (Some. v)))
```

As you can see, `Some` can contain a single value, whereas `None` contains nothing. It's simply a marker indicating the absence of content. We have also created a helper function, called `option`, which creates the appropriate record, depending on whether its argument is `nil`.

The next step is to extend the `Functor` protocol to both records, as follows:

```
(extend-protocol fkp/Functor
  Some
  (fmap [f g]
    (Some. (g (:v f))))
  None
  (fmap [_ _]
    (None.)))
```

Here's where the semantic meaning of the `option` functor becomes apparent—as `Some` contains a value, its implementation of `fmap` simply applies the function `g` to the value inside of the functor, `f`, which is of the type `Some`. Finally, we put the results inside of a new `Some` record.

Now, what does it mean to map a function over `None`? You have probably guessed that it doesn't really make sense; the `None` record holds no values. The only thing that we can do is return another `None`. As you will see shortly, this gives the `option` functor a short-circuiting semantic.

> In the `fmap` implementation of `None`, we could have returned a reference to `this`, instead of a new record instance. I haven't done so, simply to make it clear that we need to return an instance of `None`.

Now that we've implemented the functor protocol, we can try it out, as follows:

```
(->> (option (pirate-by-name "Jack Sparrow"))
     (fkc/fmap age)) ;; #library_design.option.Some{:v 40}

(->> (option (pirate-by-name "Davy Jones"))
     (fkc/fmap age)) ;; #library_design.option.None{}
```

The first example shouldn't hold any surprises. We convert the pirate map that we get by calling `pirate-by-name` into `option`, and then we `fmap` the `age` function over it.

The second example is an interesting one. As we stated previously, we have no data about Davy Jones. However, mapping `age` over it does not throw an exception any longer; instead, it returns `None`.

This might seem like a small benefit, but the bottom line is that the `option` functor makes it safe to chain operations together:

```
(->> (option (pirate-by-name "Jack Sparrow"))
     (fkc/fmap age)
     (fkc/fmap inc)
     (fkc/fmap #(* 2 %))) ;; #library_design.option.Some{:v 82}

(->> (option (pirate-by-name "Davy Jones"))
     (fkc/fmap age)
     (fkc/fmap inc)
     (fkc/fmap #(* 2 %))) ;; #library_design.option.None{}
```

At this point, some readers might be thinking about the `some->` macro (introduced in Clojure 1.5) and how it effectively achieves the same result as the `option` functor. This intuition is correct, as demonstrated in the following code snippet:

```
(some-> (pirate-by-name "Davy Jones")
        age
        inc
        (* 2)) ;; nil
```

The `some->` macro threads the result of the first expression through the first form if it is not `nil`. Then, if the result of that expression isn't `nil`, it threads it through the next form, and so on. As soon as any of the expressions evaluates to `nil`, we see that `some->` short-circuits and returns `nil` immediately.

That being said, a functor is a much more general concept; as long as we are working with this concept, our code doesn't need to change, as we are operating at a higher level of abstraction:

```
(->> (i/future (pirate-by-name "Jack Sparrow"))
     (fkc/fmap age)
     (fkc/fmap inc)
     (fkc/fmap #(* 2 %))) ;; #<Future@30518bfc: #<Success@39bd662c: 82>>
```

In the preceding example, even though we are working with a fundamentally different tool (futures), the preceding code that returns a pirate by name did not have to change. This is only possible because both options and futures are functors, and they implement the same protocol provided by `fluokitten`. We have gained composability and simplicity, as we can use the same API to work with various different abstractions.

Speaking of composability, this property is guaranteed by the second law of functors. Let's see whether our option functor respects this and the first (identity) laws:

```
;; Identity
(= (fkc/fmap identity (option 1))
   (identity (option 1))) ;; true


;; Composition
(= (fkc/fmap (comp identity inc) (option 1))
   (fkc/fmap identity (fkc/fmap inc (option 1)))) ;; true
```

We're done; our option functor is a lawful citizen. The two remaining abstractions also come paired with their own laws. We will not cover the laws in this section, but I encourage you to read about them[4].

Finding the average of ages

In this section, we will explore a different use case for the option functor. We would like to, given a number of pirates, calculate the average of their ages. This is simple enough to do:

```
(defn avg [& xs]
  (float (/ (apply + xs) (count xs))))

(let [a (some-> (pirate-by-name "Jack Sparrow") age)
      b (some-> (pirate-by-name "Blackbeard") age)
      c (some-> (pirate-by-name "Hector Barbossa") age)]
  (avg a b c)) ;; 56.666668
```

Note that we are using some-> here, to protect us from nil values. Now, what happens if there is a pirate for which we have no information? Consider the following code snippet:

```
(let [a (some-> (pirate-by-name "Jack Sparrow") age)
      b (some-> (pirate-by-name "Davy Jones") age)
      c (some-> (pirate-by-name "Hector Barbossa") age)]
  (avg a b c)) ;; NullPointerException   clojure.lang.Numbers.ops
(Numbers.java:961)
```

It seems that we're back at square one! It's worse now, because using some-> doesn't help if we need to use all of the values at once, as opposed to threading them through a chain of function calls.

Of course, not all is lost. All we need to do is check whether all of the values are present, before calculating the average:

```
(let [a (some-> (pirate-by-name "Jack Sparrow") age)
      b (some-> (pirate-by-name "Davy Jones") age)
      c (some-> (pirate-by-name "Hector Barbossa") age)]
  (when (and a b c)
    (avg a b c))) ;; nil
```

While this works perfectly fine, our implementation suddenly had to become aware that any (or all) of the values a, b, and c could be nil. The next abstraction that we will look at, applicative functors, will fix this.

Applicative functors

Like functors, **applicative functors** are a sort of container, and they define two operations:

```
(defprotocol Applicative
  (pure [av v])
  (fapply [ag av]))
```

The pure function is a generic way to put a value inside of an applicative functor. So far, we have been using the option helper function for this purpose. We will be using it a little later.

The fapply function will unwrap the function contained in the applicative ag, and will apply it to the value contained in the applicative av.

The purpose of both of the functions will become clear with an example, but first, we need to promote our option functor to an applicative functor, as follows:

```
(extend-protocol fkp/Applicative
  Some
  (pure [_ v]
    (Some. v))

  (fapply [ag av]
    (if-let [v (:v av)]
      (Some. ((:v ag) v))
      (None.)))
  None
  (pure [_ v]
    (Some. v))

  (fapply [ag av]
    (None.)))
```

The implementation of `pure` is the simplest. All it does is wrap the value, v, into an instance of `Some`. Equally simple is the implementation of `fapply` for `None`. As there is no value, we simply return `None` again.

The `fapply` implementation of `Some` ensures that both arguments have a value for the :v keyword; strictly speaking, they both have to be instances of `Some`. If :v is not `nil`, it applies the function contained in `ag` to v, finally wrapping the result. Otherwise, it returns `None`.

This should be enough to try our first example, using the applicative functor API:

```
(fkc/fapply (option inc) (option 2))
;; #library_design.option.Some{:v 3}

(fkc/fapply (option nil) (option 2))
;; #library_design.option.None{}
```

We are now able to work with functors that contain functions. Additionally, we have also preserved the semantics of what should happen when any of the functors don't have a value.

We can now revisit the average-age example from before, as follows:

```
(def age-option (comp (partial fkc/fmap age) option pirate-by-name))

(let [a (age-option "Jack Sparrow")
      b (age-option "Blackbeard")
      c (age-option "Hector Barbossa")]
  (fkc/<*> (option (fkj/curry avg 3))
           a b c))
;; #library_design.option.Some{:v 56.666668}
```

The `vararg` function, `<*>`, is defined by `fluokitten` and performs a left-associative `fapply` on its arguments. Essentially, it is a convenience function that makes `(<*> f g h)` equivalent to `(fapply (fapply f g) h)`.

We start by defining a helper function, to avoid repetition. The `age-option` function retrieves the age of a pirate for us as an option.

Next, we curry the `avg` function to 3 arguments and put it into `option`. Then, we use the `<*>` function to apply it to the options a, b, and c. We get the same result, but have the applicative functor take care of `nil` values for us.

Function currying: Currying is the technique of transforming a function of multiple arguments into a higher-order function of a single argument that returns more single-argument functions until all of the arguments have been supplied.

Roughly speaking, currying makes the following snippets equivalent:

```
(def curried-1 (fkj/curry + 2))
(def curried-2 (fn [a]
                 (fn [b]
                   (+ a b))))

((curried-1 10) 20) ;; 30
((curried-2 10) 20) ;; 30
```

Using applicative functors this way is so common that the pattern has been captured as the function `alift`, as shown in the following code snippet:

```
(defn alift
  "Lifts a n-ary function `f` into a applicative context"
  [f]
  (fn [& as]
    {:pre  [(seq as)]}
    (let [curried (fkj/curry f (count as))]
      (apply fkc/<*>
             (fkc/fmap curried (first as))
             (rest as)))))
```

The `alift` function is responsible for lifting a function in such a way that it can be used with applicative functors without much ceremony. Because of the assumptions that we are able to make about applicative functors (for instance, that it is also a functor), we can write generic code that can be reused across any applicatives.

With `alift` in place, our age average example turns into the following:

```
(let [a (age-option "Jack Sparrow")
      b (age-option "Blackbeard")
      c (age-option "Hector Barbossa")]
  ((alift avg) a b c))
;; #library_design.option.Some{:v 56.666668}
```

We lift `avg` into an applicative-compatible version, making the code look remarkably like a simple function application. And, since we are not doing anything interesting with the `let` bindings, we can simplify it further, as follows:

```
((alift avg) (age-option "Jack Sparrow")
             (age-option "Blackbeard")
             (age-option "Hector Barbossa"))
;; #library_design.option.Some{:v 56.666668}

((alift avg) (age-option "Jack Sparrow")
             (age-option "Davy Jones")
             (age-option "Hector Barbossa"))
;; #library_design.option.None{}
```

As with functors, we can take the code as it is, and we can simply replace the underlying abstraction, preventing repetition once again:

```
((alift avg) (i/future (some-> (pirate-by-name "Jack Sparrow") age))
             (i/future (some-> (pirate-by-name "Blackbeard") age))
             (i/future (some-> (pirate-by-name "Hector Barbossa") age)))
;; #<Future@17b1be96: #<Success@16577601: 56.666668>>
```

Gathering stats about ages

Now that we can safely calculate the average age of a number of pirates, it might be interesting to take this further and calculate the median and standard deviation of the pirates' ages, in addition to their average age.

We already have a function to calculate the average; so, let's just create the ones to calculate the median and the standard deviation of a list of numbers, as follows:

```
(defn median [& ns]
  (let [ns (sort ns)
        cnt (count ns)
        mid (bit-shift-right cnt 1)]
    (if (odd? cnt)
      (nth ns mid)
      (/ (+ (nth ns mid) (nth ns (dec mid))) 2))))

(defn std-dev [& samples]
  (let [n (count samples)
   mean (/ (reduce + samples) n)
   intermediate (map #(Math/pow (- %1 mean) 2) samples)]
    (Math/sqrt
     (/ (reduce + intermediate) n))))
```

With these functions in place, we can write the code that will gather all of the stats for us:

```
(let [a        (some-> (pirate-by-name "Jack Sparrow")     age)
      b        (some-> (pirate-by-name "Blackbeard")       age)
      c        (some-> (pirate-by-name "Hector Barbossa") age)
      avg      (avg a b c)
      median   (median a b c)
      std-dev  (std-dev a b c)]
  {:avg avg
   :median median
   :std-dev std-dev})

;; {:avg 56.666668,
;;  :median 60,
;;  :std-dev 12.472191289246473}
```

This implementation is fairly straightforward. First, we retrieve all of the ages that we're interested in and bind them to the locals a, b, and c. We then reuse the values when calculating the remaining stats. Finally, we gather all of the results in map, for easy access.

By now, you probably know where we're headed. What if any of those values is nil? Consider the following code:

```
(let [a        (some-> (pirate-by-name "Jack Sparrow")     age)
      b        (some-> (pirate-by-name "Davy Jones")       age)
      c        (some-> (pirate-by-name "Hector Barbossa") age)
      avg      (avg a b c)
      median   (median a b c)
      std-dev  (std-dev a b c)]
  {:avg avg
   :median median
   :std-dev std-dev})
;; NullPointerException   clojure.lang.Numbers.ops (Numbers.java:961)
```

The second binding, b, returns nil, as we don't have any information about Davy Jones. As such, it causes the calculations to fail. Like before, we can change our implementation to protect us from such failures, as follows:

```
(let [a        (some-> (pirate-by-name "Jack Sparrow")     age)
      b        (some-> (pirate-by-name "Davy Jones")       age)
      c        (some-> (pirate-by-name "Hector Barbossa") age)
      avg      (when (and a b c) (avg a b c))
      median   (when (and a b c) (median a b c))
      std-dev  (when (and a b c) (std-dev a b c))]
  (when (and a b c)
    {:avg avg
     :median median
```

```
        :std-dev std-dev}))
;; nil
```

This time, it's even worse than when we only had to calculate the average. The code is checking for `nil` values in four extra spots—before calling the three stats functions, and just before gathering the stats into the resulting `map`.

Can we do better?

Monads

Our last abstraction will solve the very problem that we raised in the previous section—how to safely perform intermediate calculations by preserving the semantics of the abstractions that we're working with (in this case, options).

It should be no surprise by now that `fluokitten` also provides a protocol for monads, simplified and shown as follows:

```
(defprotocol Monad (bind [mv g]))
```

If you think in terms of a class hierarchy, monads would be at the bottom of it, inheriting from applicative functors, which, in turn, inherit from functors. That is, if you're working with a monad, you can assume that it is also an applicative and a functor.

The `bind` function of monads takes a function, g, as its second argument. This function receives as input the value contained in `mv`, and returns another monad containing its result. This is a crucial part of the contract—g has to return a monad.

The reason why will become clearer after a number of examples. But first, let's promote our option abstraction to a monad; at this point, `option` is already an applicative functor and a functor:

```
(extend-protocol fkp/Monad
  Some
  (bind [mv g]
    (g (:v mv)))

  None
  (bind [_ _]
    (None.)))
```

The implementation is fairly simple. In the `None` version, we can't really do anything; so, just like we have been doing so far, we return an instance of `None`.

The `Some` implementation extracts the value from the monad `mv` and applies the function `g` to it. Note that this time, we don't need to wrap the result, as the function `g` already returns a monad instance.

Using the monad API, we could sum the ages of our pirates as follows:

```
(def opt-ctx (None.))

(fkc/bind (age-option "Jack Sparrow")
          (fn [a]
            (fkc/bind (age-option "Blackbeard")
                      (fn [b]
                        (fkc/bind (age-option "Hector Barbossa")
                                  (fn [c]
                                    (fkc/pure opt-ctx
                                              (+ a b c)))))))))
;; #library_design.option.Some{:v 170.0}
```

First, we make use of the applicative's `pure` function in the innermost function. Remember that the role of `pure` is to provide a generic way to put a value into an applicative functor. Since monads are also applicative, we make use of them here.

However, since Clojure is a dynamically typed language, we need to hint `pure` with a type of context we wish to use. This context is simply an instance of either `Some` or `None`. They both have the same pure implementation.

While we do get the right answer, the preceding example is far from what we would like to write, due to its excessive nesting. It is also hard to read.

Thankfully, `fluokitten` provides a much better way to write monadic code, called the **do-notation**, as follows:

```
(fkc/mdo [a (age-option "Jack Sparrow")
          b (age-option "Blackbeard")
          c (age-option "Hector Barbossa")]
         (fkc/pure opt-ctx  (+ a b c)))
;; #library_design.option.Some{:v 170.0}
```

Suddenly, the same code becomes a lot cleaner and easier to read, without losing any of the semantics of the `option` monad. This is because `mdo` is a macro that expands to the code equivalent of the nested version, as we can verify by expanding the macro, as follows:

```
(require '[clojure.walk :as w])

(w/macroexpand-all '(fkc/mdo [a (age-option "Jack Sparrow")
                              b (age-option "Blackbeard")
```

```
                              c (age-option "Hector Barbossa")]
                            (option  (+ a b c))))
;; (uncomplicate.fluokitten.core/bind
;;  (age-option "Jack Sparrow")
;;  (fn*
;;    ([a]
;;     (uncomplicate.fluokitten.core/bind
;;       (age-option "Blackbeard")
;;       (fn*
;;         ([b]
;;          (uncomplicate.fluokitten.core/bind
;;            (age-option "Hector Barbossa")
;;            (fn* ([c] (fkc/pure opt-ctx (+ a b c)))))))))))))
```

> **TIP**
>
> It is important to stop for a moment and appreciate the power of Clojure (and Lisp, in general). Languages such as Haskell and Scala, which make heavy use of abstractions, such as functors, applicatives, and monads, also have their own versions of the do-notation. However, this support is baked into the compiler itself.
>
> As an example, when Haskell added do-notation to the language, a new version of the compiler was released, and developers wishing to use the new feature had to upgrade. In Clojure, on the other hand, this new feature can be shipped as a library, due to the power and flexibility of macros. This is exactly what fluokitten has done.

Now, we are ready to go back to our original problem—gathering stats about the pirates' ages.

First, we will define a couple of helper functions that will convert the result of our stats functions into the option monad:

```
(def avg-opt      (comp option avg))
(def median-opt  (comp option median))
(def std-dev-opt (comp option std-dev))
```

Here, we take advantage of function composition in order to create monadic versions of existing functions.

Next, we will rewrite our solution by using the monadic do-notation that we learned earlier:

```
(fkc/mdo [a       (age-option "Jack Sparrow")
          b       (age-option "Blackbeard")
          c       (age-option "Hector Barbossa")
          avg     (avg-opt a b c)
          median  (median-opt a b c)
```

```
                  std-dev (std-dev-opt a b c)]
               (option {:avg avg
                        :median median
                        :std-dev std-dev}))
 ;; #library_design.option.Some{:v {:avg 56.666668,
 ;;                                  :median 60,
 ;;                                  :std-dev 12.472191289246473}}
```

This time, we were able to write the function as we normally would, without having to worry about whether any values in the intermediate computations are empty. This semantic (that is the very essence of the `option` monad) is still preserved, and can be seen as follows:

```
(fkc/mdo [a        (age-option "Jack Sparrow")
          b        (age-option "Blackbeard")
          c        (age-option "Hector Barbossa")
          avg      (avg-opt a b c)
          median   (median-opt a b c)
          std-dev  (std-dev-opt a b c)]
         (fkc/pure opt-ctx {:avg avg
                            :median median
                            :std-dev std-dev}))
 ;; #library_design.option.None{}
```

For the sake of completeness, we will use futures to demonstrate how the do-notation works for any monad:

```
(def avg-fut     (comp i/future-call avg))
(def median-fut  (comp i/future-call median))
(def std-dev-fut (comp i/future-call std-dev))

(fkc/mdo [a (i/future (some-> (pirate-by-name "Jack Sparrow") age))
          b (i/future (some-> (pirate-by-name "Blackbeard") age))
          c (i/future (some-> (pirate-by-name "Hector Barbossa") age))
          avg      (avg-fut a b c)
          median   (median-fut a b c)
          std-dev  (std-dev-fut a b c)]
         (i/const-future {:avg avg
                          :median median
                          :std-dev std-dev}))
 ;; #<Future@3fd0b0d0: #<Success@1e08486b: {:avg 56.666668,
 ;;                                         :median 60,
 ;;                                         :std-dev 12.472191289246473}>>
```

Please note that the preceding code snippet generates a varying result.

Summary

This appendix has taken you on a brief tour of the world of category theory. You learned about three of its abstractions—functors, applicative functors, and monads. They are the guiding principles behind the `imminent` API.

To deepen your knowledge and understanding, we implemented our own `option` monad—a common abstraction used to safely handle the absence of values.

You also saw that using these abstractions allows us to make some assumptions about our code, as seen in functions such as `alift`. There are many other functions that we would normally rewrite over and over again for different purposes, but that can be reused if we recognize that our code fits into one of the abstractions that were covered.

Finally, we hope that this encourages you to explore category theory more, as it will undoubtedly change the way that you think. And, if we can be so bold, we hope that this will also change the way that you design libraries in the future.

Further reading

Here is a list of information you can refer to:

1. *Basic Category Theory for Computer Scientists (Foundations of Computing)*, Benjamin C. Pierce:
   `http://www.amazon.com/Category-Computer-Scientists-FoundationsComputing-ebook/dp/B00MG7E5WE/ref=sr_1_7?ie=UTF8&qid=1423484917&sr=8-7&keywords=category+theory`

2. *Category Theory (Oxford Logic Guides)*, Steve Awodey:
   `http://www.amazon.com/Category-Theory-Oxford-Logic-Guides/dp/0199237182/ref=sr_1_2?ie=UTF8&qid=1423484917&sr=8-2&keywords=category+theory`

3. *Null References: The Billion Dollar Mistake*, Tony Hoare: `http://www.infoq.com/presentations/Null-References-The-Billion-Dollar-Mistake-Tony-Hoare`

4. *Monads in Small Bites*, Leonardo Borges: `http://www.leonardoborges.com/writings/2012/11/30/monads-in-small-bites-part-i-functors`

Other Books You May Enjoy

If you enjoyed this book, you may be interested in these other books by Packt:

Hands-On Reactive Programming in Spring 5
Oleh Dokuka, Igor Lozynskyi

ISBN: 978-1-78728-495-1

- Discover the difference between a reactive system and reactive programming
- Explore the benefits of a reactive system and understand its applications
- Get to grips with using reactive programming in Spring 5
- Gain an understanding of Project Reactor
- Build a reactive system using Spring 5 and Project Reactor
- Create a highly efficient reactive microservice with Spring Cloud
- Test, monitor, and release reactive applications

Hands-On Reactive Programming with Reactor

Rahul Sharma

ISBN: 978-1-78913-579-4

- Explore benefits of the Reactive paradigm and the Reactive Streams API
- Discover the impact of Flux and Mono implications in Reactor
- Expand and repeat data in stream processing
- Get to grips with various types of processors and choose the best one
- Understand how to map errors to make corrections easier
- Create robust tests using testing utilities offered by Reactor
- Find the best way to schedule the execution of code

Leave a review - let other readers know what you think

Please share your thoughts on this book with others by leaving a review on the site that you bought it from. If you purchased the book from Amazon, please leave us an honest review on this book's Amazon page. This is vital so that other potential readers can see and use your unbiased opinion to make purchasing decisions, we can understand what our customers think about our products, and our authors can see your feedback on the title that they have worked with Packt to create. It will only take a few minutes of your time, but is valuable to other potential customers, our authors, and Packt. Thank you!

Index

R

race condition 238
React.js
  about 130
  functional programming 131, 132
Reactive Extensions (Rx) 23, 26, 31, 124
Reactive Programming
  about 7, 8, 9, 10, 11
  colors 13, 14
  dataflow programming 17, 18
  exercise 16
  Functional Reactive Programming (FRP) 23
  higher-order FRP 23, 24
  history 16, 17
  object-oriented Reactive Programming 18, 19,
    20, 21
  Observer design pattern 22, 23
  reactive animation, creating 14, 15
  usage 21, 22
ReactiveCocoa
  about 26
  reference 23
Reagi
  comparing, with other CES frameworks 124
refs
  about 244
  alter function 246
  commute 247
  dereferencing 244
  mutating 245
  ref-set function 246
  Software Transactional Memory (STM) 245
  using 239
Relational Database Service (RDS)
  about 176
  describeDBInstances endpoint 177
reset! function 241
respondent application 102, 103
RESTful microservices
  implementing 201
RESTful services 201
retry 47, 48
rolling average
  displaying 56, 57, 59

root binding 248
RxClojure
  about 33
  incidental complexity, removing 60, 61
  observable rolling averages 62, 63, 64
  reference 33
RxJava
  reference 23, 33
RxJS
  reference 8
  time 11, 12, 13

S

sample combinator 49, 50
send function 243
send-off function 244
service separation
  build dependencies 200
  services communication 200
  services contracts 200
signals 24, 25
sliding buffer 83
software testing
  about 211
  benefits 212
Software Transactional Memory (STM) 245
Speclj framework
  about 226
  reference 226
  should-be-a macro 230
  should-contain macro 229
  should-throw macro 230
  should= macro 229
  should== macro 229
starvation 237
state, problems
  about 235
  lost updates 236
  phantom reads 236
  unrepeatable reads 236
state
  about 234, 235
  traditional solution 237
stock market monitoring application
  building 53, 54, 56